# Hendrix

## Electric Requiem

# BY MATTIA COLOMBARA
# & GIANLUCA MACONI

**COLORS:**
**TENTACLE**

**TRANSLATION:**
**MICOL BELTRAMINI**

**LETTERING:**
**A LARGER WORLD STUDIOS' TROY PETERI**

**COVER AND LOGO DESIGN:**
**GIOVANNI MARINOVICH**

**SPECIAL THANKS:**
**MARCO SCHIAVONE, FEDERICO SALVAN, JEFF & BENITA WEBBER**

**FOR ABLAZE**

**Managing Editor**
RICH YOUNG

**Editor**
KEVIN KETNER

**Designers**
RODOLFO MURAGUCHI
CINTHIA TAKEDA CAETANO

Publisher's Cataloging-in-Publication data

Names: Colombara, Mattia, author. | Maconi, Gianluca, artist.
Title: Hendrix : Electric Requiem / Mattia Colombara; Gianluca Maconi.
Description: Portland, OR: Ablaze, 2022.
Identifiers: ISBN: 978-1-950912-65-0
Subjects: LCSH Hendrix, Jimi—Comic books, strips, etc. | Rock musicians—United States—
Biography—Comic books, strips, etc. | Graphic novels. | BISAC COMICS & GRAPHIC
NOVELS / Nonfiction / Biography & Memoir | BIOGRAPHY & AUTOBIOGRAPHY /
Entertainment & Performing Arts | BIOGRAPHY & AUTOBIOGRAPHY / Music
Classification: LCC ML410.H476 C65 2022 | DDC 784/.092—dc23

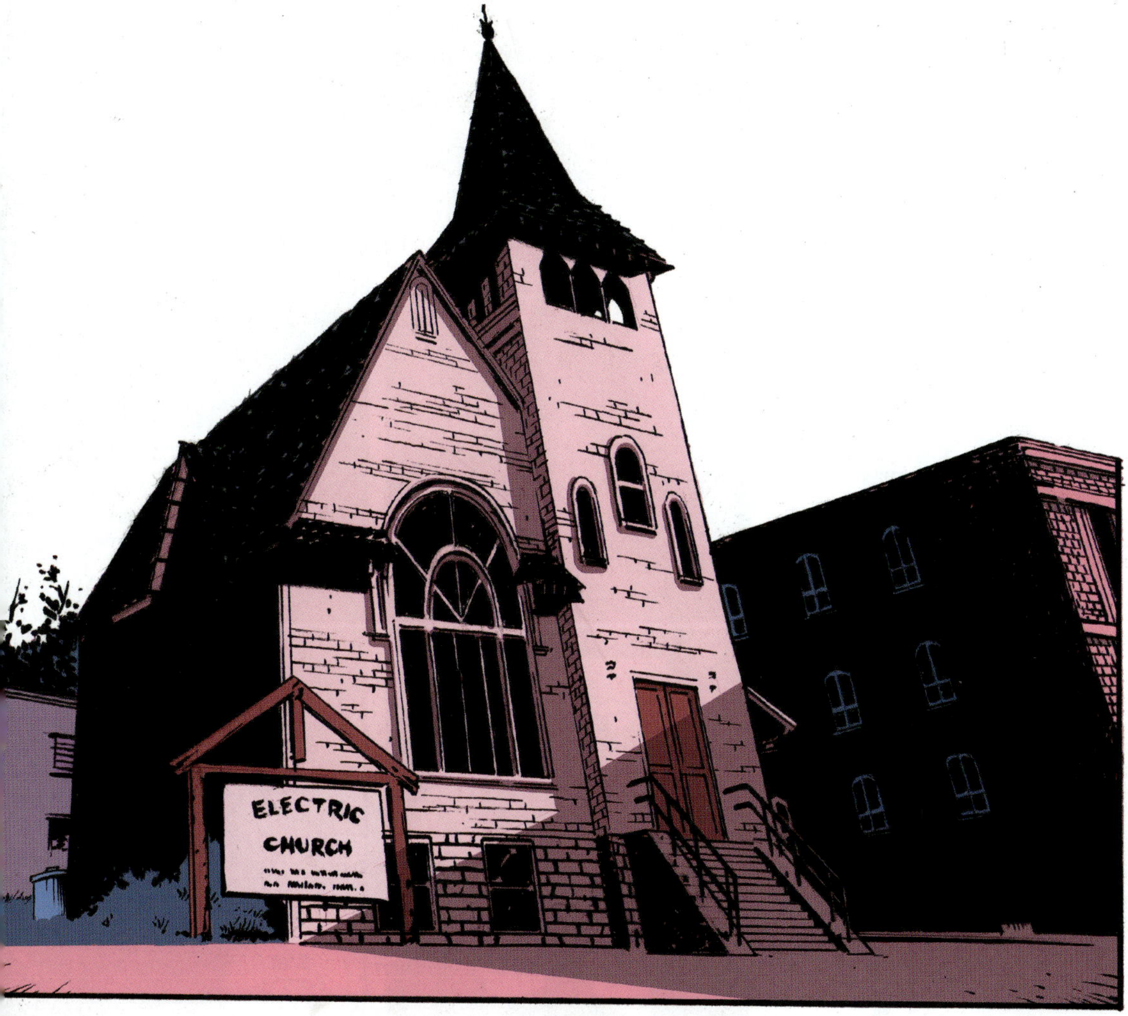
ELECTRIC
CHURCH

# EXP-introduction

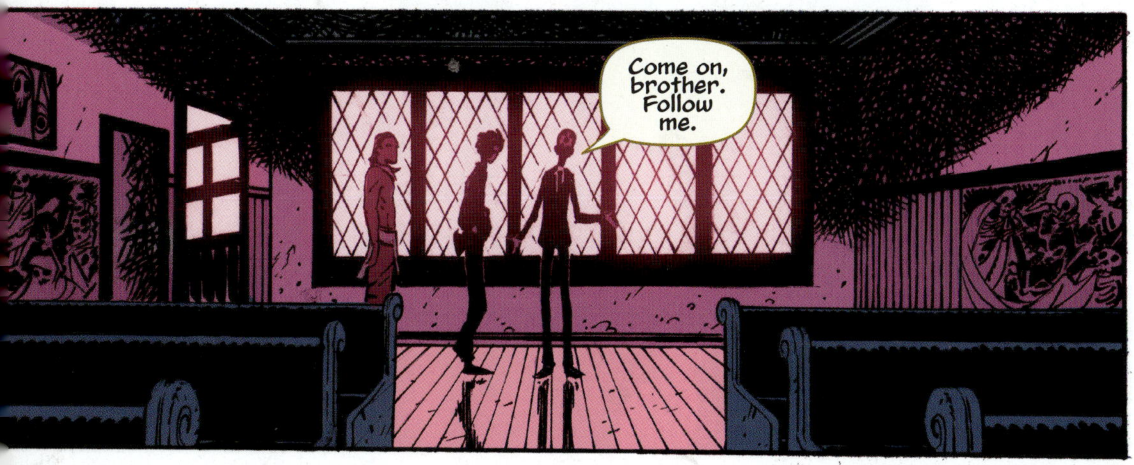
Come on, brother. Follow me.

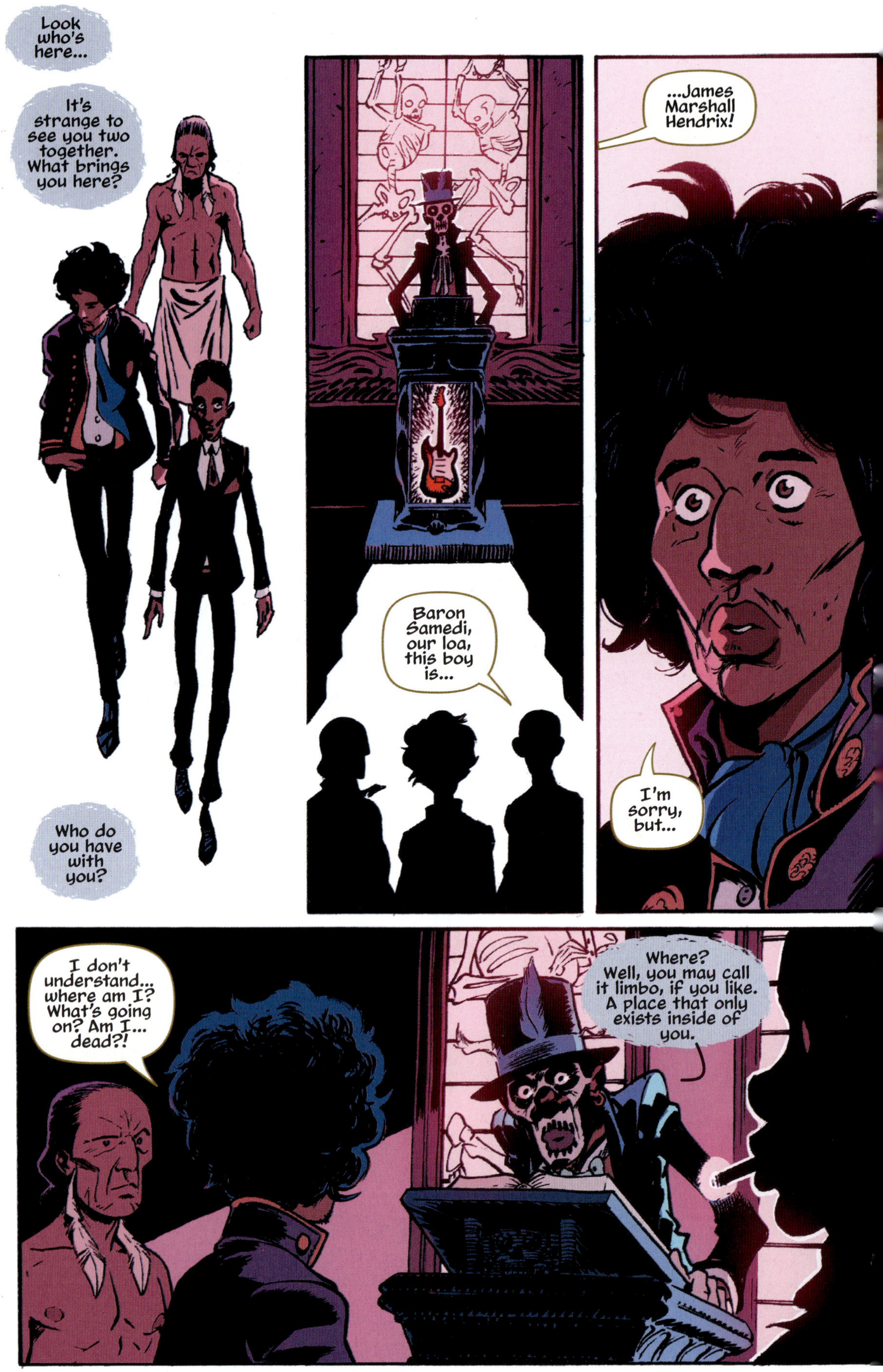
Look who's here...
It's strange to see you two together. What brings you here?
Who do you have with you?
Baron Samedi, our loa, this boy is...
...James Marshall Hendrix!
I'm sorry, but...
I don't understand... where am I? What's going on? Am I... dead?!
Where? Well, you may call it limbo, if you like. A place that only exists inside of you.

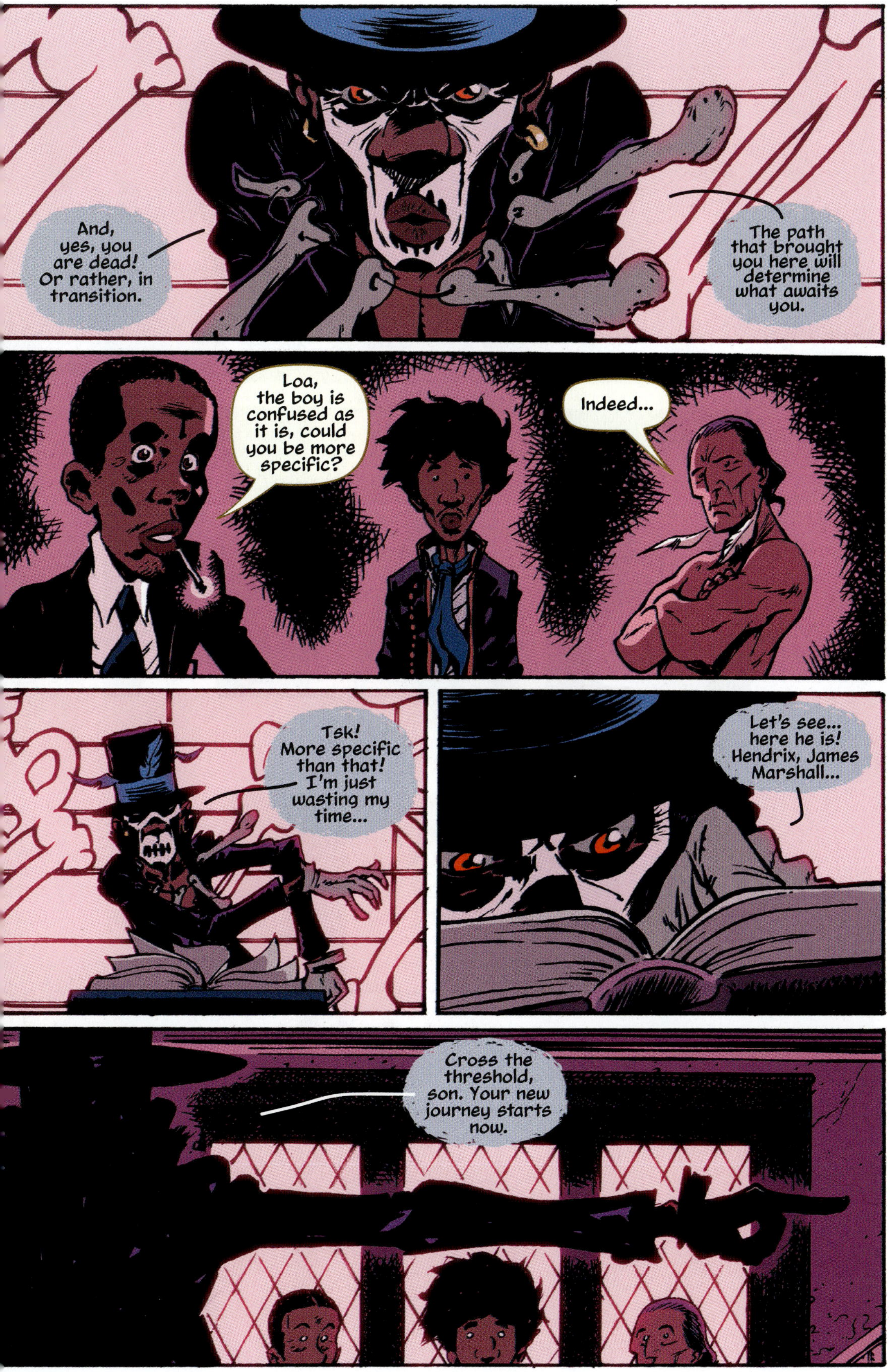
And, yes, you are dead! Or rather, in transition.
The path that brought you here will determine what awaits you.
Loa, the boy is confused as it is, could you be more specific?
Indeed...
Tsk! More specific than that! I'm just wasting my time...
Let's see... here he is! Hendrix, James Marshall...
Cross the threshold, son. Your new journey starts now.

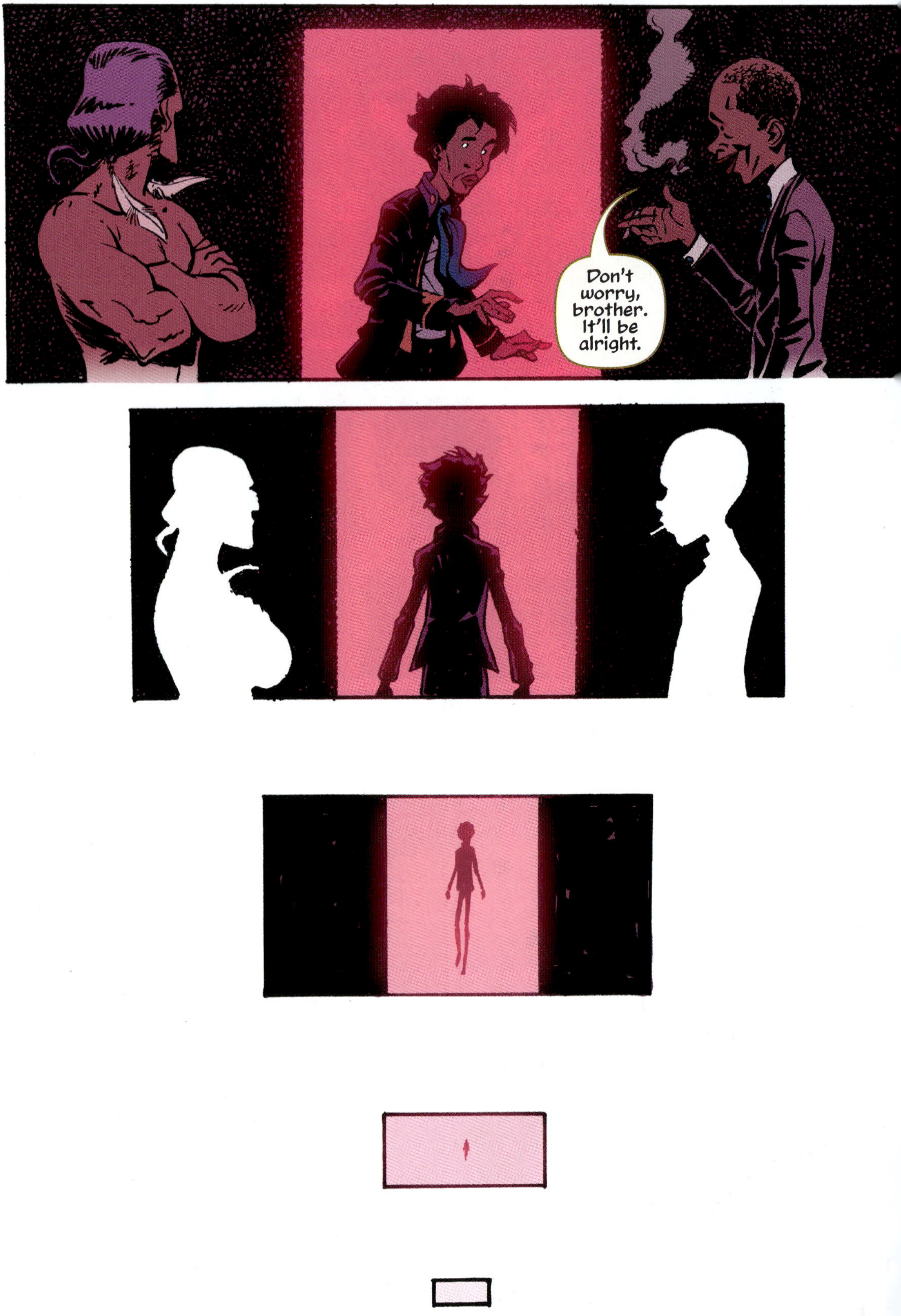
Don't worry, brother. It'll be alright.

# 01.

# VooDoo
# CHILE

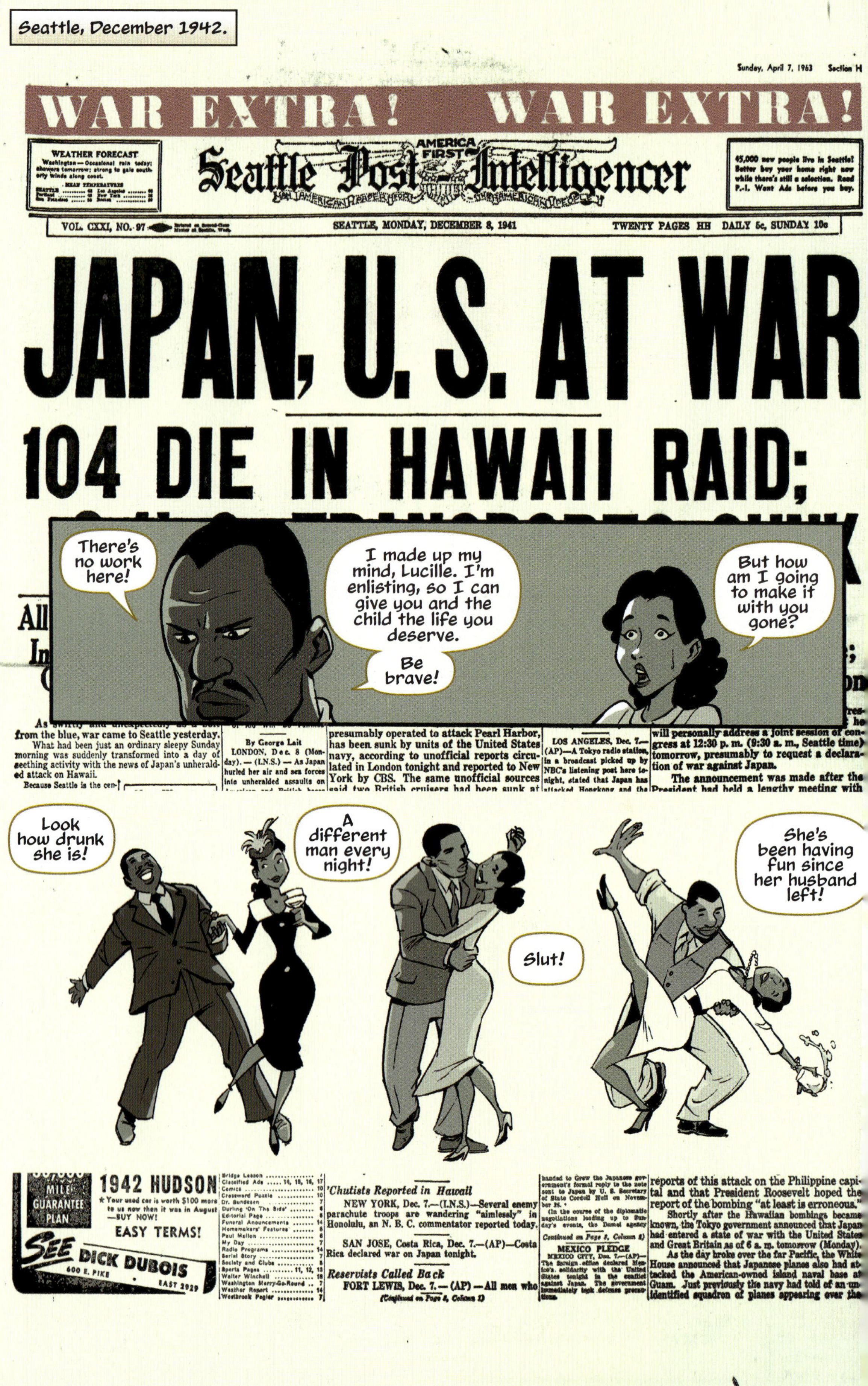
Seattle, December 1942.
Sunday, April 7, 1963 Section H
WAR EXTRA! WAR EXTRA!
Seattle Post-Intelligencer
AMERICA FIRST
WEATHER FORECAST
45,000 new people live in Seattle! Better buy your home right now while there's still a selection. Read P.-I. Want Ads before you buy.
VOL. CXXI, NO. 97
SEATTLE, MONDAY, DECEMBER 8, 1941
TWENTY PAGES HH DAILY 5c, SUNDAY 10c
JAPAN, U.S. AT WAR
104 DIE IN HAWAII RAID;
There's no work here!
I made up my mind, Lucille. I'm enlisting, so I can give you and the child the life you deserve.
Be brave!
But how am I going to make it with you gone?
from the blue, war came to Seattle yesterday.
What had been just an ordinary sleepy Sunday morning was suddenly transformed into a day of seething activity with the news of Japan's unheralded attack on Hawaii.
By George Lait
LONDON, Dec. 8 (Monday). — (I.N.S.) — As Japan hurled her air and sea forces into unheralded assaults on
presumably operated to attack Pearl Harbor, has been sunk by units of the United States navy, according to unofficial reports circulated in London tonight and reported to New York by CBS. The same unofficial sources
LOS ANGELES, Dec. 7.—(AP)—A Tokyo radio station, in a broadcast picked up by NBC's listening post here tonight, stated that Japan has
will personally address a joint session of congress at 12:30 p.m. (9:30 a.m., Seattle time) tomorrow, presumably to request a declaration of war against Japan.
The announcement was made after the
Look how drunk she is!
A different man every night!
Slut!
She's been having fun since her husband left!
MILE GUARANTEE PLAN
1942 HUDSON
★ Your used car is worth $100 more to us now than it was in August —BUY NOW!
EASY TERMS!
SEE DICK DUBOIS
600 E. PIKE EAST 2929
'Chutists Reported in Hawaii
NEW YORK, Dec. 7.—(I.N.S.)—Several enemy parachute troops are wandering "aimlessly" in Honolulu, an N. B. C. commentator reported today.
SAN JOSE, Costa Rica, Dec. 7.—(AP)—Costa Rica declared war on Japan tonight.
Reservists Called Back
FORT LEWIS, Dec. 7. — (AP) — All men who
(Continued on Page 4, Column 1)
MEXICO PLEDGE
reports of this attack on the Philippine capital and that President Roosevelt hoped the report of the bombing "at least is erroneous."
Shortly after the Hawaiian bombings became known, the Tokyo government announced that Japan had entered a state of war with the United States and Great Britain as of 6 a. m. tomorrow (Monday).
As the day broke over the far Pacific, the White House announced that Japanese planes also had attacked the American-owned island naval base at Guam. Just previously the navy had told of an unidentified squadron of planes appearing over the

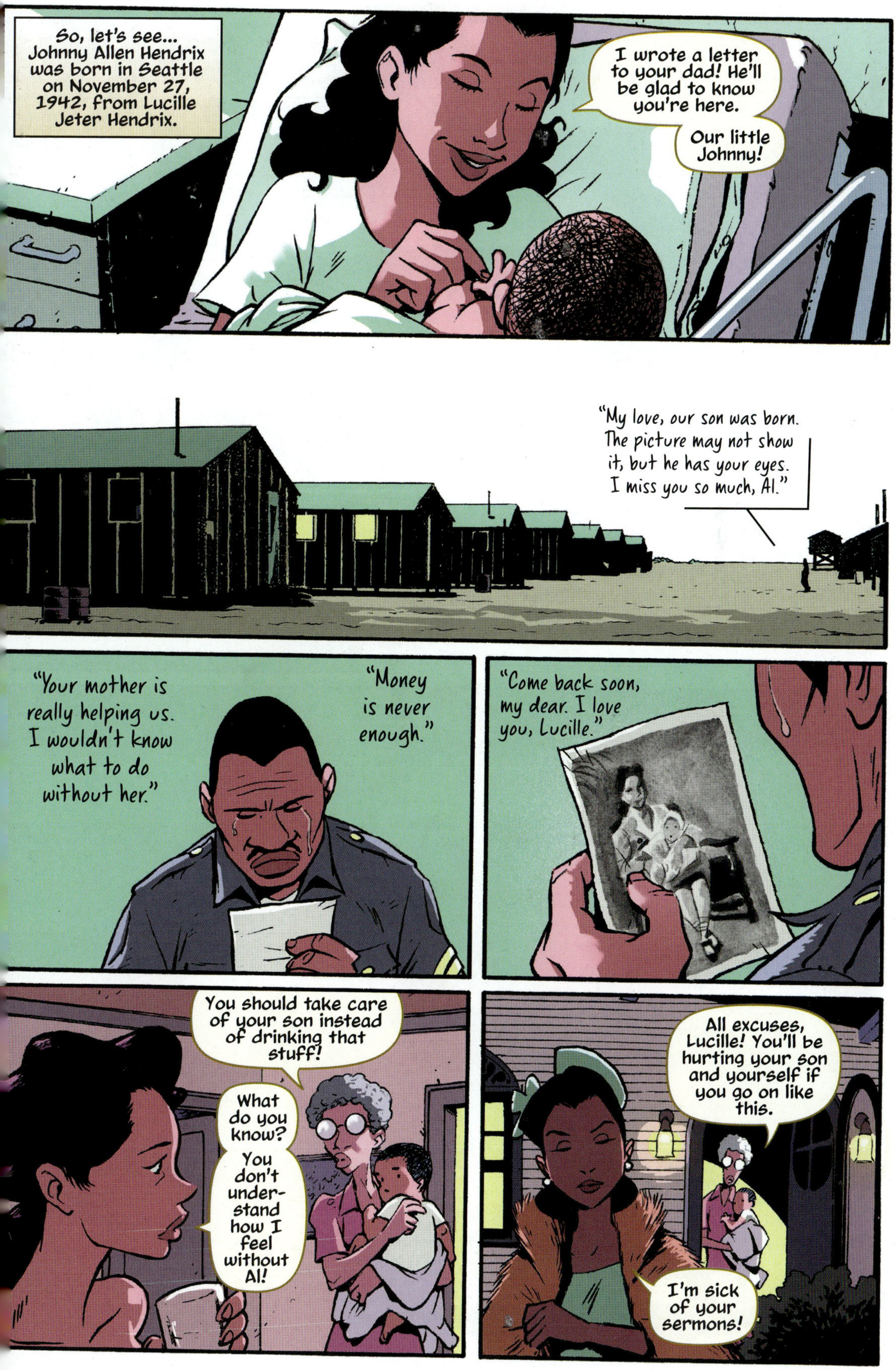
So, let's see... Johnny Allen Hendrix was born in Seattle on November 27, 1942, from Lucille Jeter Hendrix.
I wrote a letter to your dad! He'll be glad to know you're here.
Our little Johnny!
"My love, our son was born. The picture may not show it, but he has your eyes. I miss you so much, Al."
"Your mother is really helping us. I wouldn't know what to do without her."
"Money is never enough."
"Come back soon, my dear. I love you, Lucille."
You should take care of your son instead of drinking that stuff!
What do you know?
You don't under-stand how I feel without Al!
All excuses, Lucille! You'll be hurting your son and yourself if you go on like this.
I'm sick of your sermons!

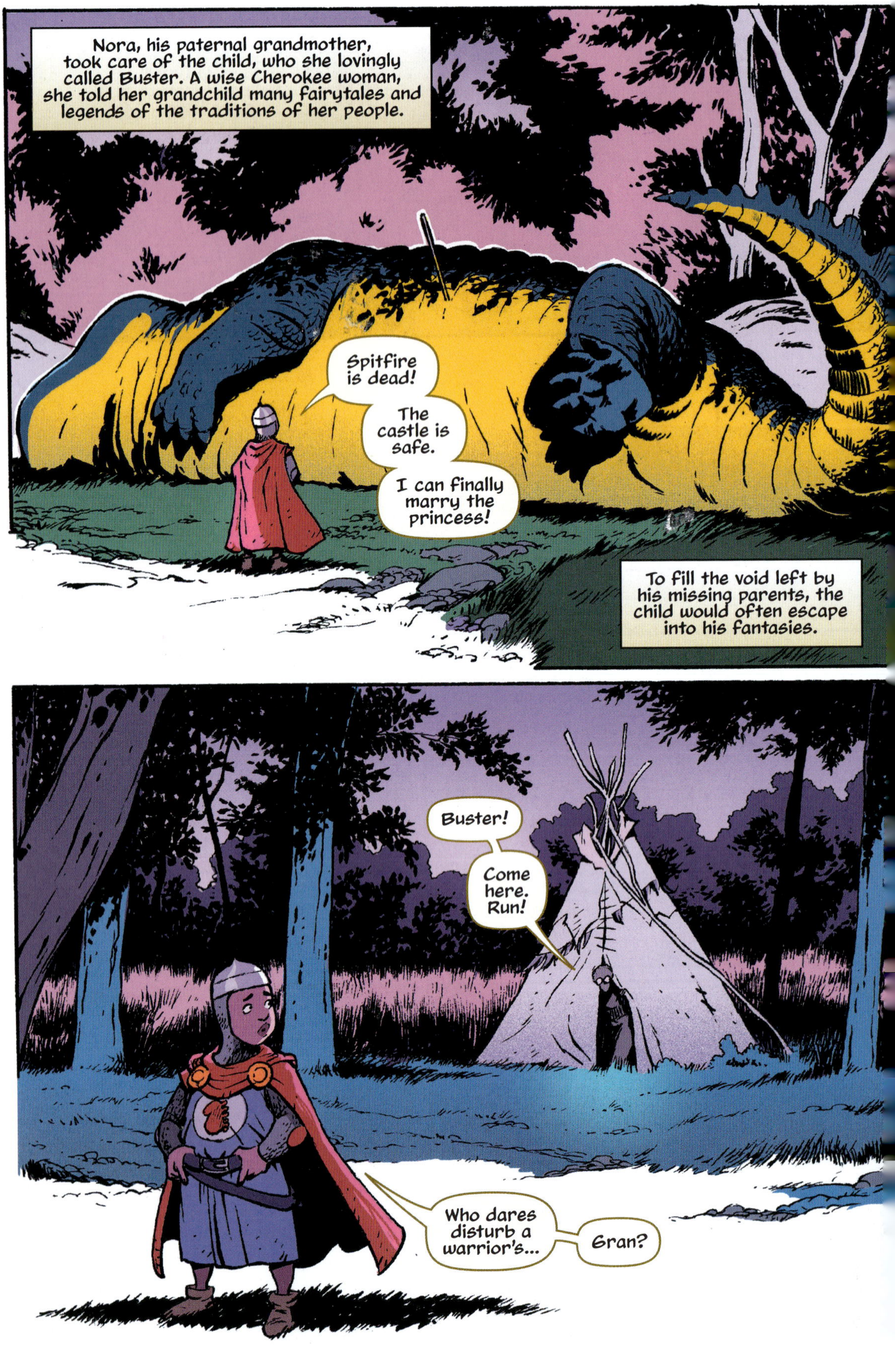

Nora, his paternal grandmother, took care of the child, who she lovingly called Buster. A wise Cherokee woman, she told her grandchild many fairytales and legends of the traditions of her people.
Spitfire is dead!
The castle is safe.
I can finally marry the princess!
To fill the void left by his missing parents, the child would often escape into his fantasies.
Buster!
Come here. Run!
Who dares disturb a warrior's...
Gran?

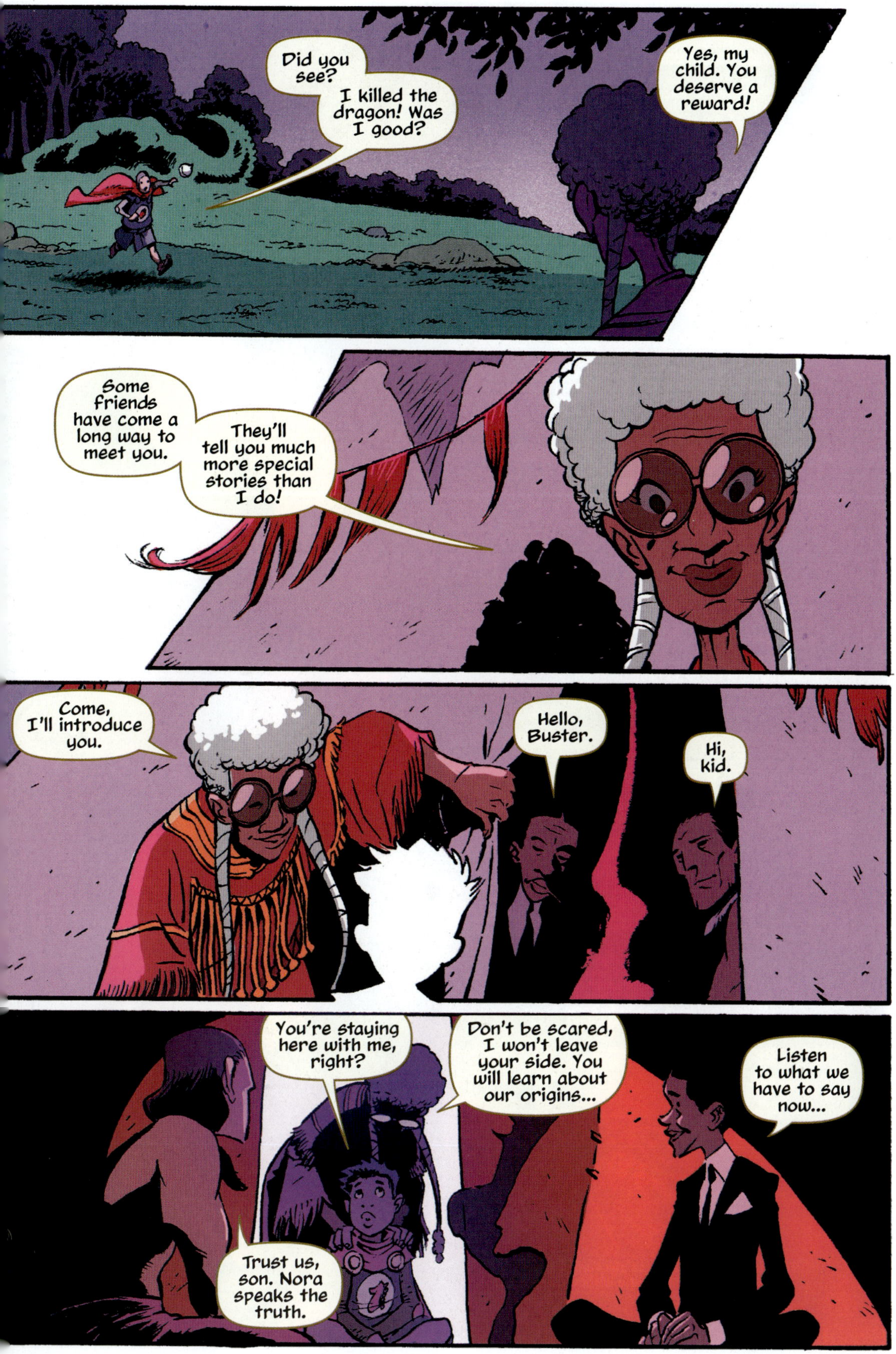
Did you see?
I killed the dragon! Was I good?
Yes, my child. You deserve a reward!
Some friends have come a long way to meet you.
They'll tell you much more special stories than I do!
Come, I'll introduce you.
Hello, Buster.
Hi, kid.
You're staying here with me, right?
Don't be scared, I won't leave your side. You will learn about our origins...
Listen to what we have to say now...
Trust us, son. Nora speaks the truth.

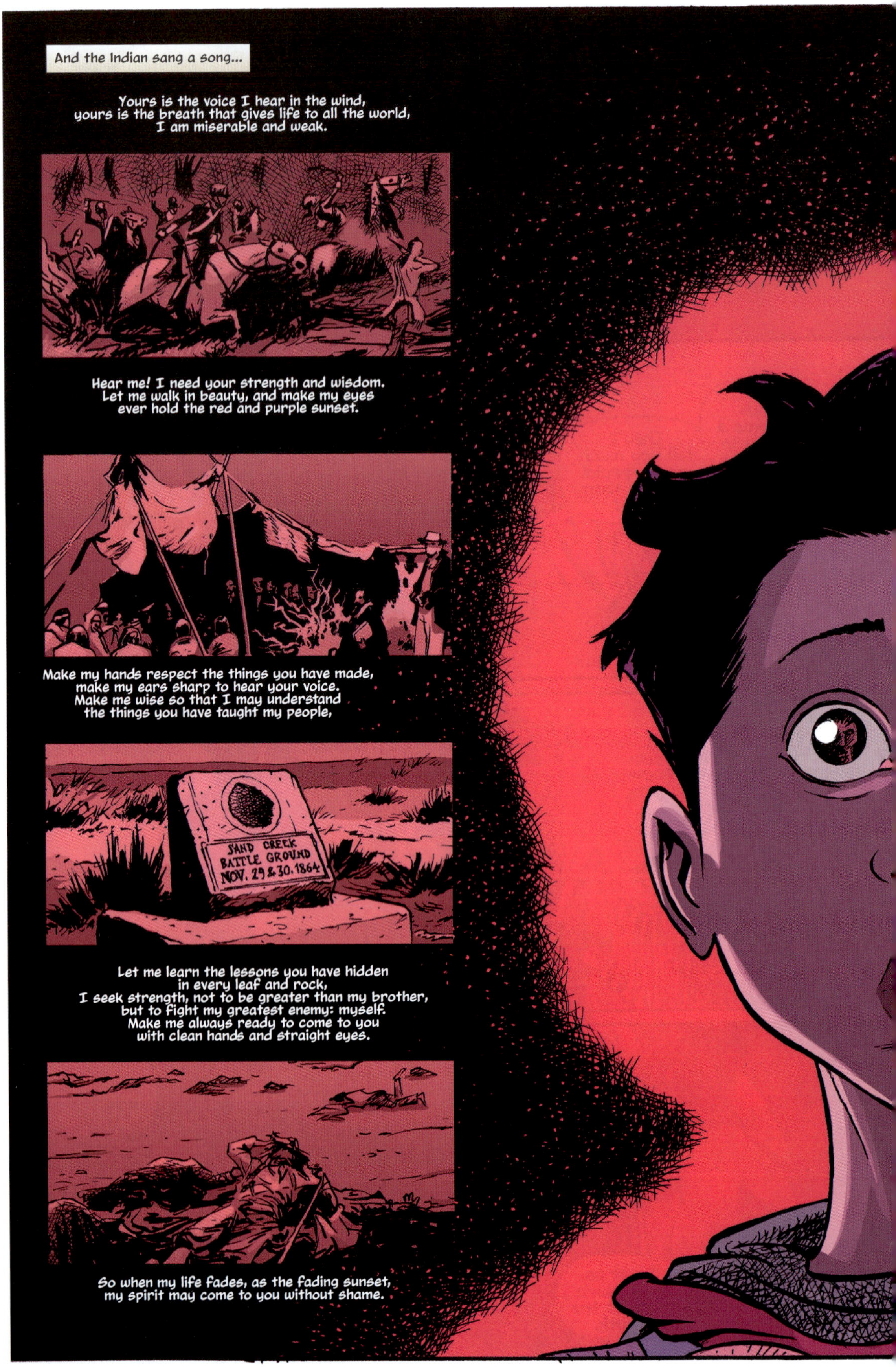
And the Indian sang a song...
Yours is the voice I hear in the wind, yours is the breath that gives life to all the world, I am miserable and weak.
Hear me! I need your strength and wisdom. Let me walk in beauty, and make my eyes ever hold the red and purple sunset.
Make my hands respect the things you have made, make my ears sharp to hear your voice. Make me wise so that I may understand the things you have taught my people,
SAND CREEK BATTLE GROUND NOV. 29 & 30. 1864
Let me learn the lessons you have hidden in every leaf and rock, I seek strength, not to be greater than my brother, but to fight my greatest enemy: myself. Make me always ready to come to you with clean hands and straight eyes.
So when my life fades, as the fading sunset, my spirit may come to you without shame.

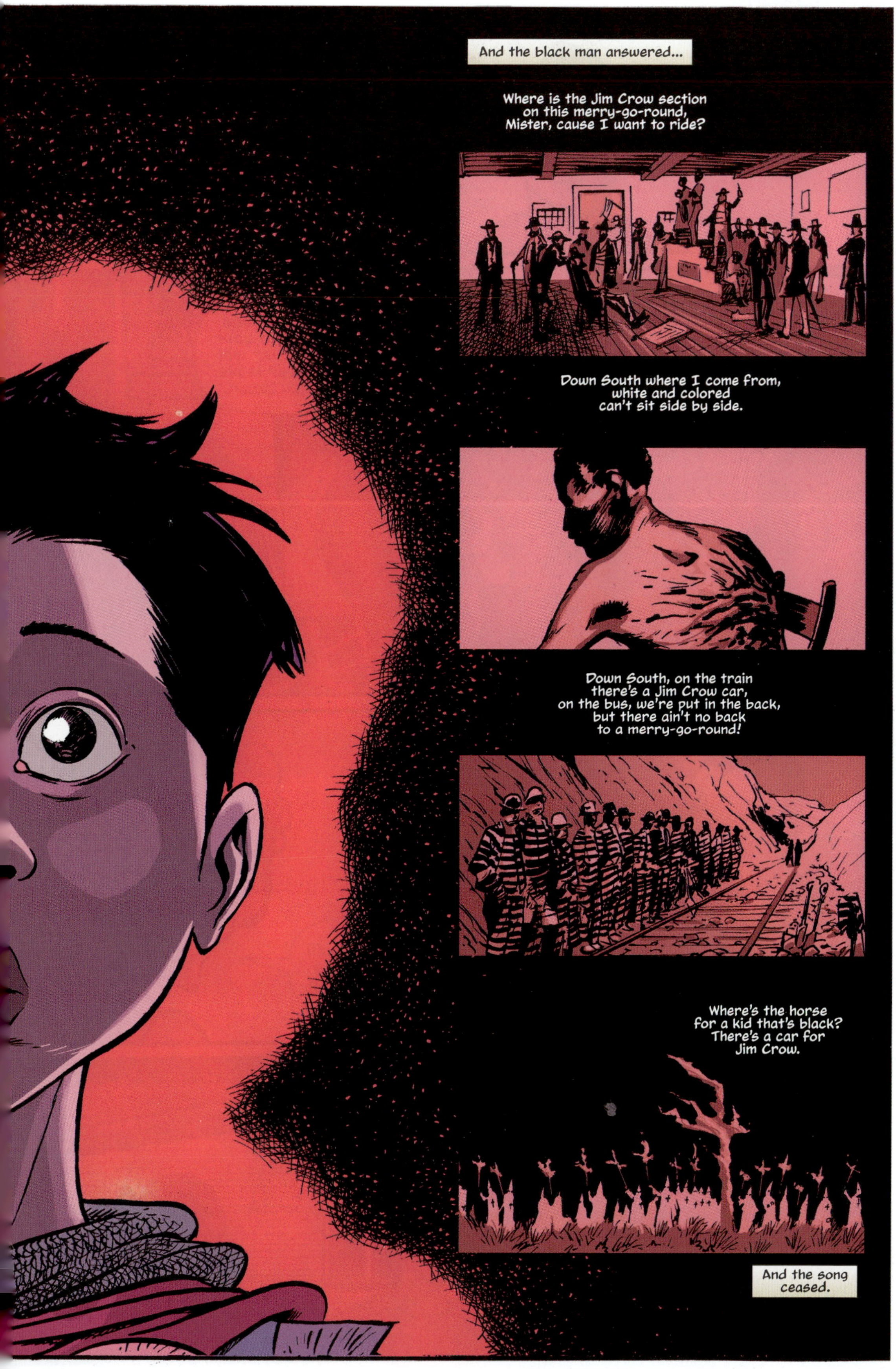
And the black man answered...
Where is the Jim Crow section on this merry-go-round, Mister, cause I want to ride?
Down South where I come from, white and colored can't sit side by side.
Down South, on the train there's a Jim Crow car, on the bus, we're put in the back, but there ain't no back to a merry-go-round!
Where's the horse for a kid that's black? There's a car for Jim Crow.
And the song ceased.

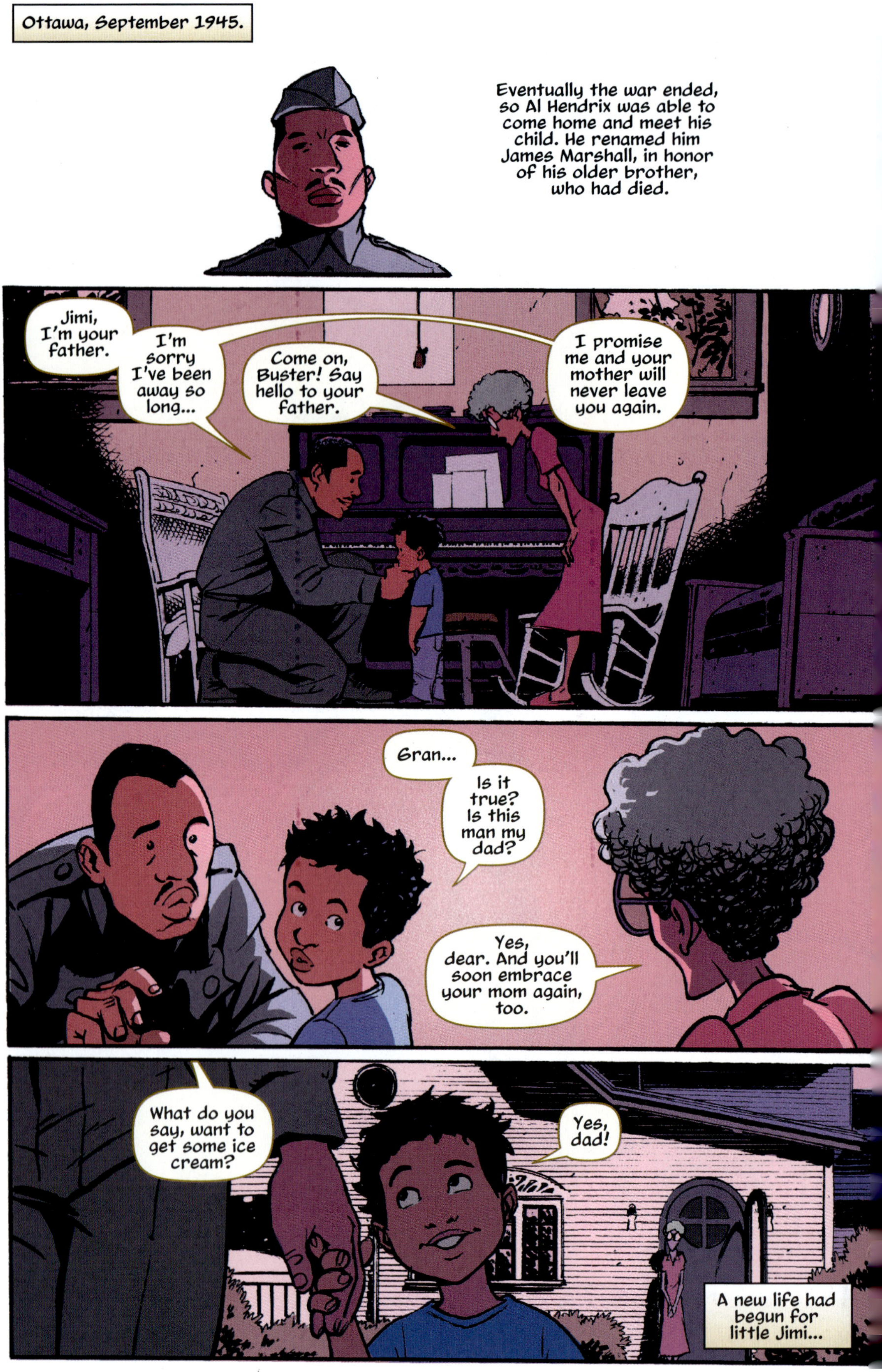
Ottawa, September 1945.
Eventually the war ended, so Al Hendrix was able to come home and meet his child. He renamed him James Marshall, in honor of his older brother, who had died.
Jimi, I'm your father.
I'm sorry I've been away so long...
Come on, Buster! Say hello to your father.
I promise me and your mother will never leave you again.
Gran...
Is it true? Is this man my dad?
Yes, dear. And you'll soon embrace your mom again, too.
What do you say, want to get some ice cream?
Yes, dad!
A new life had begun for little Jimi...

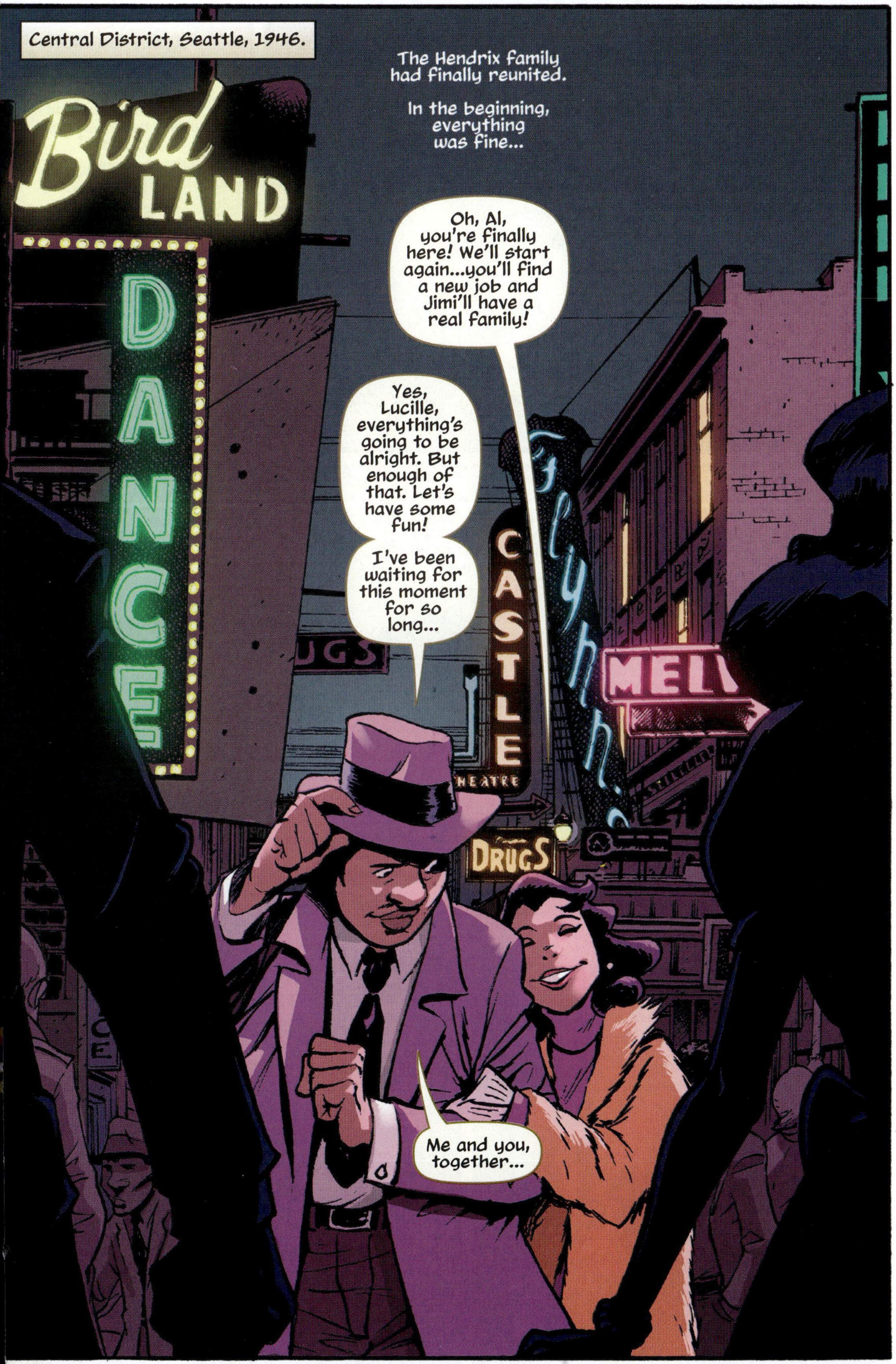
Central District, Seattle, 1946.
The Hendrix family had finally reunited.
In the beginning, everything was fine...
Bird LAND
DANCE
Oh, Al, you're finally here! We'll start again...you'll find a new job and Jimi'll have a real family!
Yes, Lucille, everything's going to be alright. But enough of that. Let's have some fun!
I've been waiting for this moment for so long...
CASTLE
DRUGS
MEL
Me and you, together...

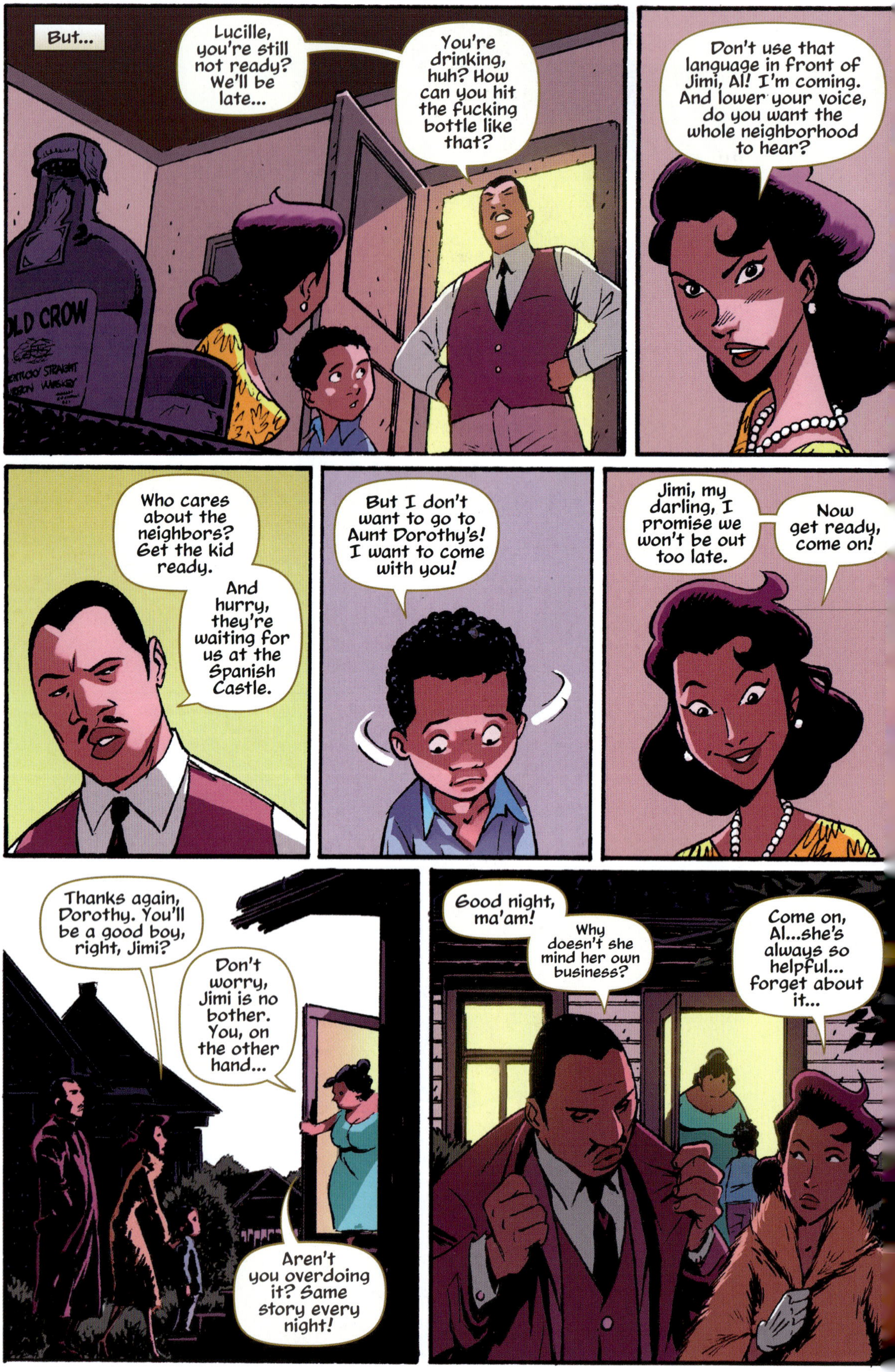
But...
Lucille, you're still not ready? We'll be late...
You're drinking, huh? How can you hit the fucking bottle like that?
Don't use that language in front of Jimi, Al! I'm coming. And lower your voice, do you want the whole neighborhood to hear?
Who cares about the neighbors? Get the kid ready.
And hurry, they're waiting for us at the Spanish Castle.
But I don't want to go to Aunt Dorothy's! I want to come with you!
Jimi, my darling, I promise we won't be out too late.
Now get ready, come on!
Thanks again, Dorothy. You'll be a good boy, right, Jimi?
Don't worry, Jimi is no bother. You, on the other hand...
Aren't you overdoing it? Same story every night!
Good night, ma'am!
Why doesn't she mind her own business?
Come on, Al...she's always so helpful... forget about it...

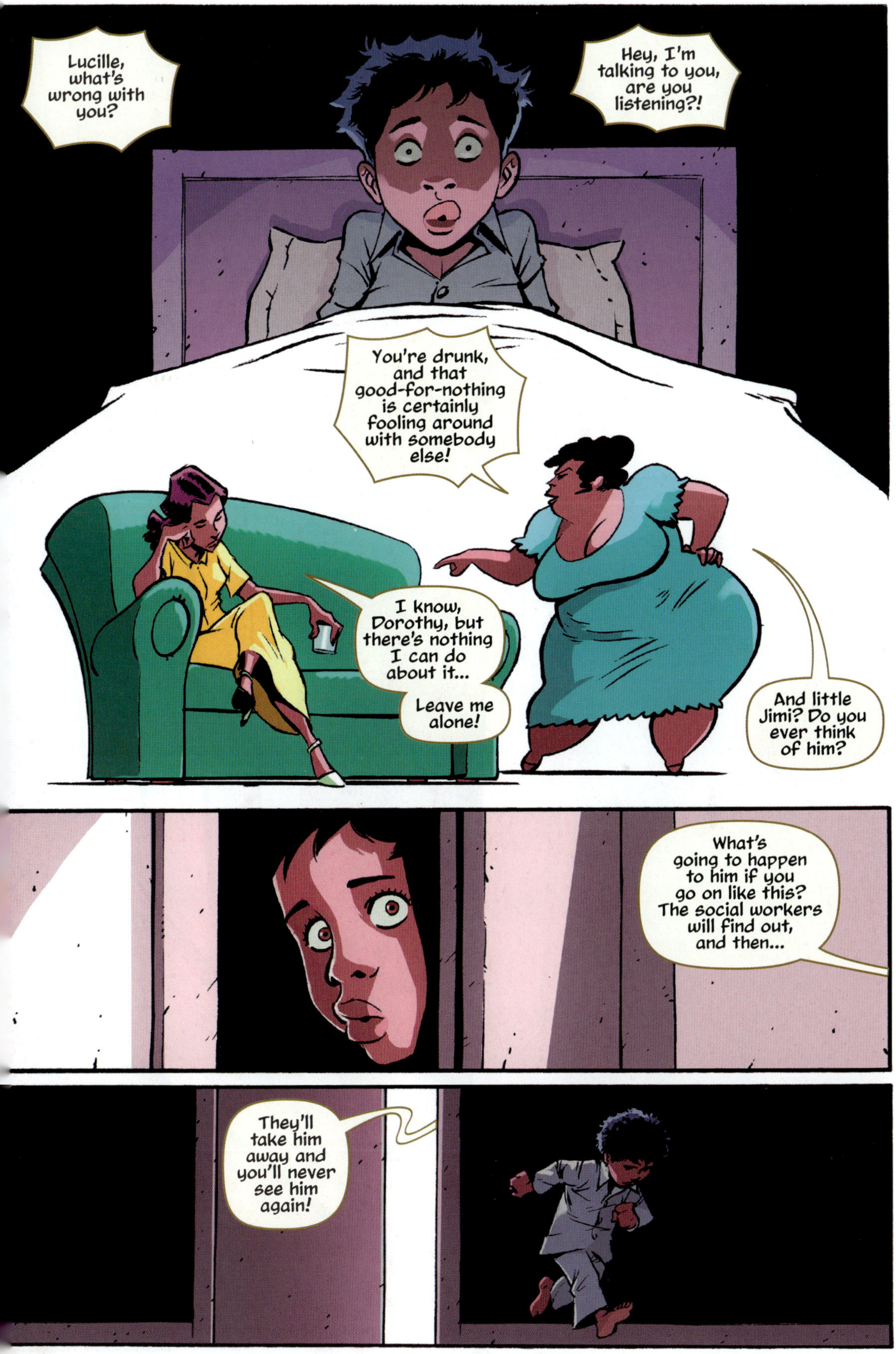
Lucille, what's wrong with you?
Hey, I'm talking to you, are you listening?!
You're drunk, and that good-for-nothing is certainly fooling around with somebody else!
I know, Dorothy, but there's nothing I can do about it...
Leave me alone!
And little Jimi? Do you ever think of him?
What's going to happen to him if you go on like this? The social workers will find out, and then...
They'll take him away and you'll never see him again!

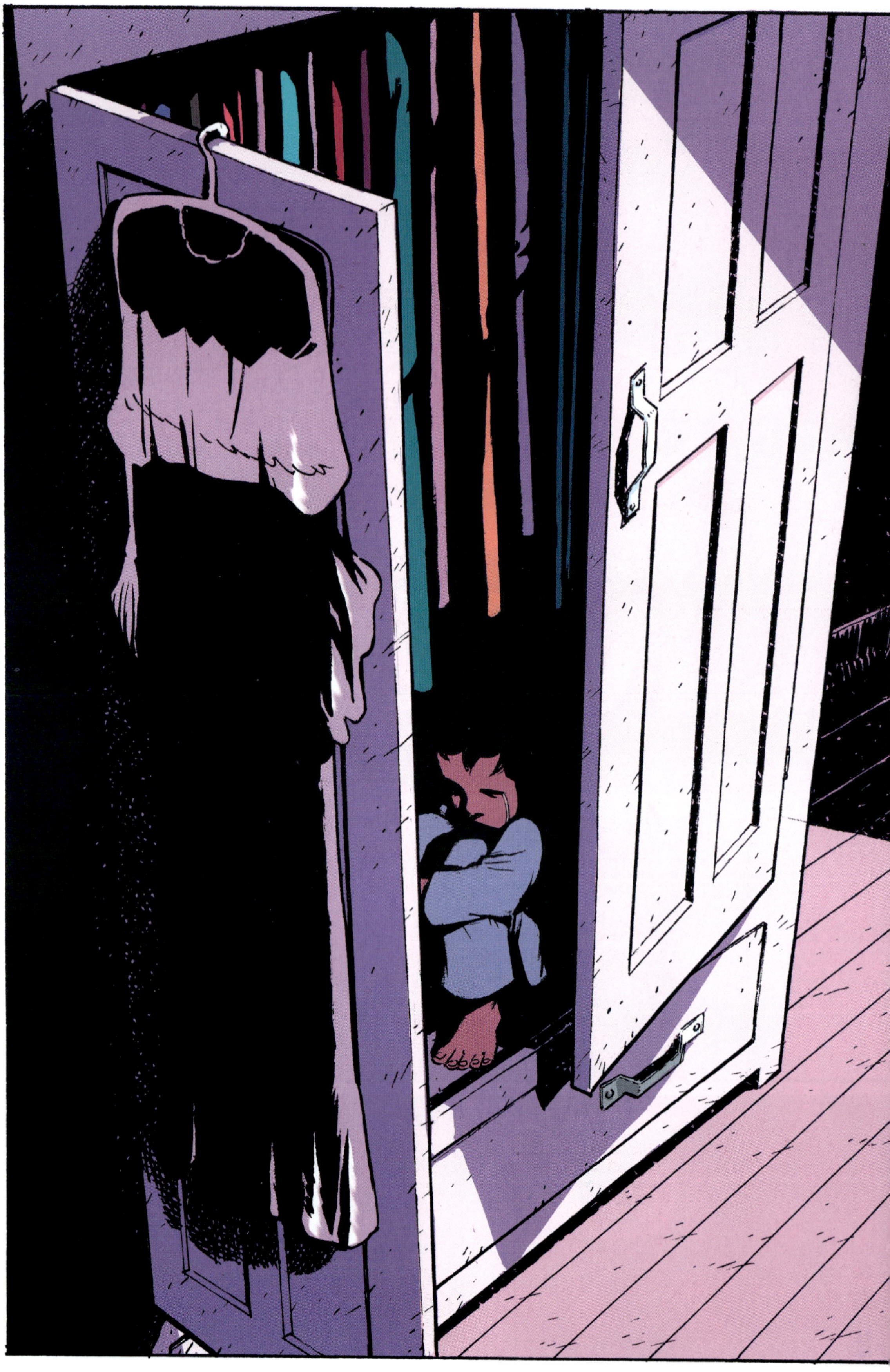

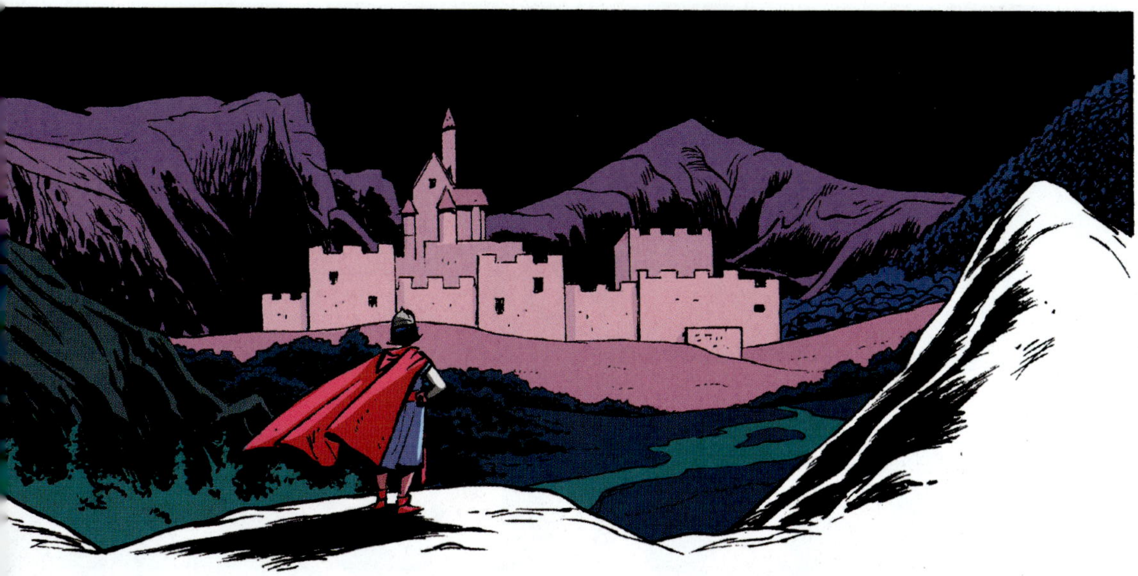

So one night our hero escaped his neighbor's care to find out what could be so special about the place that was keeping his mom away from him. Young Jimi was looking for his family, but didn't expect to find so much more at the end of the quest that would take him to the...

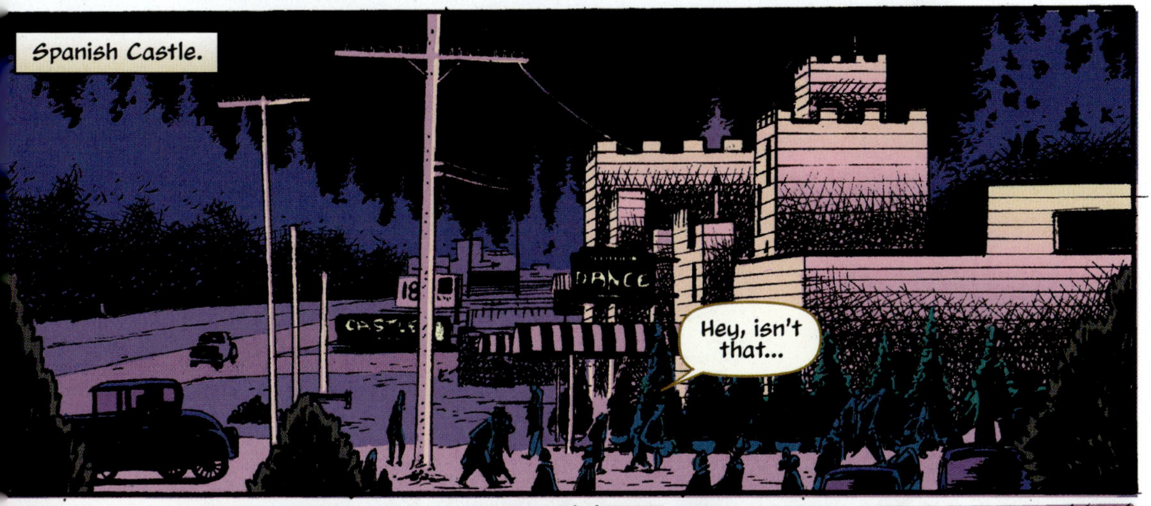
Spanish Castle.
DANCE
CASTLE
Hey, isn't that...

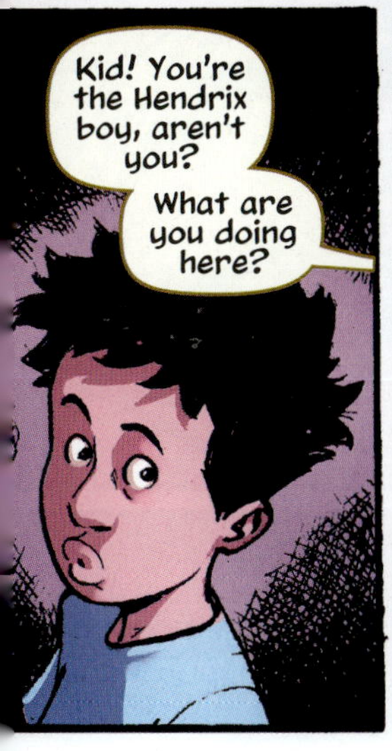
Kid! You're the Hendrix boy, aren't you?
What are you doing here?

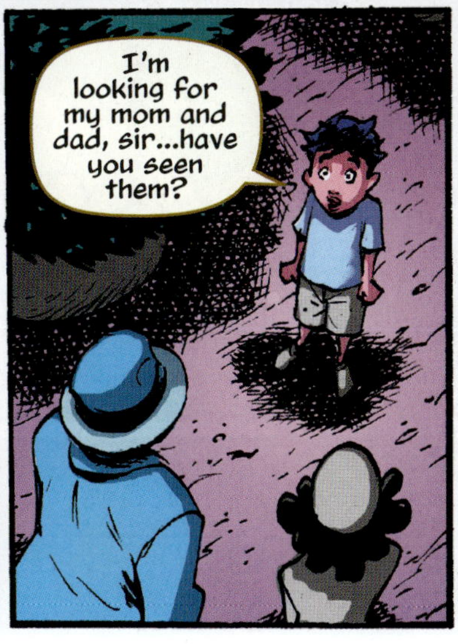
I'm looking for my mom and dad, sir...have you seen them?

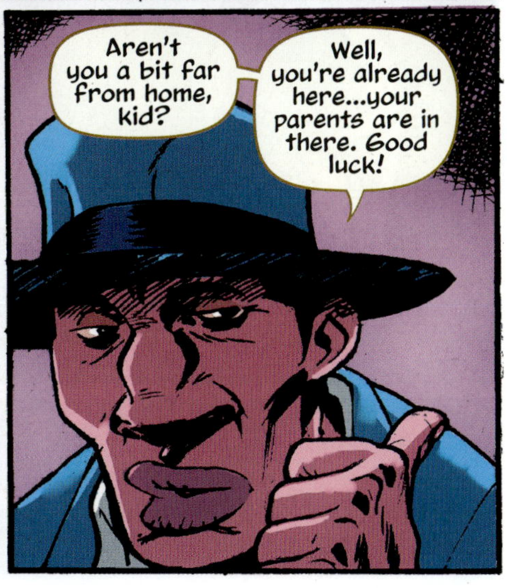
Aren't you a bit far from home, kid?
Well, you're already here...your parents are in there. Good luck!

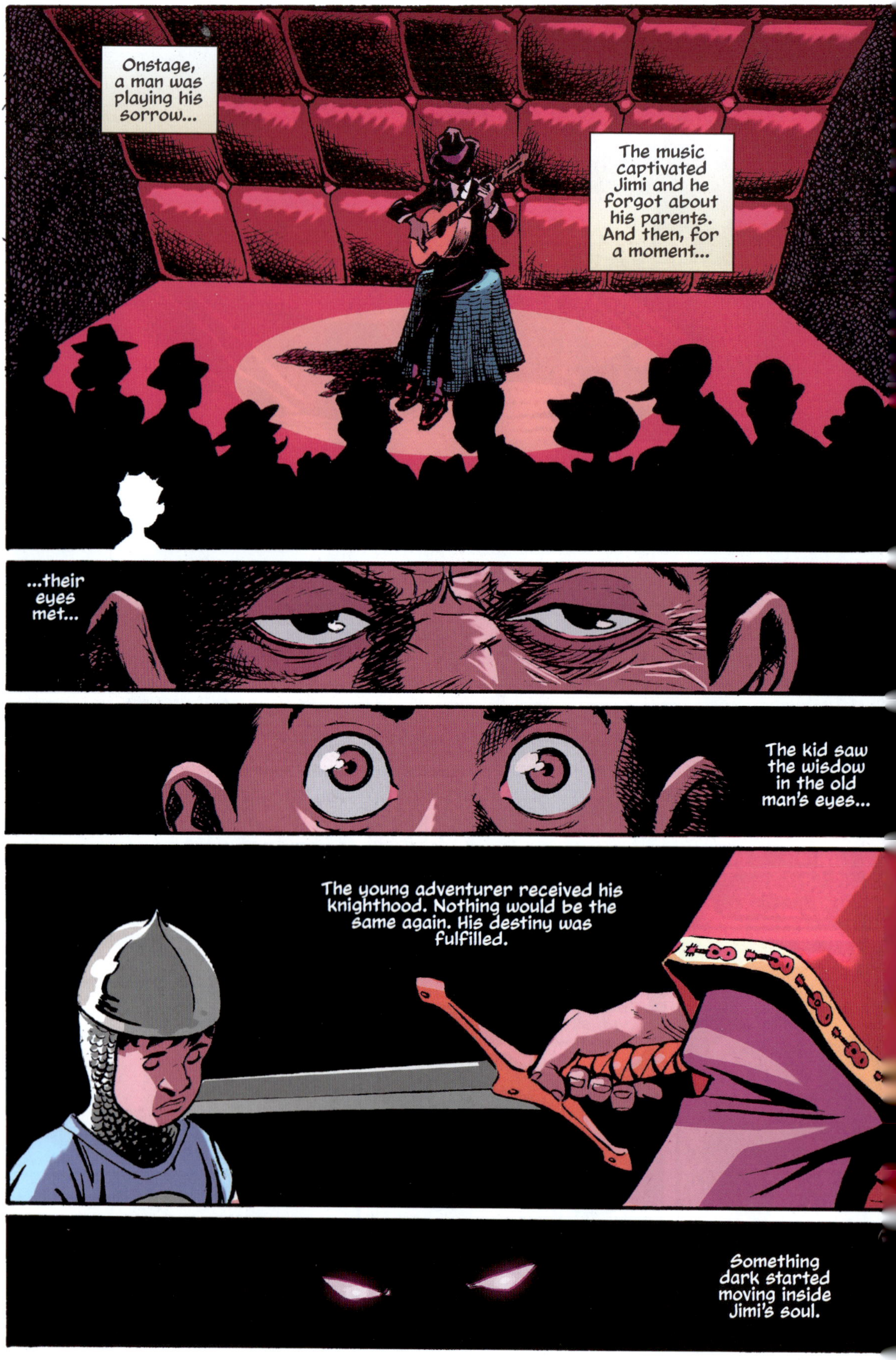
Onstage, a man was playing his sorrow...
The music captivated Jimi and he forgot about his parents. And then, for a moment...
...their eyes met...
The kid saw the wisdow in the old man's eyes...
The young adventurer received his knighthood. Nothing would be the same again. His destiny was fulfilled.
Something dark started moving inside Jimi's soul.

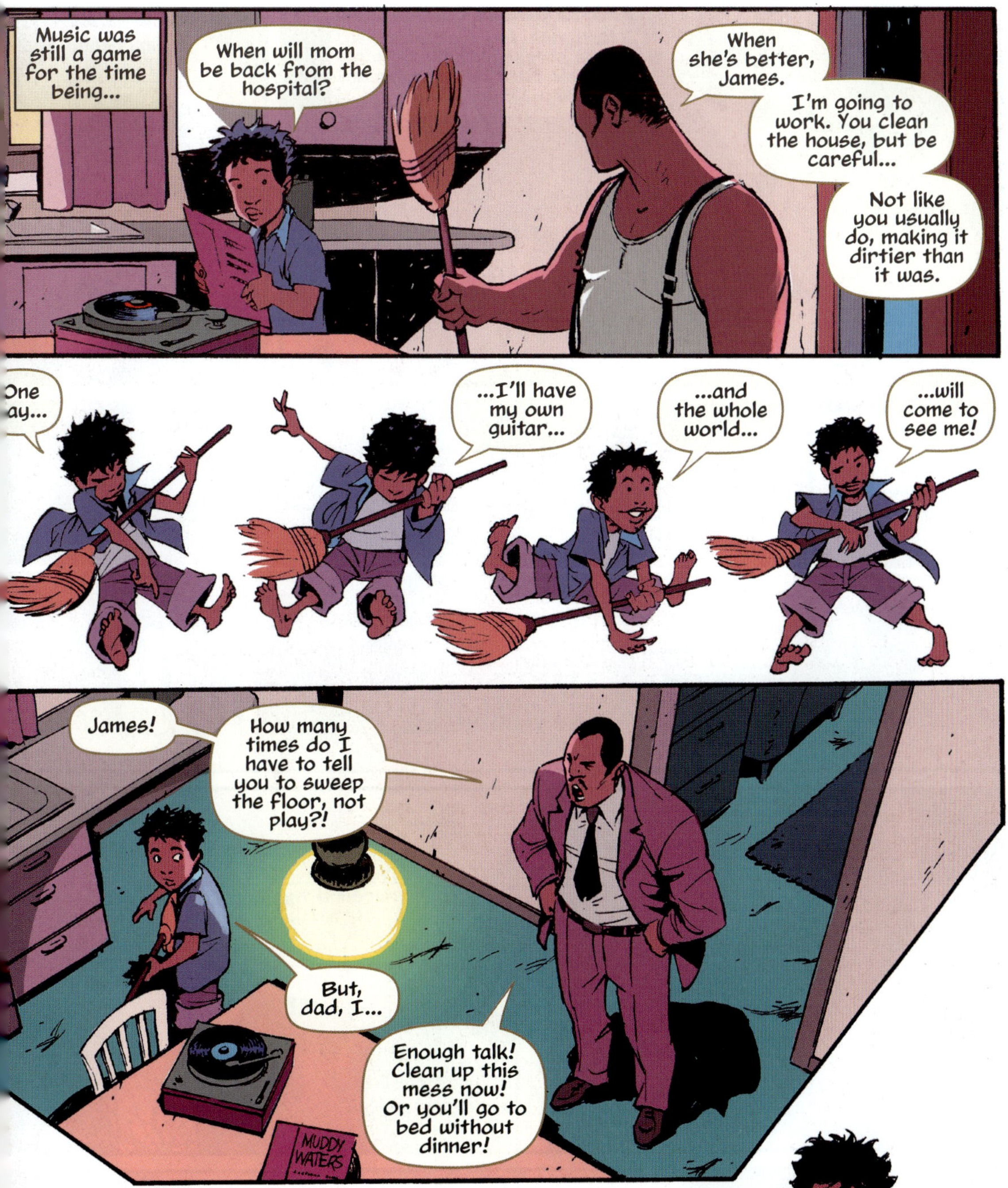

Music was still a game for the time being...
When will mom be back from the hospital?
When she's better, James.
I'm going to work. You clean the house, but be careful...
Not like you usually do, making it dirtier than it was.
One ay...
...I'll have my own guitar...
...and the whole world...
...will come to see me!
James!
How many times do I have to tell you to sweep the floor, not play?!
But, dad, I...
Enough talk! Clean up this mess now! Or you'll go to bed without dinner!
MUDDY WATERS


Eventually, Al did give his son a guitar. He taught him the basics and played along with his sax. They were trying to cure the pain of the absence of Jimi's mother, who was hospitalized because of her drinking problem.

She would never fully recover. But Jimi didn't know that yet. And day after day, music became his best friend, and his weapon of choice...

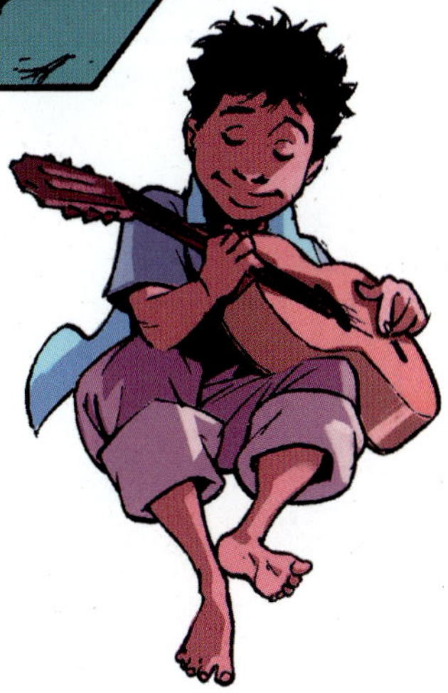

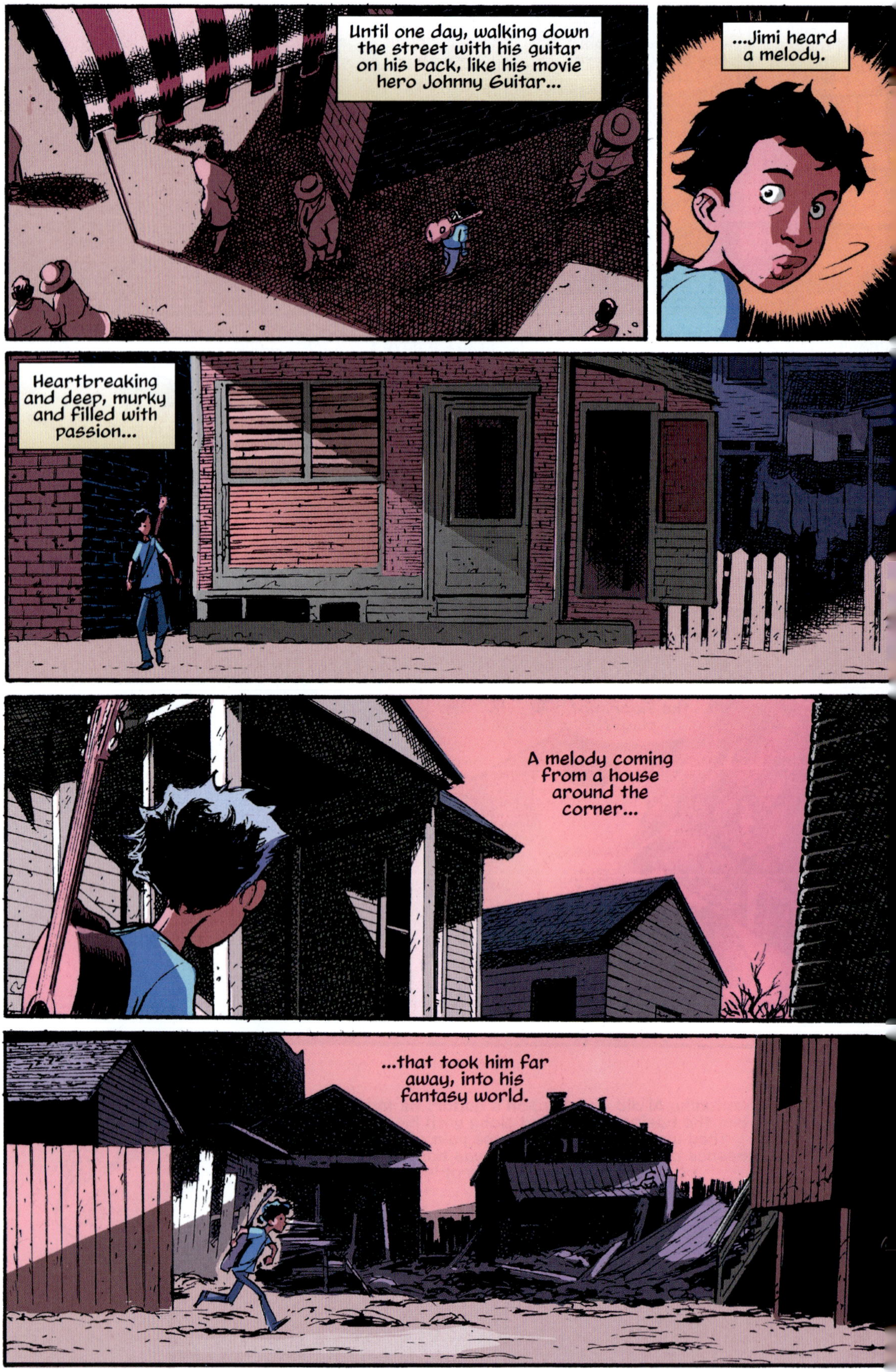
Until one day, walking down the street with his guitar on his back, like his movie hero Johnny Guitar...
...Jimi heard a melody.
Heartbreaking and deep, murky and filled with passion...
A melody coming from a house around the corner...
...that took him far away, into his fantasy world.

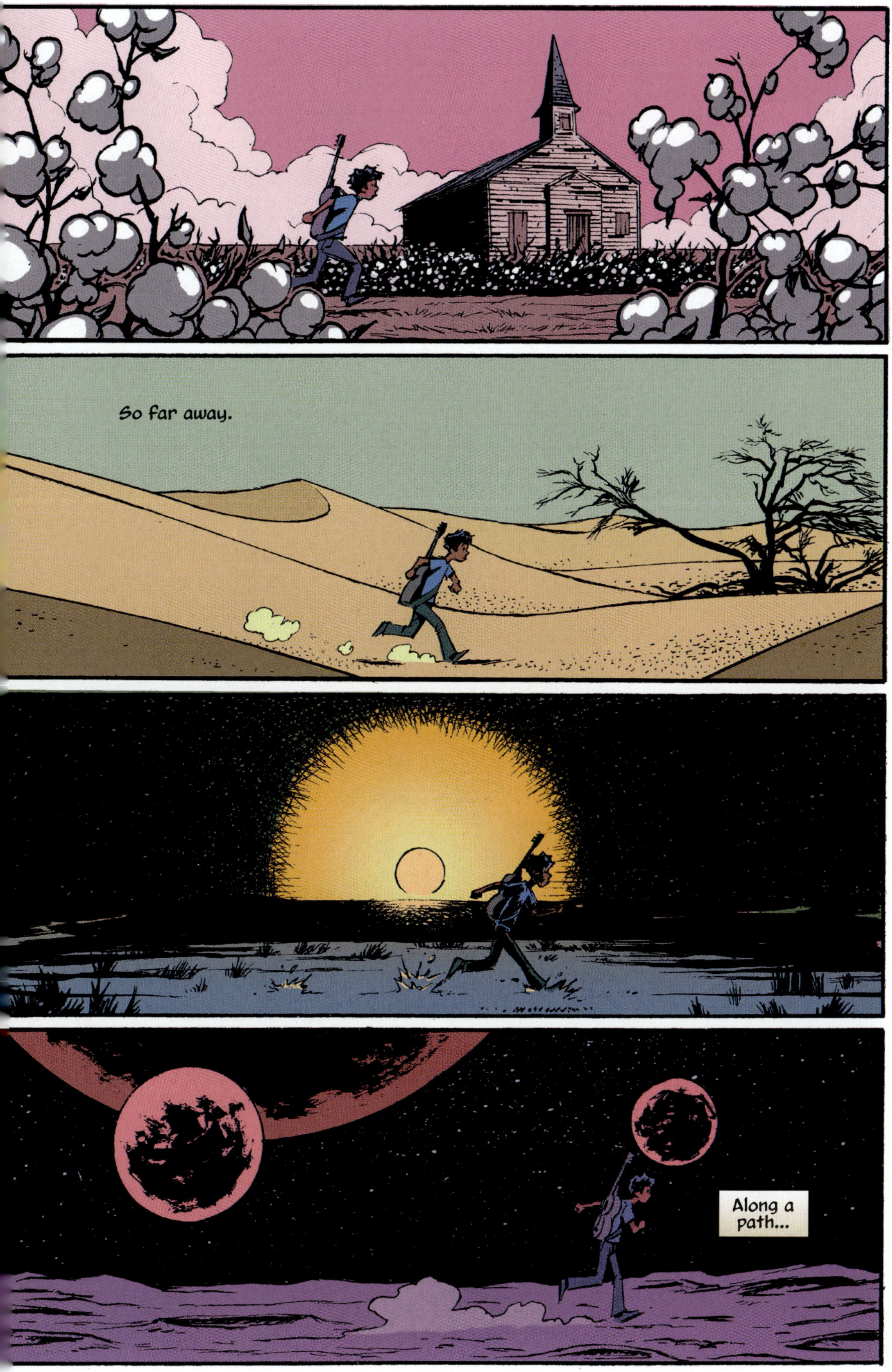
So far away.
Along a path...

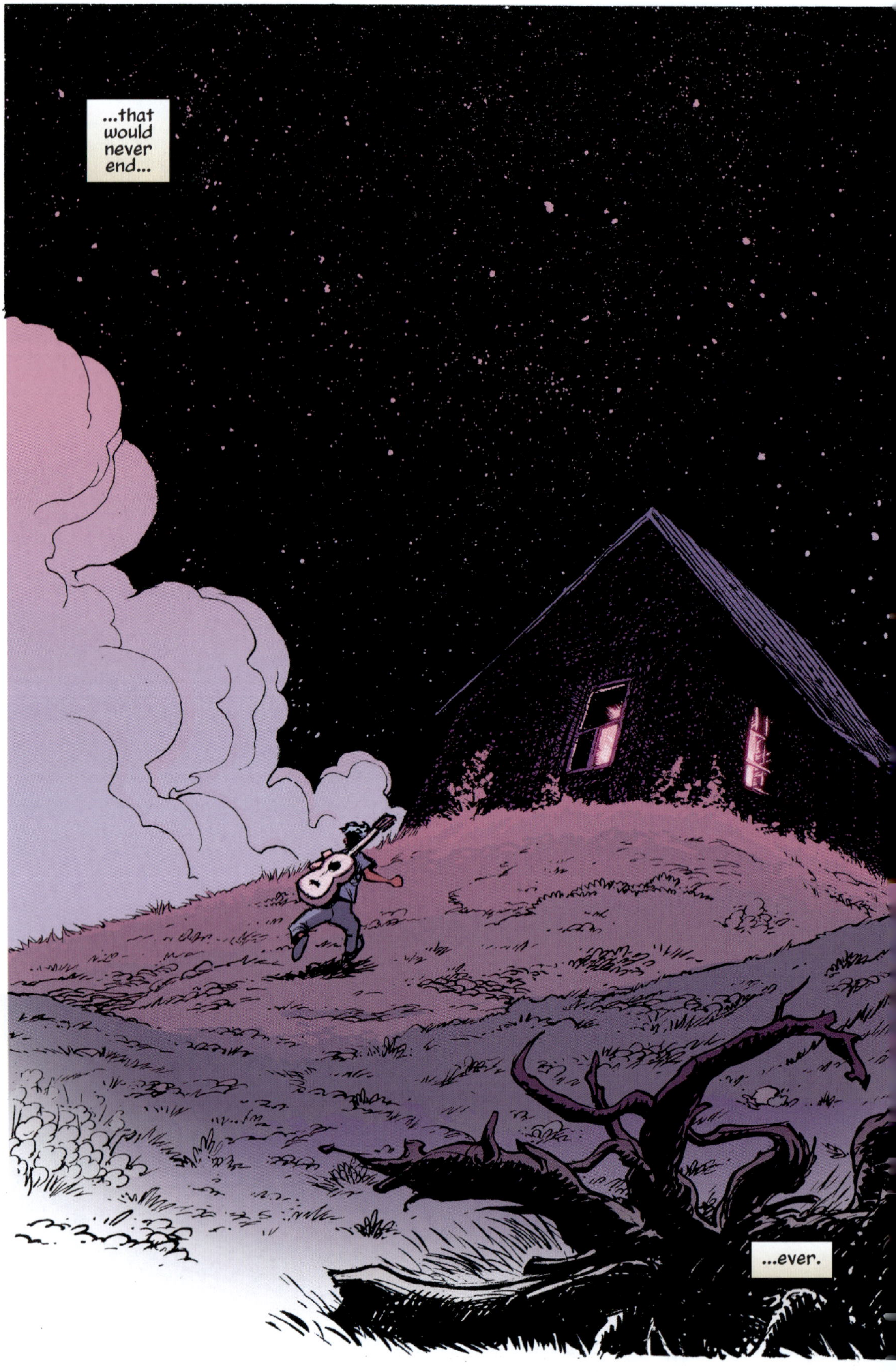
...that would never end...
...ever.

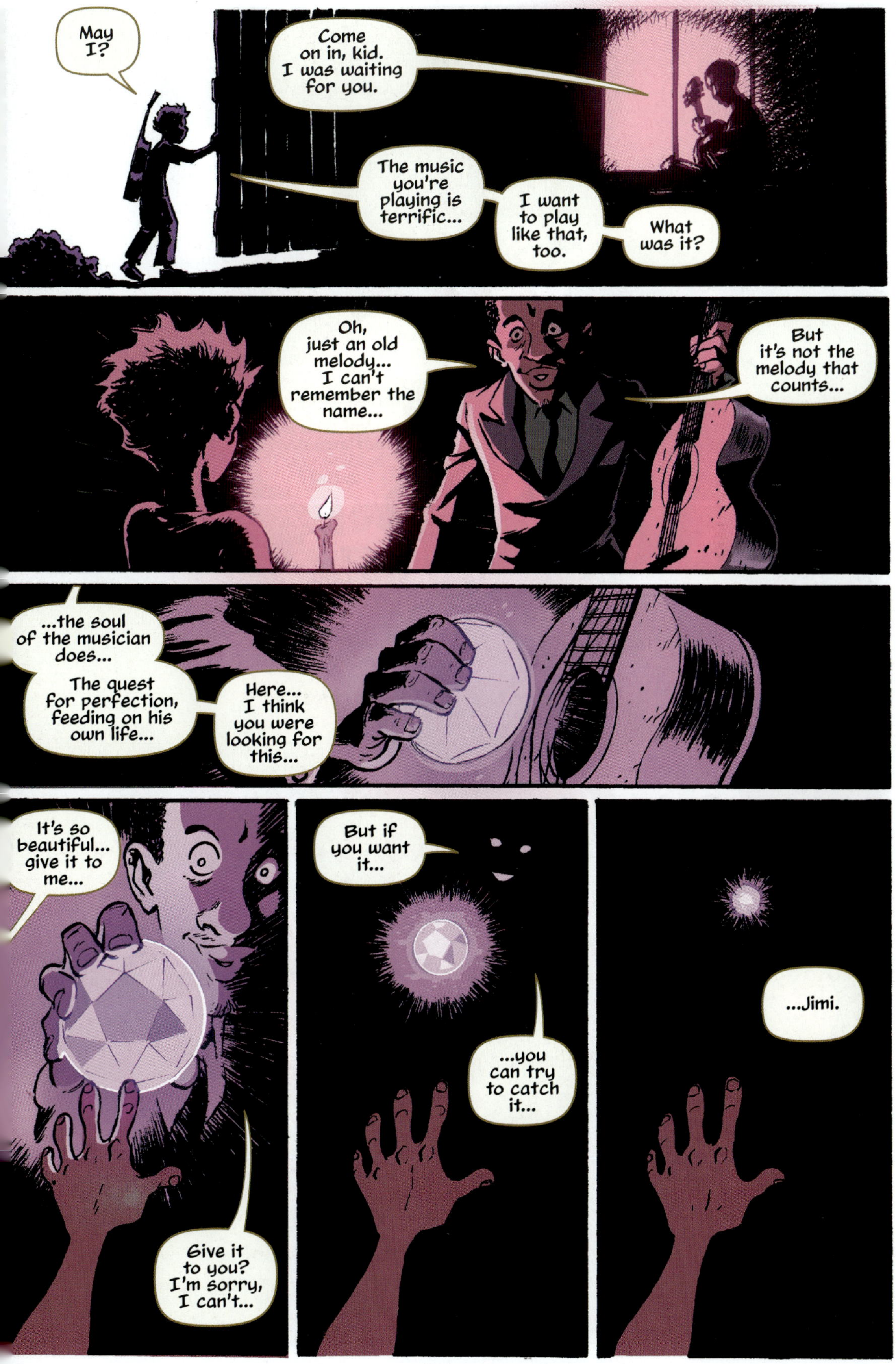
May I?
Come on in, kid. I was waiting for you.
The music you're playing is terrific...
I want to play like that, too.
What was it?
Oh, just an old melody... I can't remember the name...
But it's not the melody that counts...
...the soul of the musician does...
The quest for perfection, feeding on his own life...
Here... I think you were looking for this...
It's so beautiful... give it to me...
Give it to you? I'm sorry, I can't...
But if you want it...
...you can try to catch it...
...Jimi.

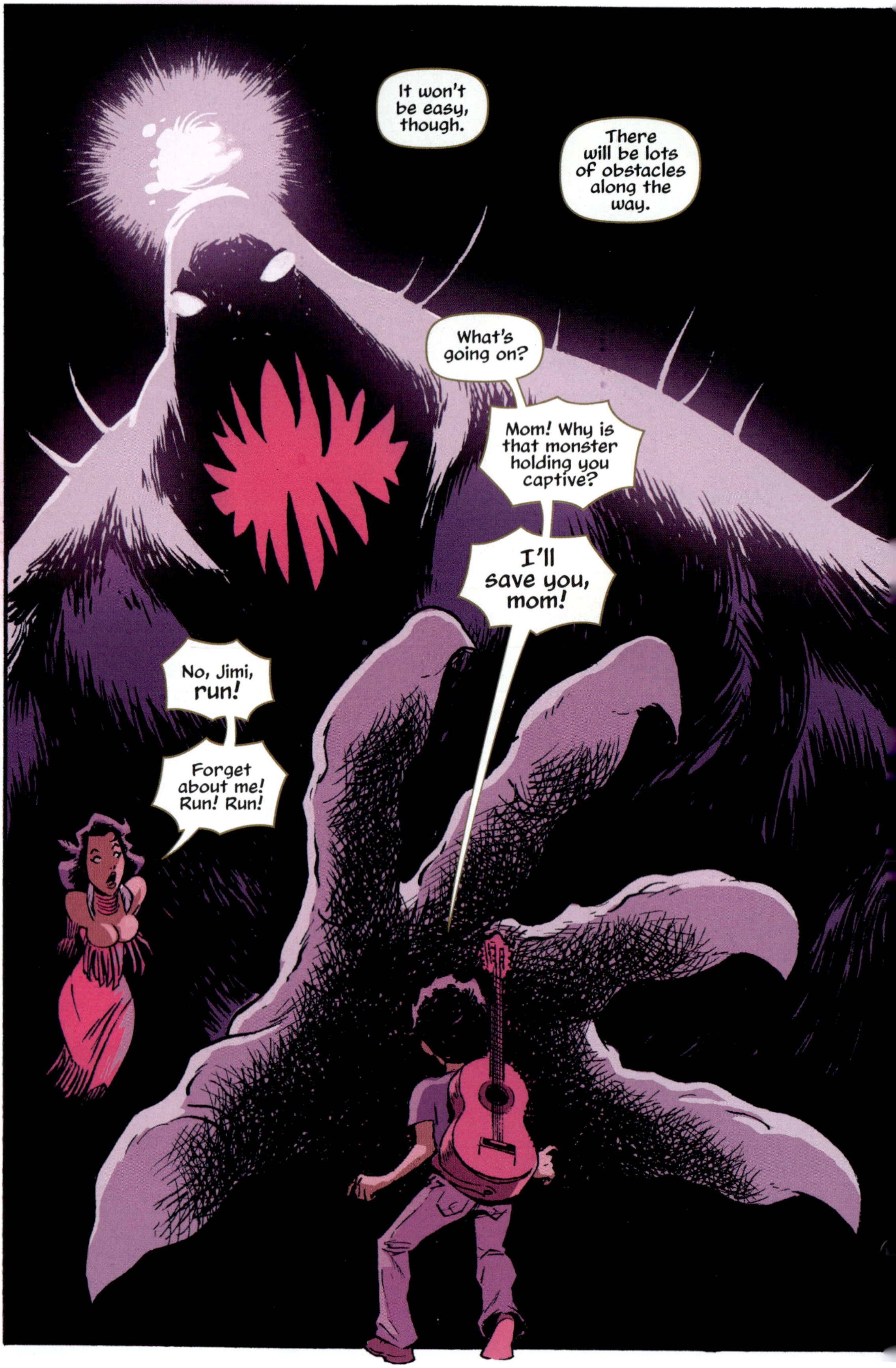
It won't be easy, though.
There will be lots of obstacles along the way.
What's going on?
Mom! Why is that monster holding you captive?
I'll save you, mom!
No, Jimi, run!
Forget about me! Run! Run!

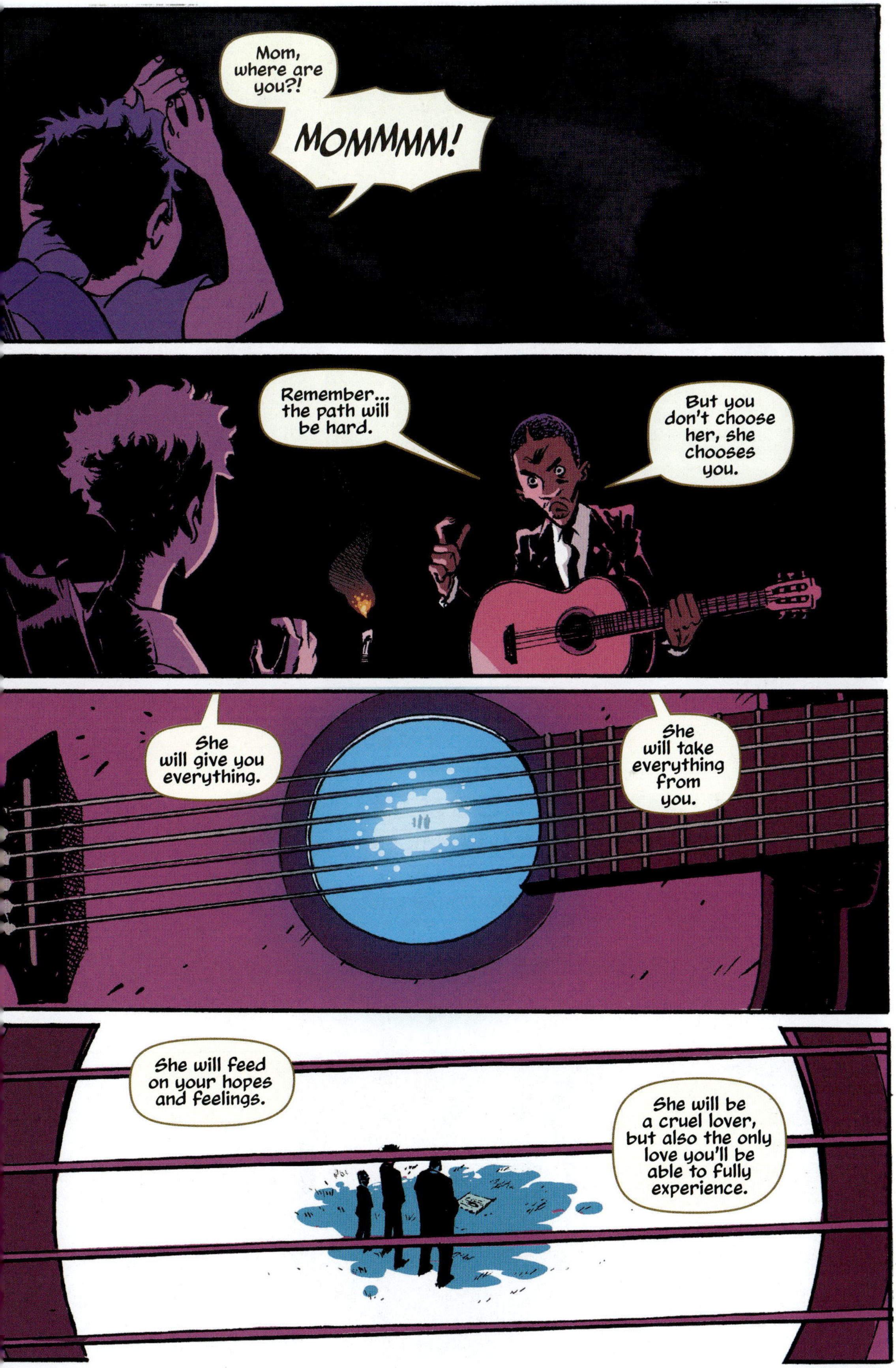
Mom, where are you?!
MOMMMM!
Remember... the path will be hard.
But you don't choose her, she chooses you.
She will give you everything.
She will take everything from you.
She will feed on your hopes and feelings.
She will be a cruel lover, but also the only love you'll be able to fully experience.

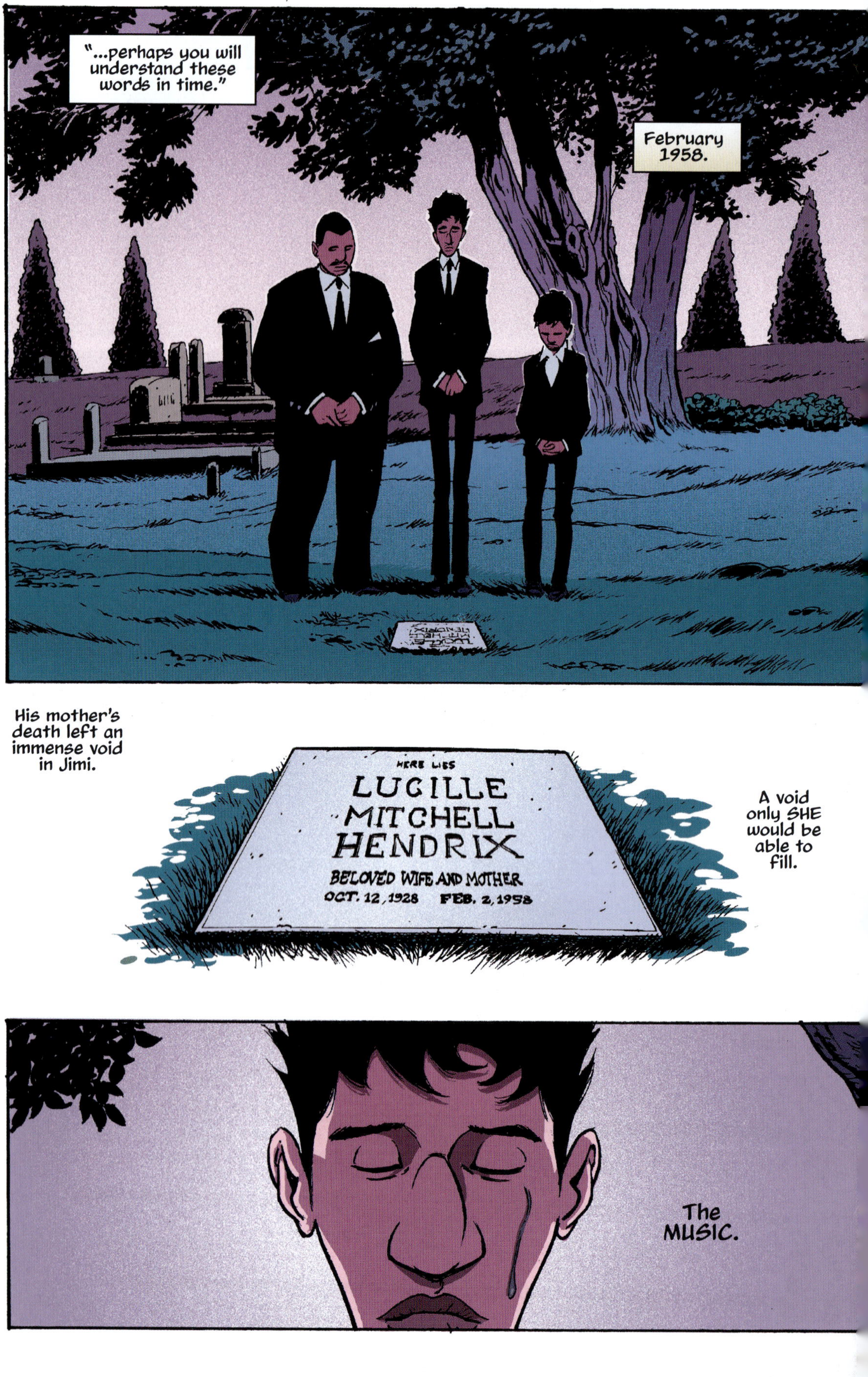
"...perhaps you will understand these words in time."
February 1958.
His mother's death left an immense void in Jimi.
HERE LIES
LUCILLE
MITCHELL
HENDRIX
BELOVED WIFE AND MOTHER
OCT. 12, 1928 FEB. 2, 1958
A void only SHE would be able to fill.
The MUSIC.

# 02.

# CROSSTOWN TRAFFIC

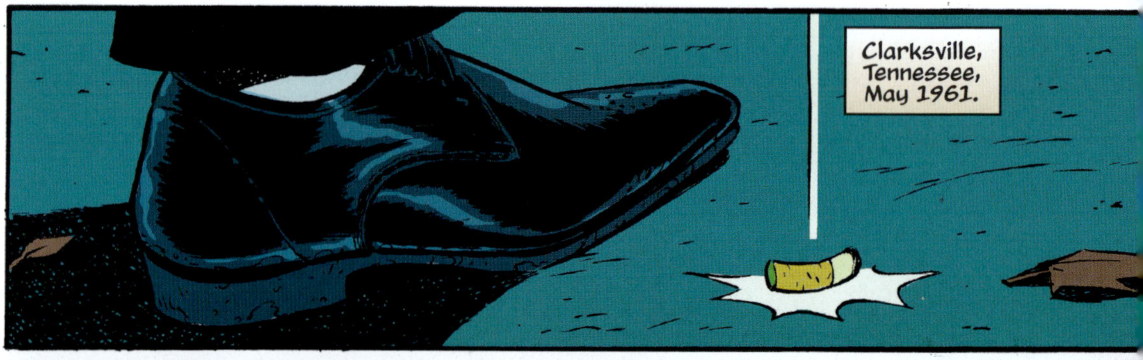
Clarksville, Tennessee, May 1961.

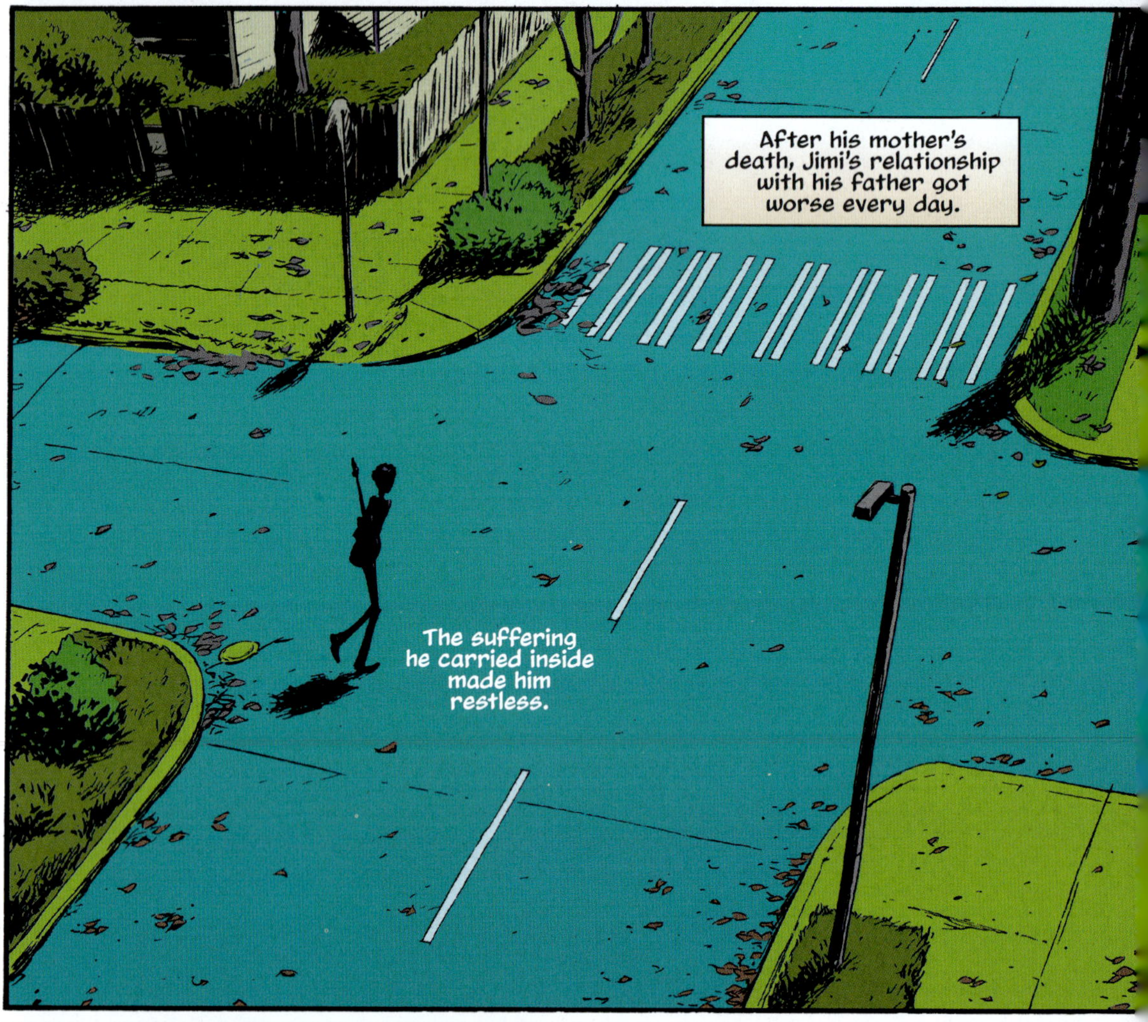
After his mother's death, Jimi's relationship with his father got worse every day.
The suffering he carried inside made him restless.

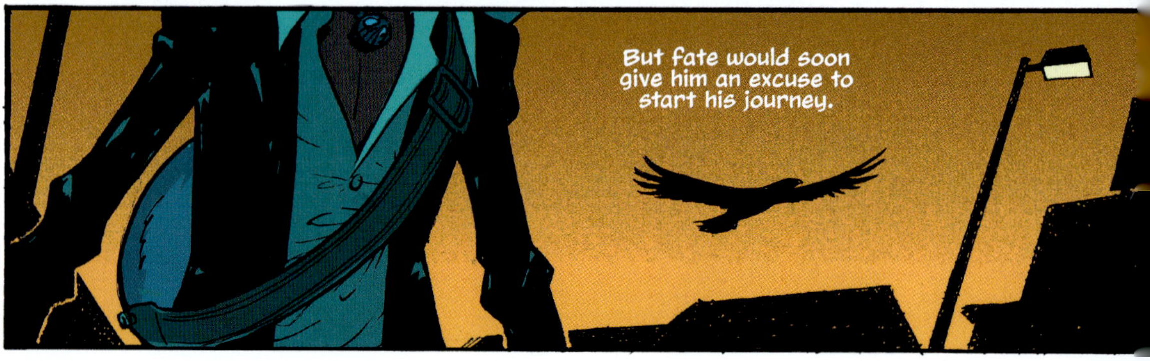
But fate would soon give him an excuse to start his journey.

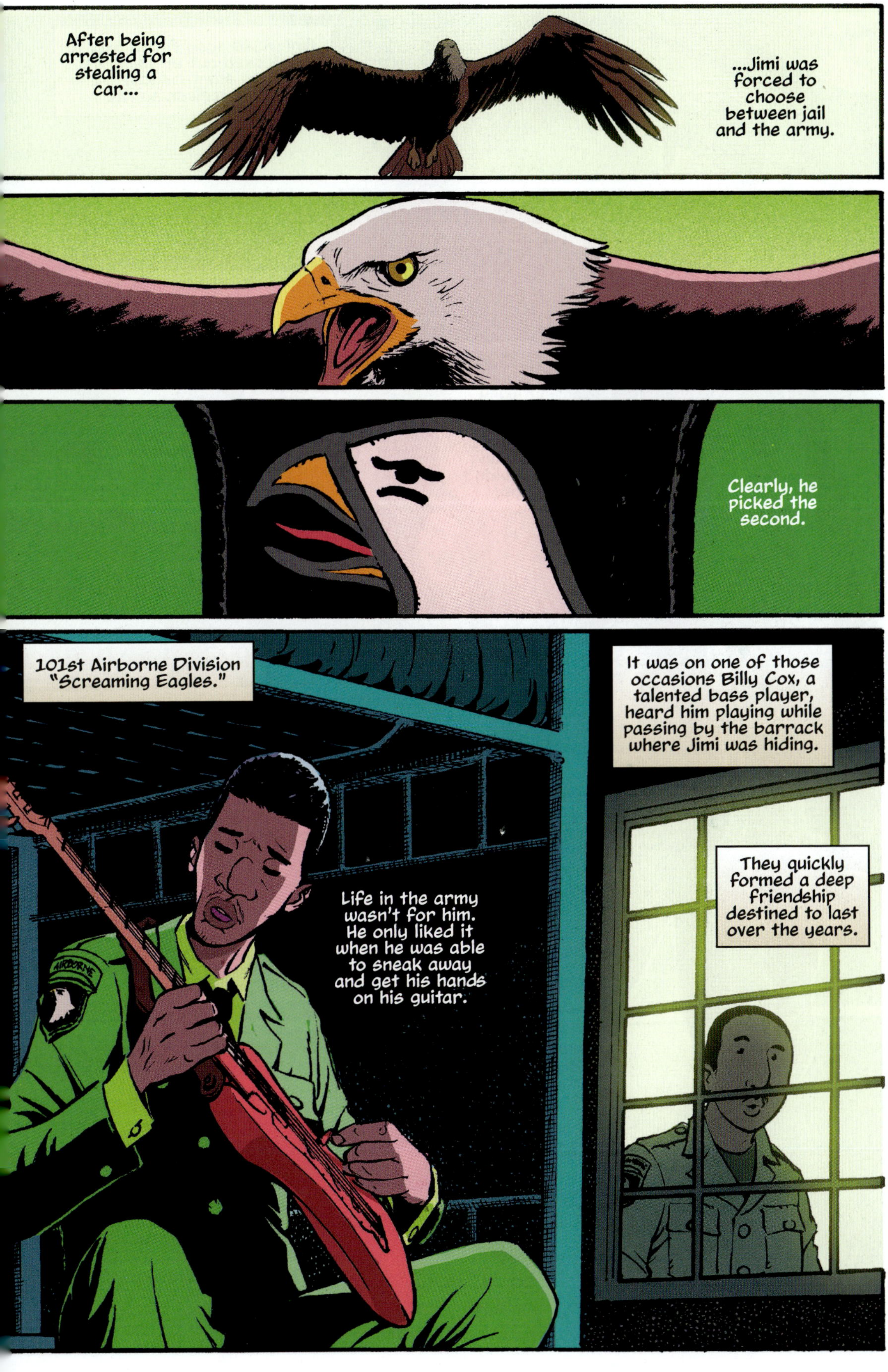
After being arrested for stealing a car...
...Jimi was forced to choose between jail and the army.
Clearly, he picked the second.
101st Airborne Division "Screaming Eagles."
Life in the army wasn't for him. He only liked it when he was able to sneak away and get his hands on his guitar.
It was on one of those occasions Billy Cox, a talented bass player, heard him playing while passing by the barrack where Jimi was hiding.
They quickly formed a deep friendship destined to last over the years.
AIRBORNE

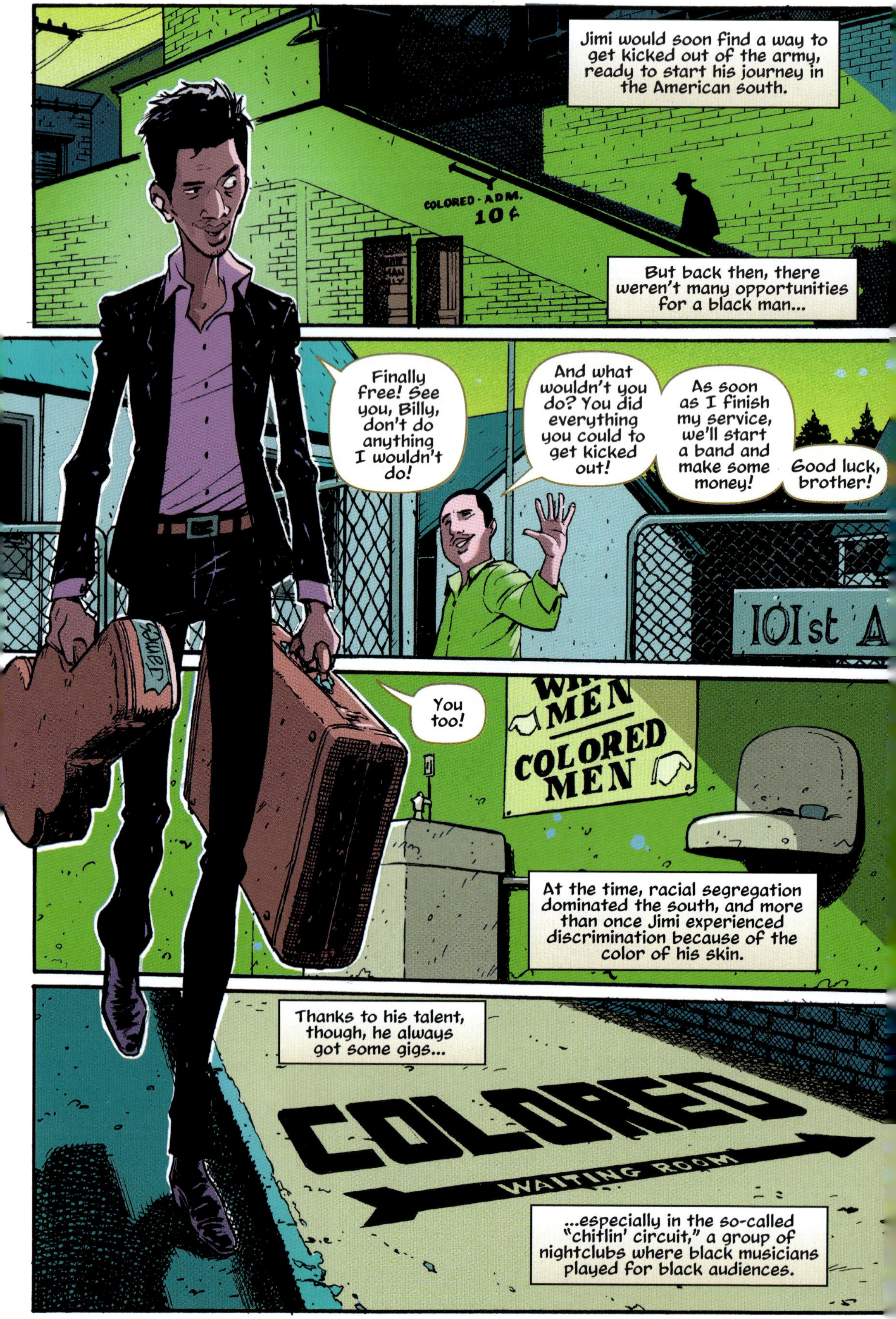
Jimi would soon find a way to get kicked out of the army, ready to start his journey in the American south.
COLORED - ADM. 10¢
But back then, there weren't many opportunities for a black man...
Finally free! See you, Billy, don't do anything I wouldn't do!
And what wouldn't you do? You did everything you could to get kicked out!
As soon as I finish my service, we'll start a band and make some money!
Good luck, brother!
101st A
You too!
MEN
COLORED MEN
At the time, racial segregation dominated the south, and more than once Jimi experienced discrimination because of the color of his skin.
Thanks to his talent, though, he always got some gigs...
COLORED
WAITING ROOM
...especially in the so-called "chitlin' circuit," a group of nightclubs where black musicians played for black audiences.

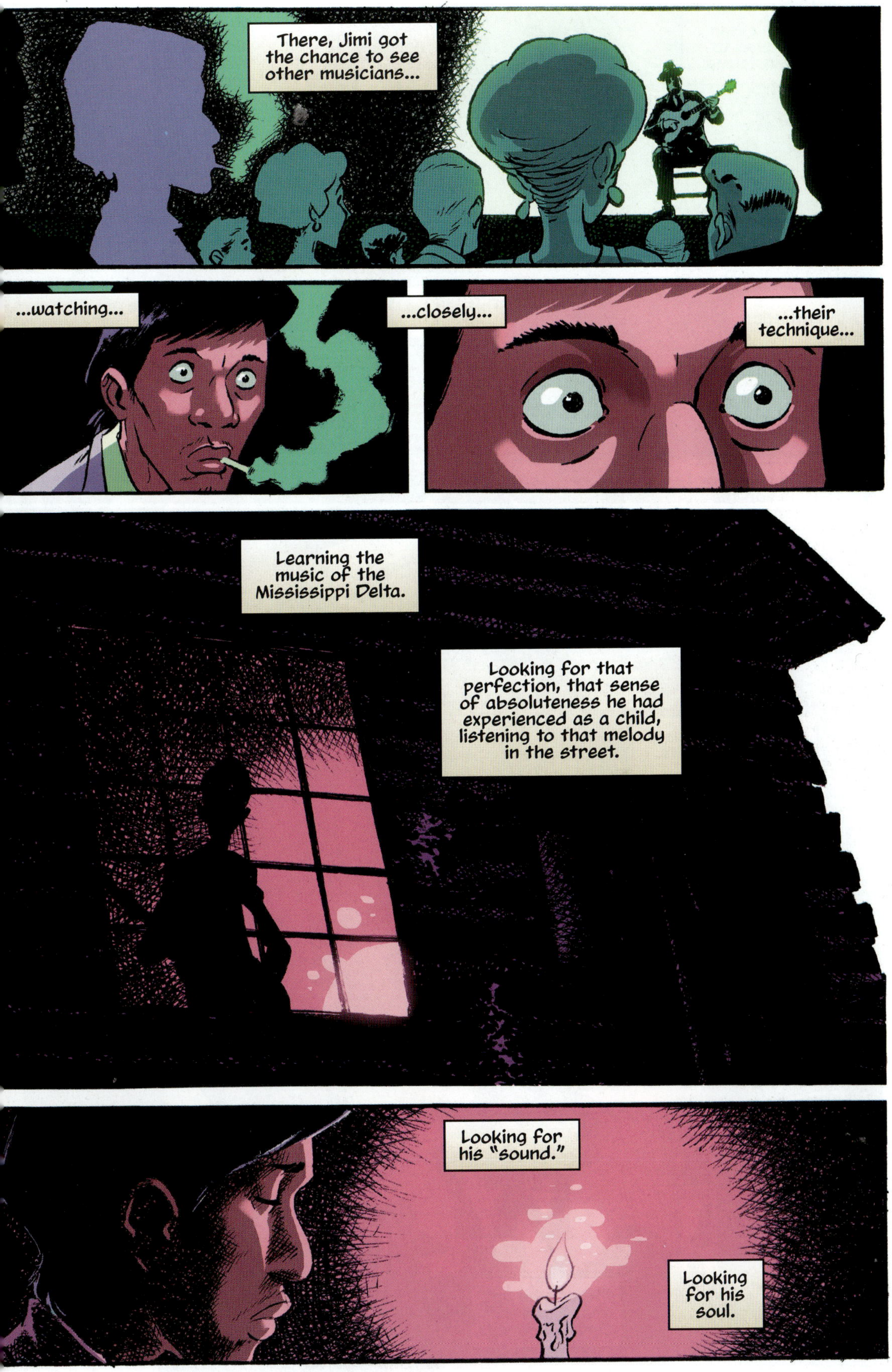
There, Jimi got the chance to see other musicians...
...watching...
...closely...
...their technique...
Learning the music of the Mississippi Delta.
Looking for that perfection, that sense of absoluteness he had experienced as a child, listening to that melody in the street.
Looking for his "sound."
Looking for his soul.

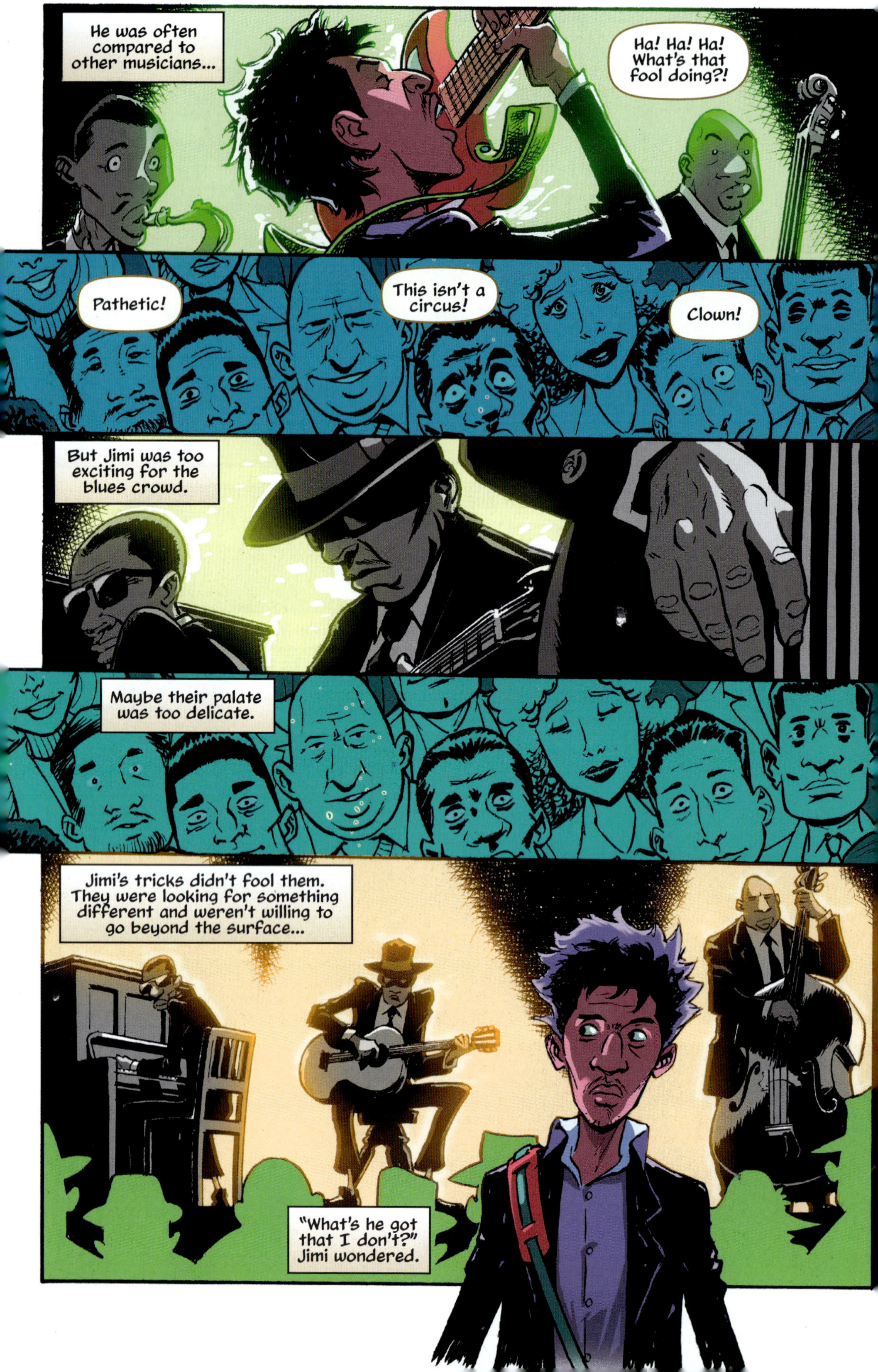
He was often compared to other musicians...
Ha! Ha! Ha! What's that fool doing?!
Pathetic!
This isn't a circus!
Clown!
But Jimi was too exciting for the blues crowd.
Maybe their palate was too delicate.
Jimi's tricks didn't fool them. They were looking for something different and weren't willing to go beyond the surface...
"What's he got that I don't?" Jimi wondered.

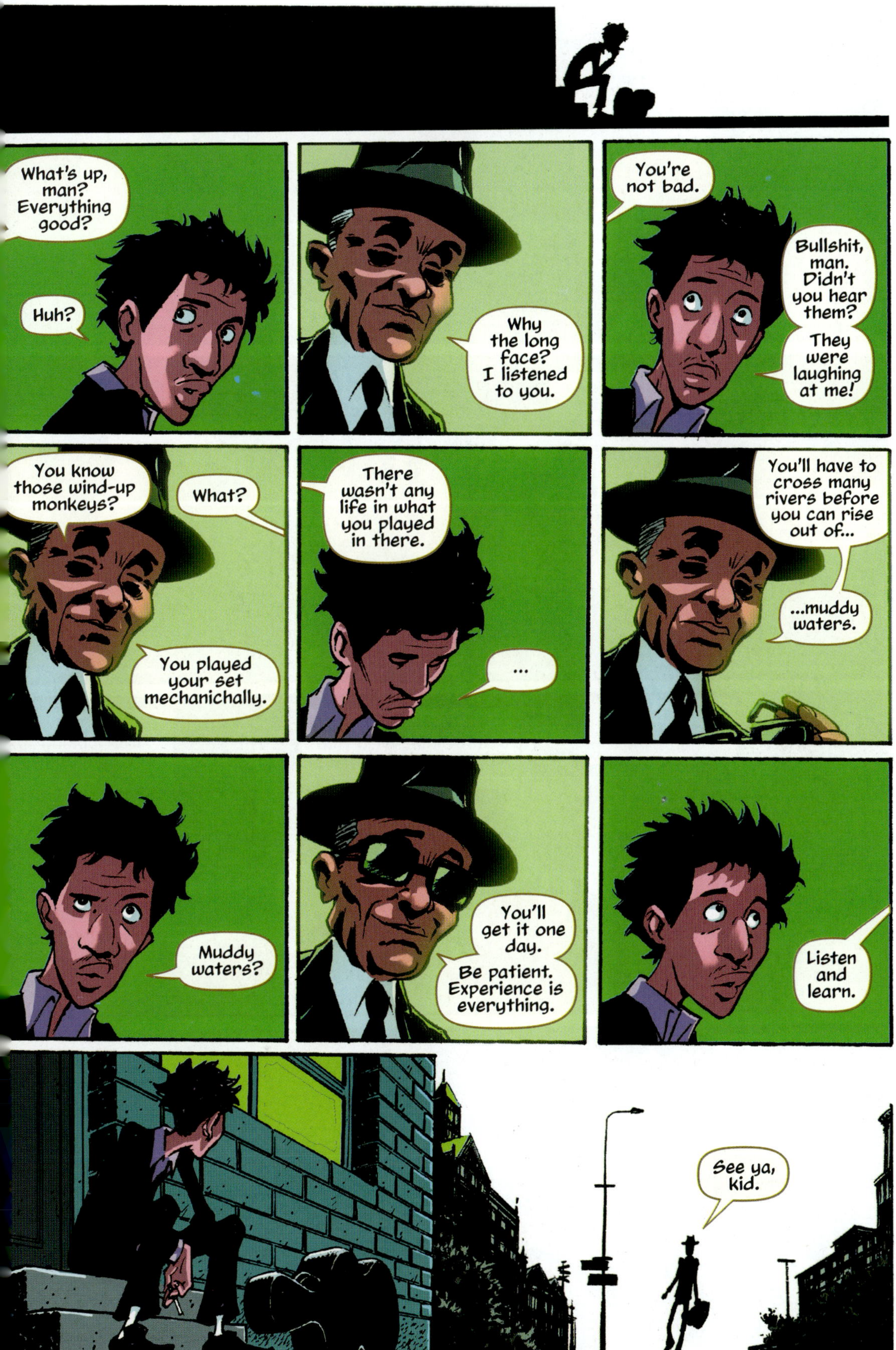
What's up, man? Everything good?
Huh?
Why the long face? I listened to you.
You're not bad.
Bullshit, man. Didn't you hear them?
They were laughing at me!
You know those wind-up monkeys?
What?
You played your set mechanichally.
There wasn't any life in what you played in there.
...
You'll have to cross many rivers before you can rise out of...
...muddy waters.
Muddy waters?
You'll get it one day.
Be patient. Experience is everything.
Listen and learn.
See ya, kid.

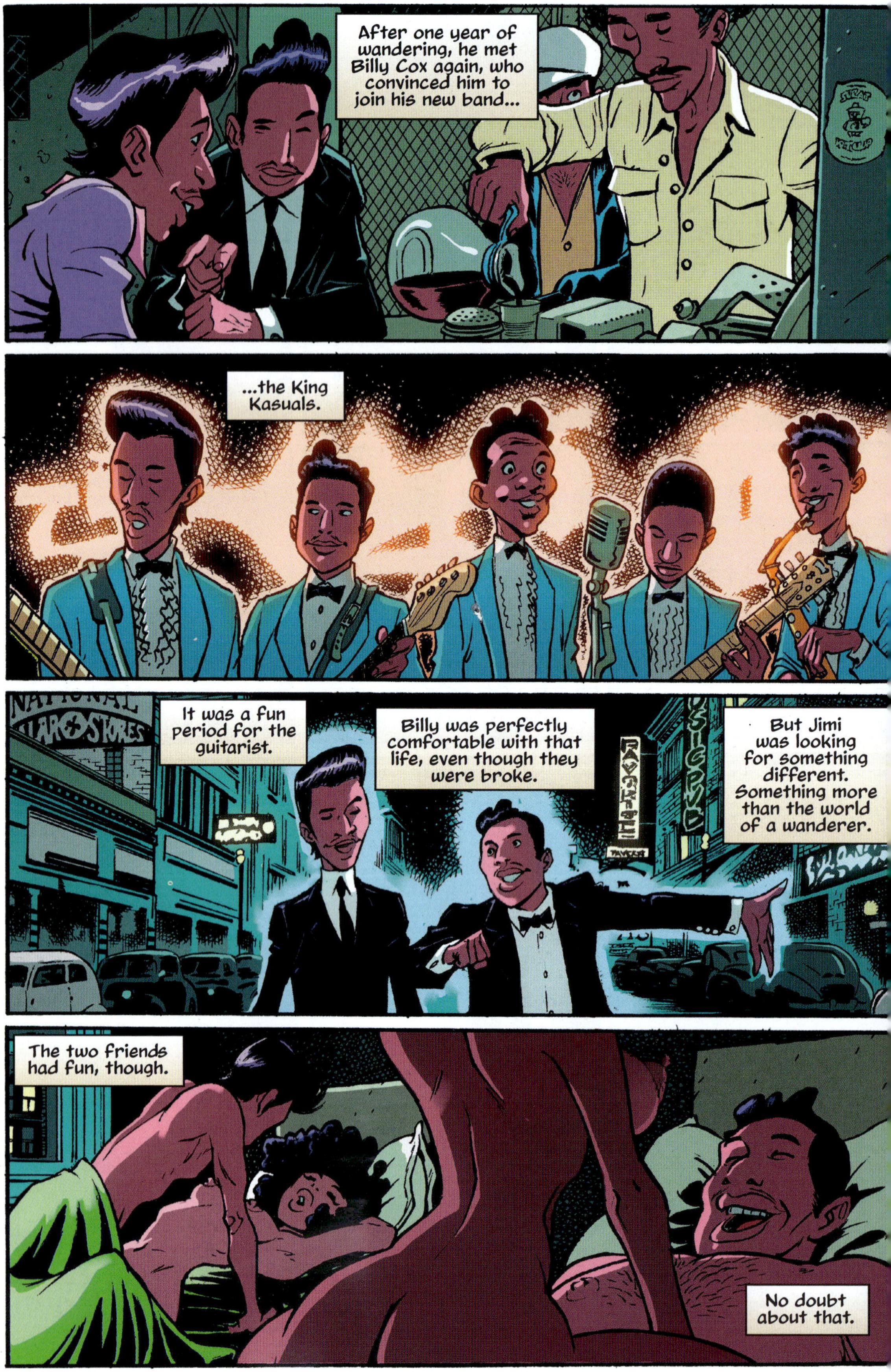
After one year of wandering, he met Billy Cox again, who convinced him to join his new band...
...the King Kasuals.
NATIONAL
STORES
It was a fun period for the guitarist.
Billy was perfectly comfortable with that life, even though they were broke.
But Jimi was looking for something different. Something more than the world of a wanderer.
The two friends had fun, though.
No doubt about that.

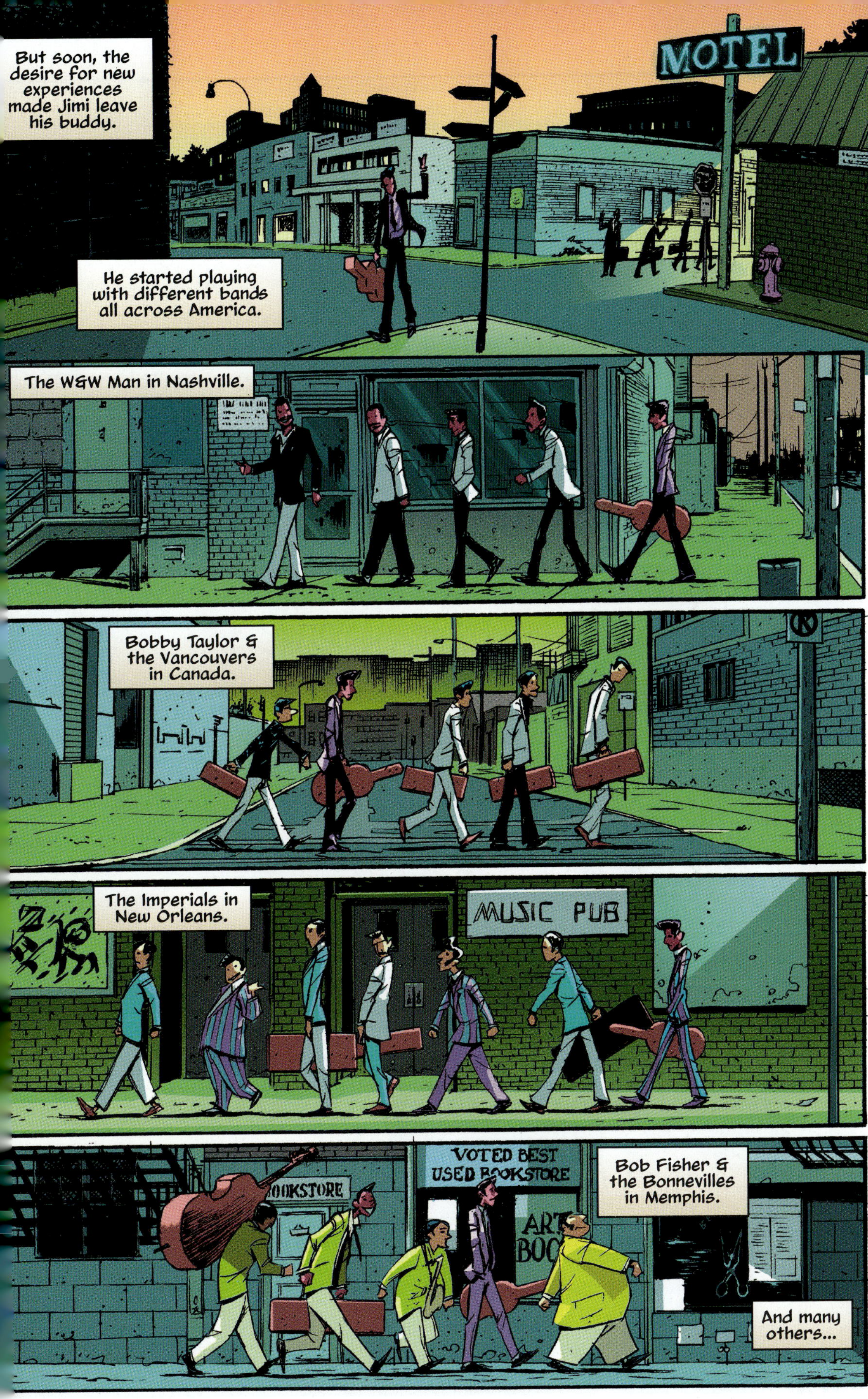
But soon, the desire for new experiences made Jimi leave his buddy.
MOTEL
He started playing with different bands all across America.
The W&W Man in Nashville.
Bobby Taylor & the Vancouvers in Canada.
The Imperials in New Orleans.
MUSIC PUB
VOTED BEST USED BOOKSTORE
BOOKSTORE
ART BOO
Bob Fisher & the Bonnevilles in Memphis.
And many others...

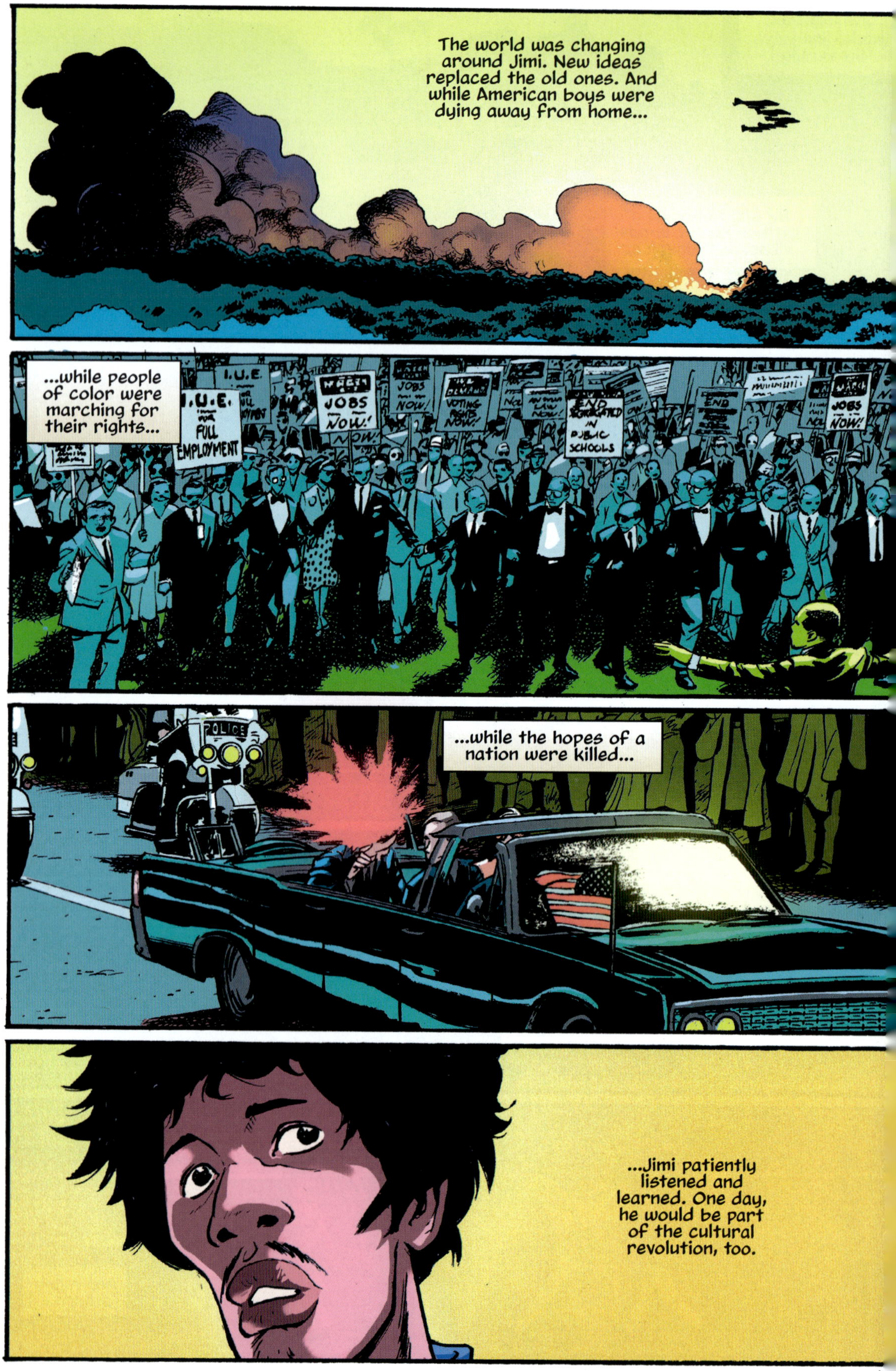
The world was changing around Jimi. New ideas replaced the old ones. And while American boys were dying away from home...
...while people of color were marching for their rights...
I.U.E.
I.U.E.
FULL EMPLOYMENT
JOBS NOW!
VOTING RIGHTS NOW!
END SEGREGATED IN PUBLIC SCHOOLS
JOBS NOW!
POLICE
...while the hopes of a nation were killed...
...Jimi patiently listened and learned. One day, he would be part of the cultural revolution, too.

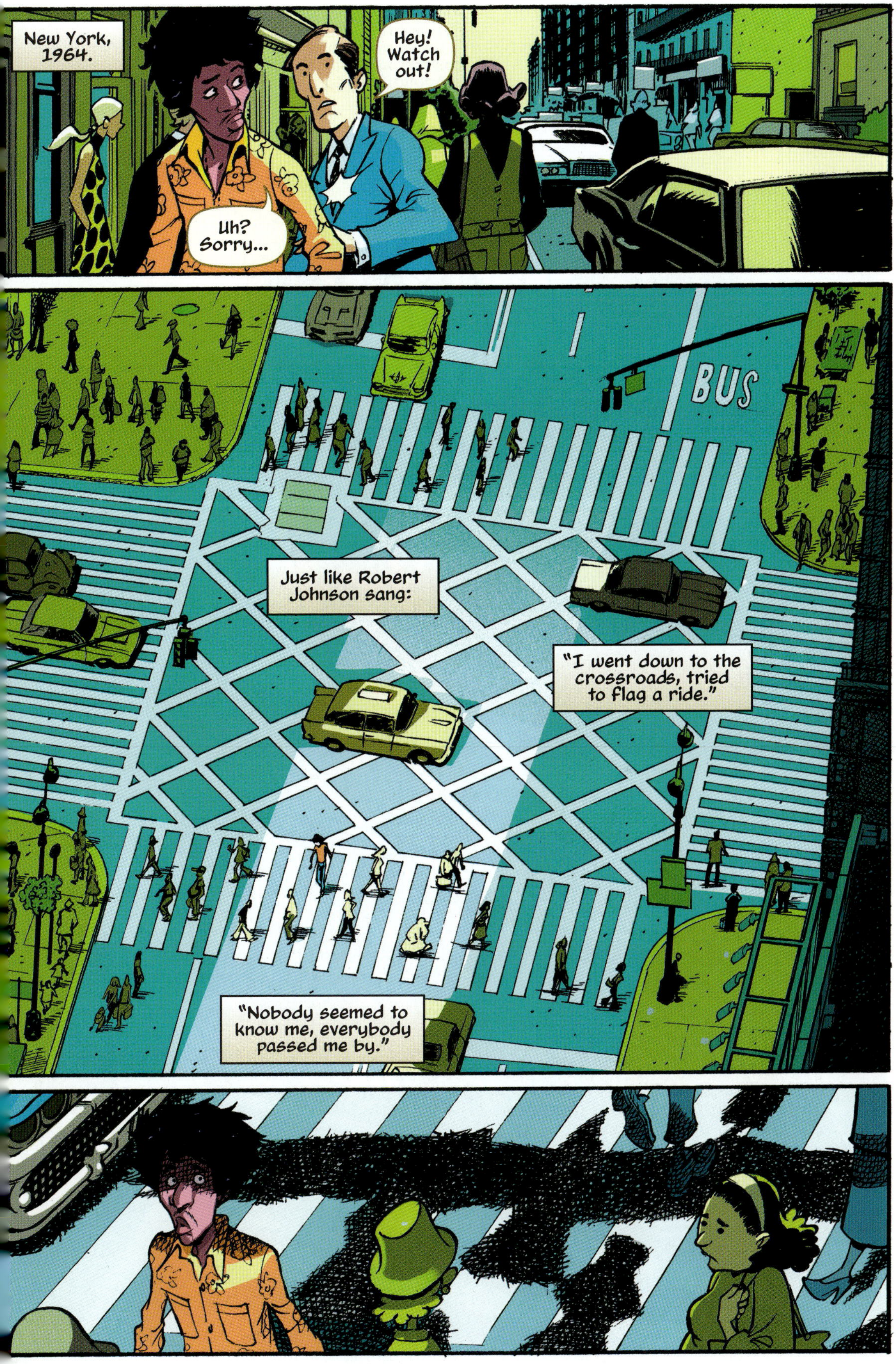
New York, 1964.
Hey! Watch out!
Uh? Sorry...
BUS
Just like Robert Johnson sang:
"I went down to the crossroads, tried to flag a ride."
"Nobody seemed to know me, everybody passed me by."

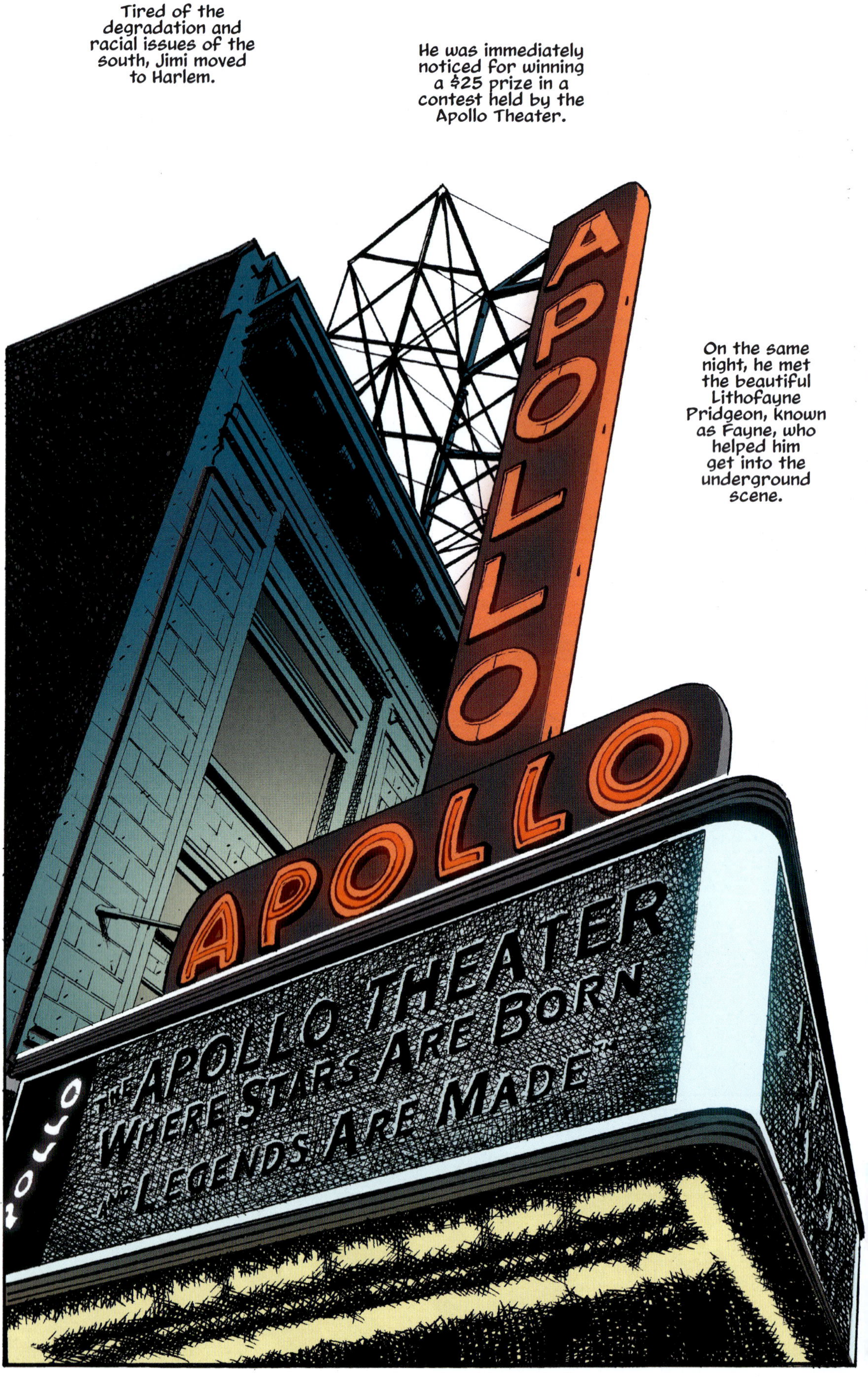
Tired of the degradation and racial issues of the south, Jimi moved to Harlem.
He was immediately noticed for winning a $25 prize in a contest held by the Apollo Theater.
APOLLO
On the same night, he met the beautiful Lithofayne Pridgeon, known as Fayne, who helped him get into the underground scene.
APOLLO
THE APOLLO THEATER
WHERE STARS ARE BORN
AND LEGENDS ARE MADE
APOLLO

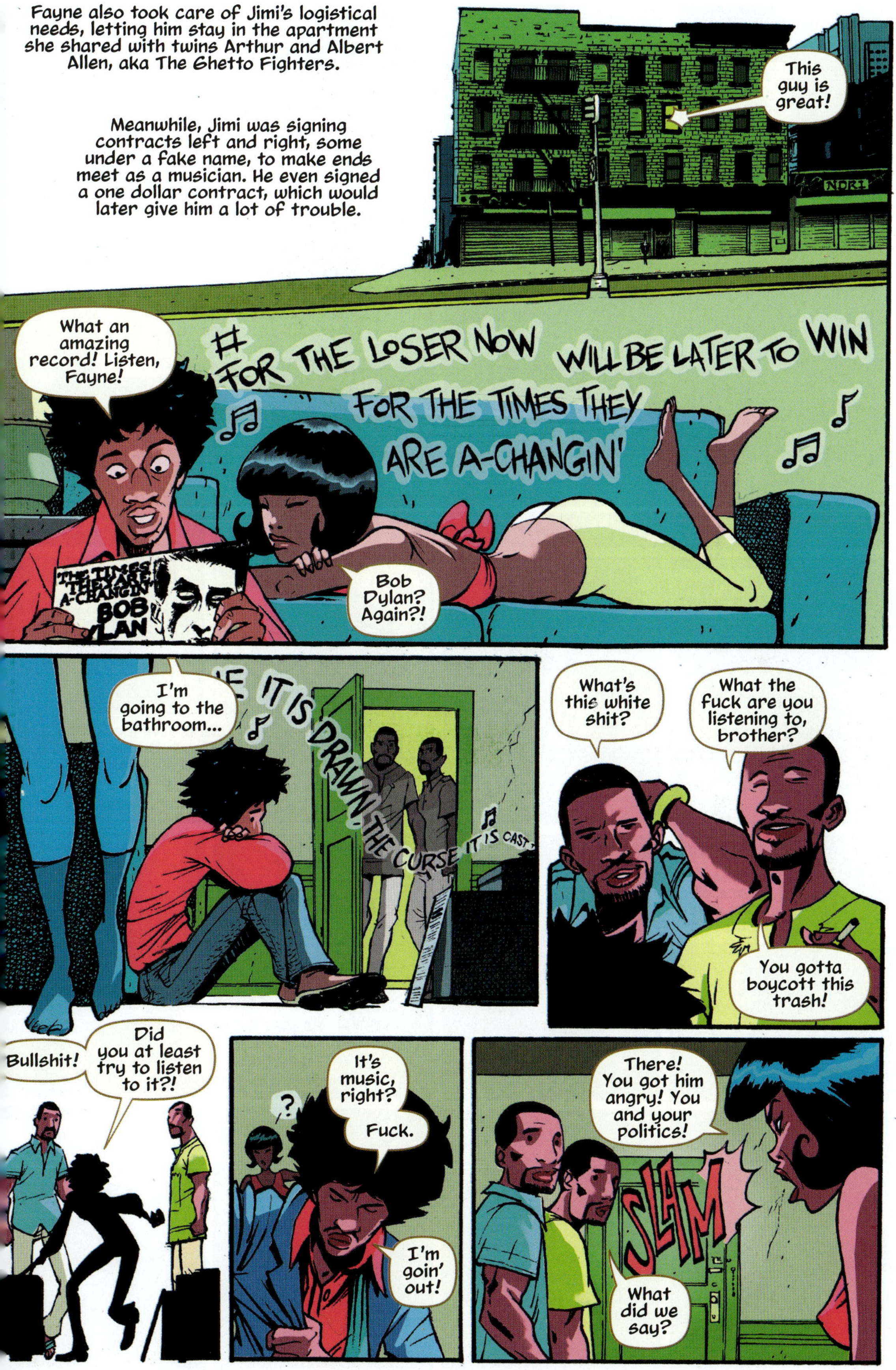
Fayne also took care of Jimi's logistical needs, letting him stay in the apartment she shared with twins Arthur and Albert Allen, aka The Ghetto Fighters.
Meanwhile, Jimi was signing contracts left and right, some under a fake name, to make ends meet as a musician. He even signed a one dollar contract, which would later give him a lot of trouble.
This guy is great!
NORI
What an amazing record! Listen, Fayne!
FOR THE LOSER NOW WILL BE LATER TO WIN
FOR THE TIMES THEY ARE A-CHANGIN'
THE TIMES THEY ARE A-CHANGIN' BOB LAN
Bob Dylan? Again?!
I'm going to the bathroom...
IT IS DRAWN, THE CURSE IT IS CAST
What's this white shit?
What the fuck are you listening to, brother?
You gotta boycott this trash!
Bullshit!
Did you at least try to listen to it?!
?
It's music, right?
Fuck.
I'm goin' out!
There! You got him angry! You and your politics!
SLAM
What did we say?

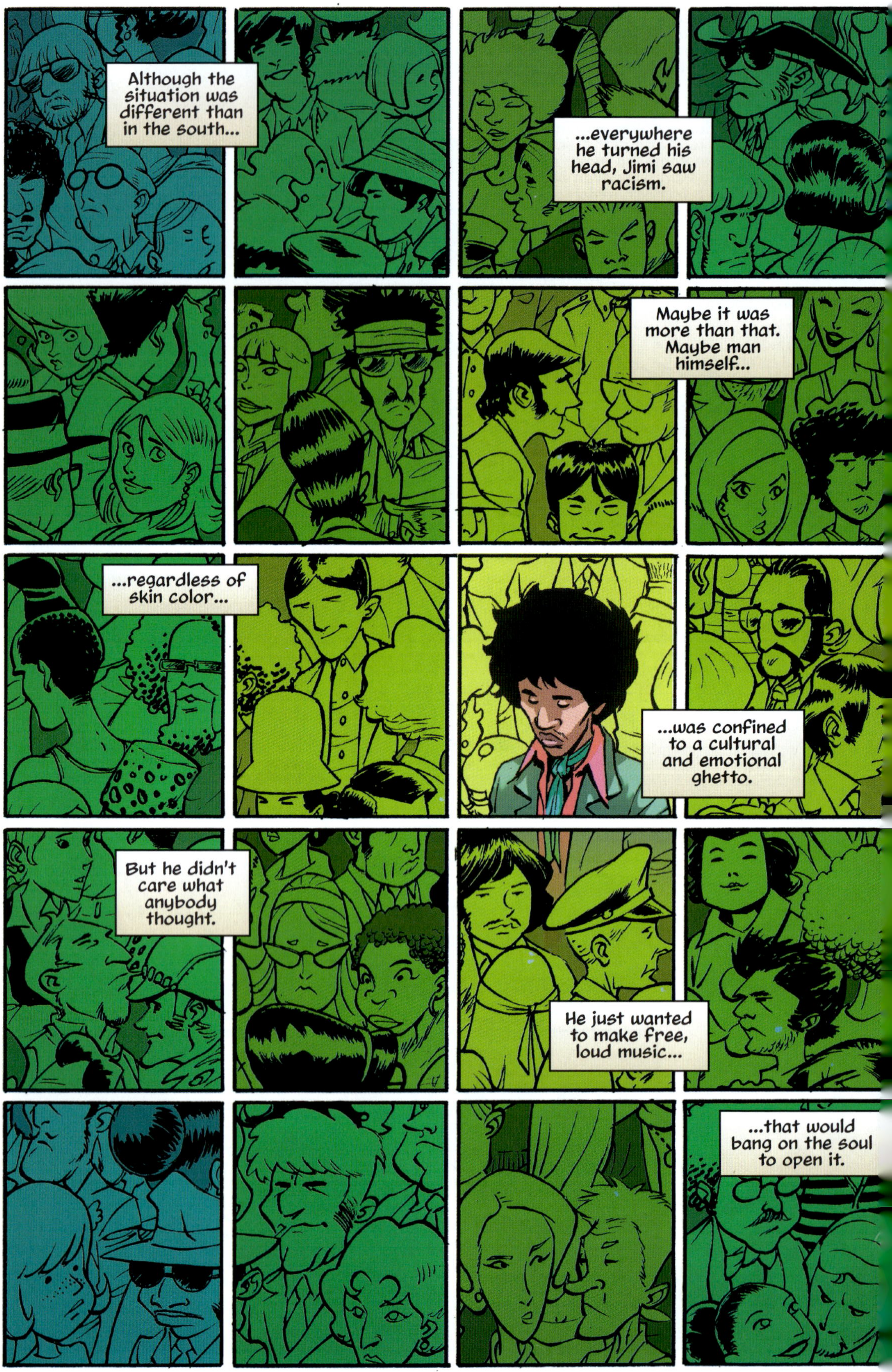
Although the situation was different than in the south...
...everywhere he turned his head, Jimi saw racism.
Maybe it was more than that. Maybe man himself...
...regardless of skin color...
...was confined to a cultural and emotional ghetto.
But he didn't care what anybody thought.
He just wanted to make free, loud music...
...that would bang on the soul to open it.

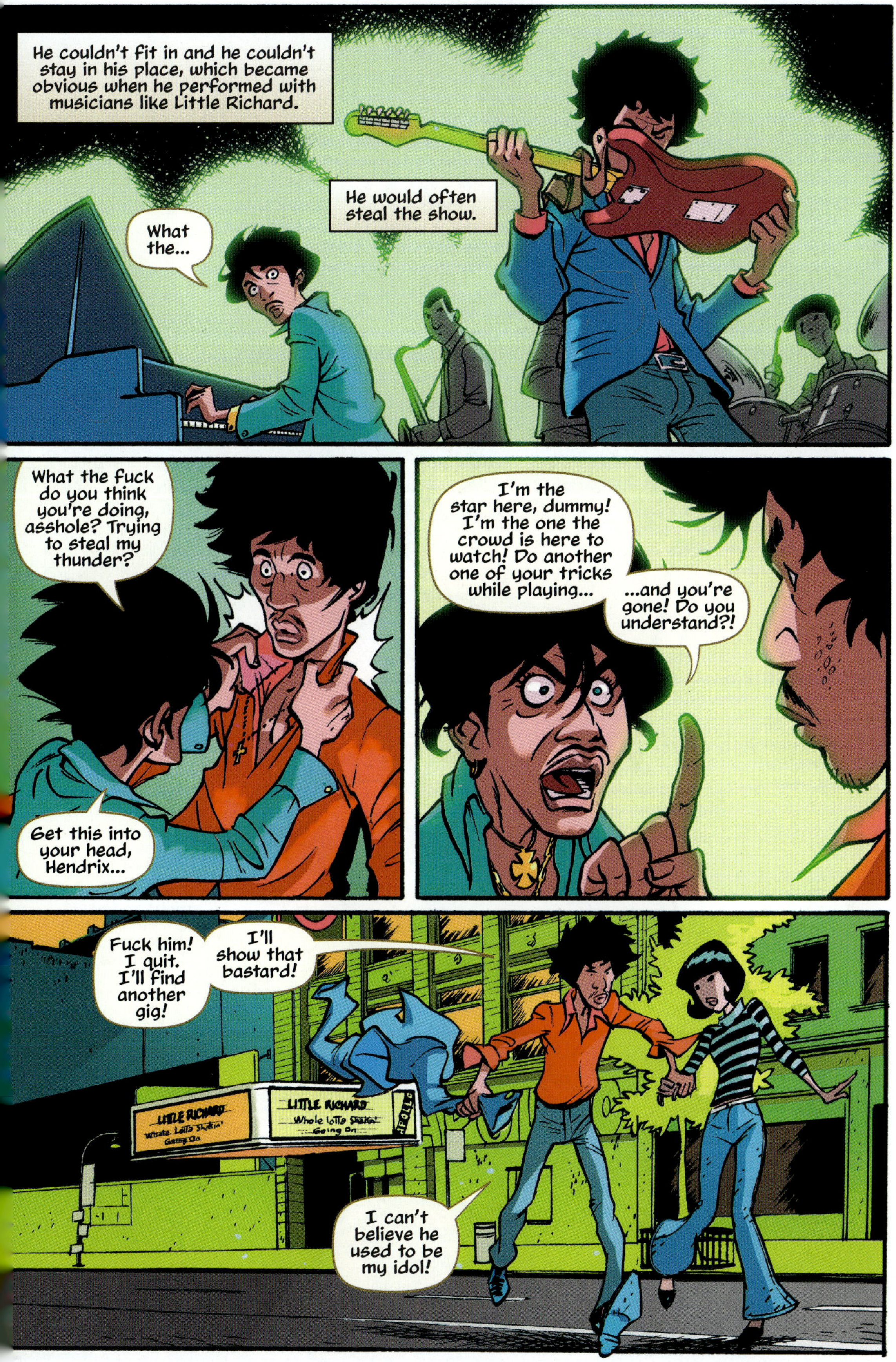
He couldn't fit in and he couldn't stay in his place, which became obvious when he performed with musicians like Little Richard.
What the...
He would often steal the show.
What the fuck do you think you're doing, asshole? Trying to steal my thunder?
Get this into your head, Hendrix...
I'm the star here, dummy! I'm the one the crowd is here to watch! Do another one of your tricks while playing...
...and you're gone! Do you understand?!
Fuck him! I quit. I'll find another gig!
I'll show that bastard!
LITTLE RICHARD
I can't believe he used to be my idol!

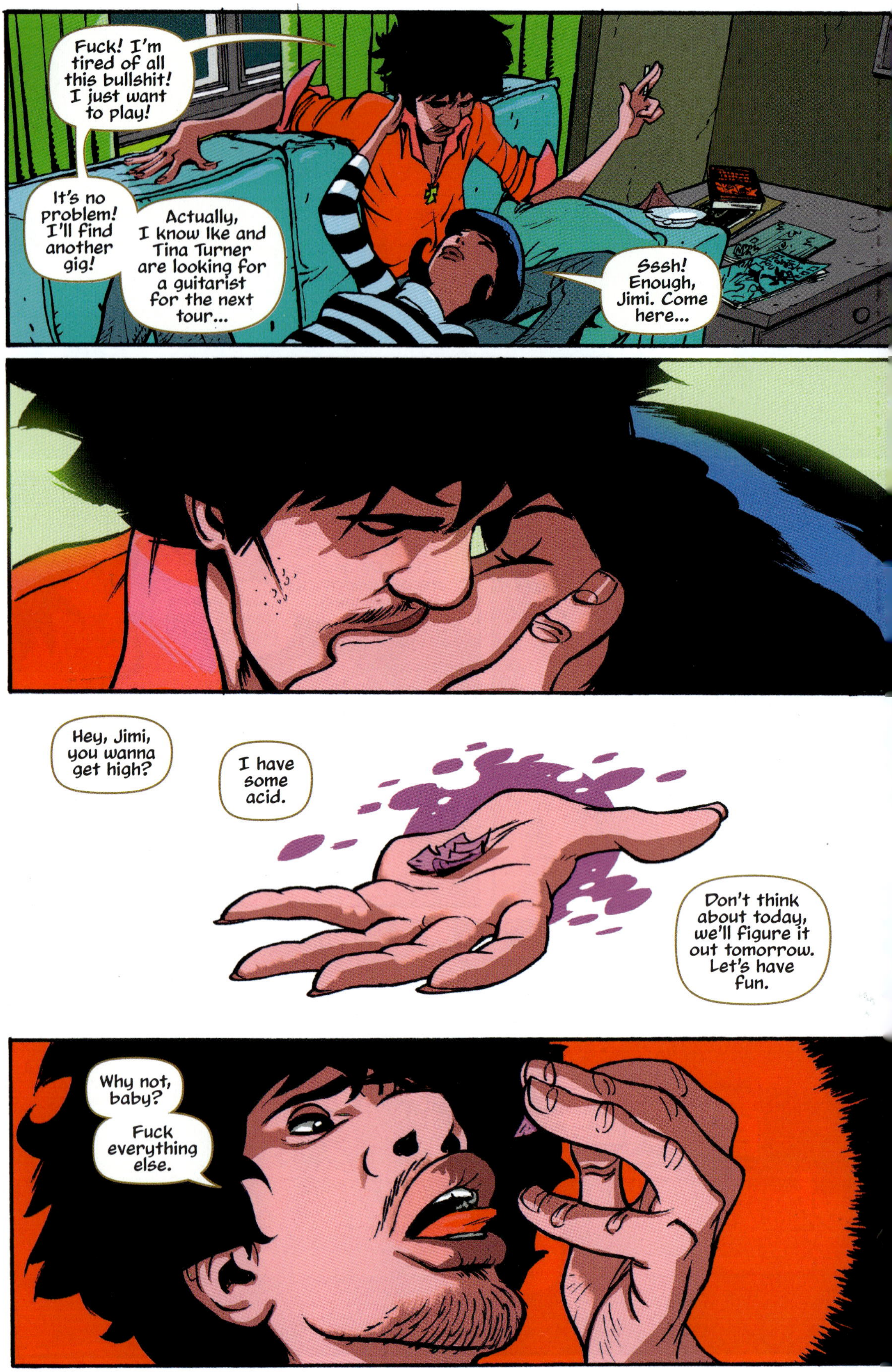
Fuck! I'm tired of all this bullshit! I just want to play!
It's no problem! I'll find another gig!
Actually, I know Ike and Tina Turner are looking for a guitarist for the next tour...
Sssh! Enough, Jimi. Come here...
Hey, Jimi, you wanna get high?
I have some acid.
Don't think about today, we'll figure it out tomorrow. Let's have fun.
Why not, baby?
Fuck everything else.

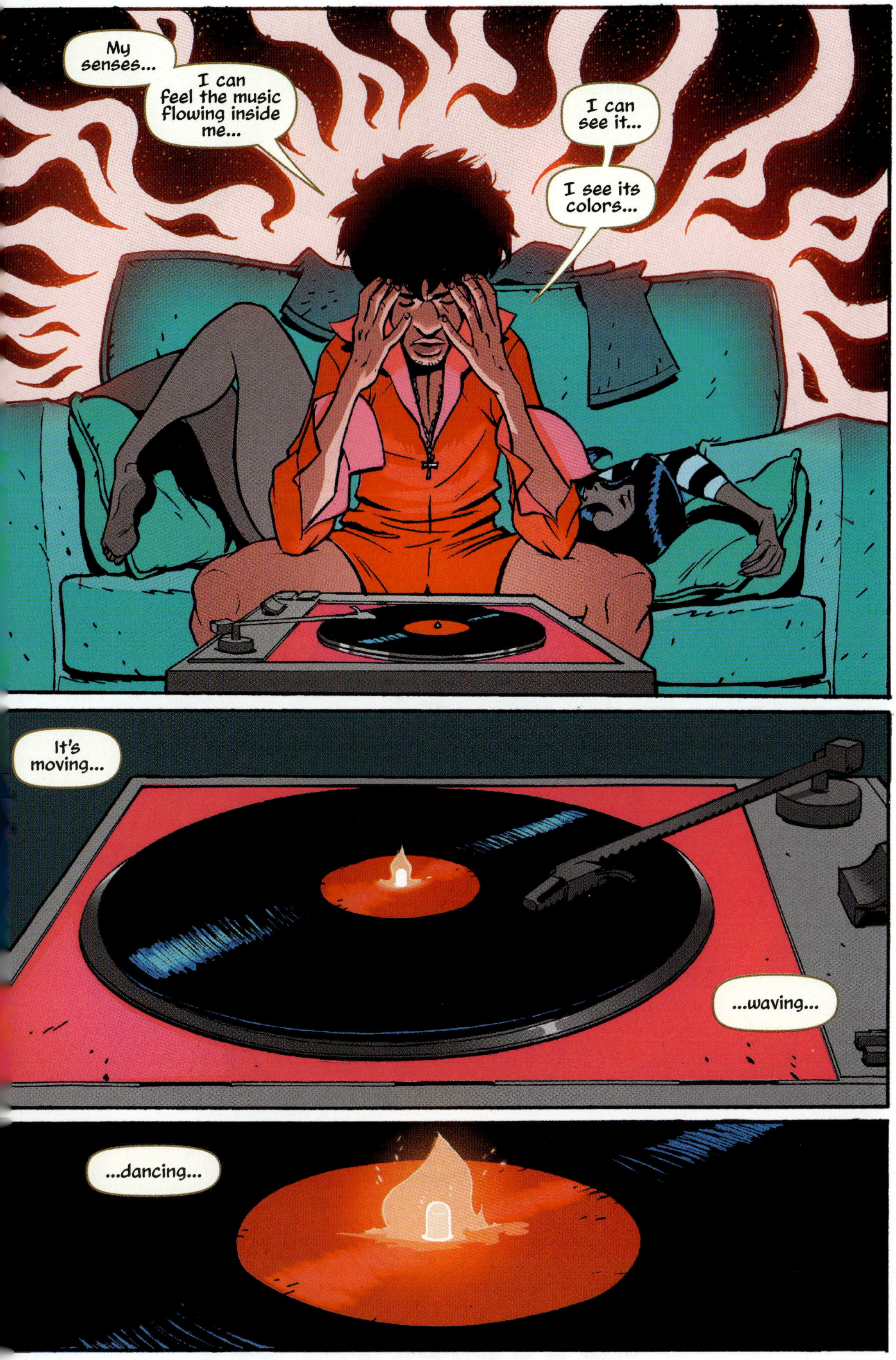
My senses...
I can feel the music flowing inside me...
I can see it...
I see its colors...
It's moving...
...waving...
...dancing...

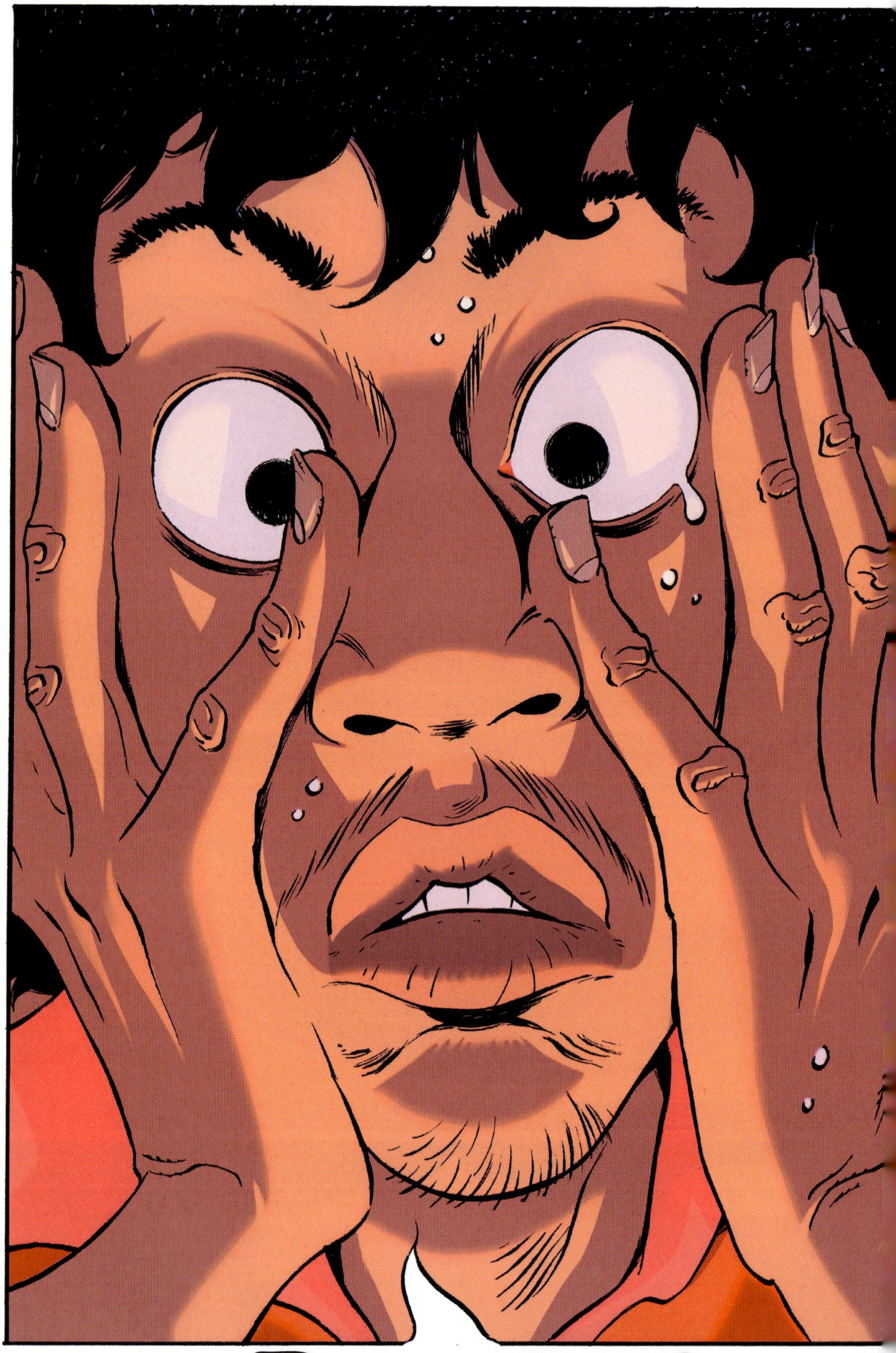

Burning!

# 03.

# BURNING
## of the
# MIDNIGHT
# LAMP

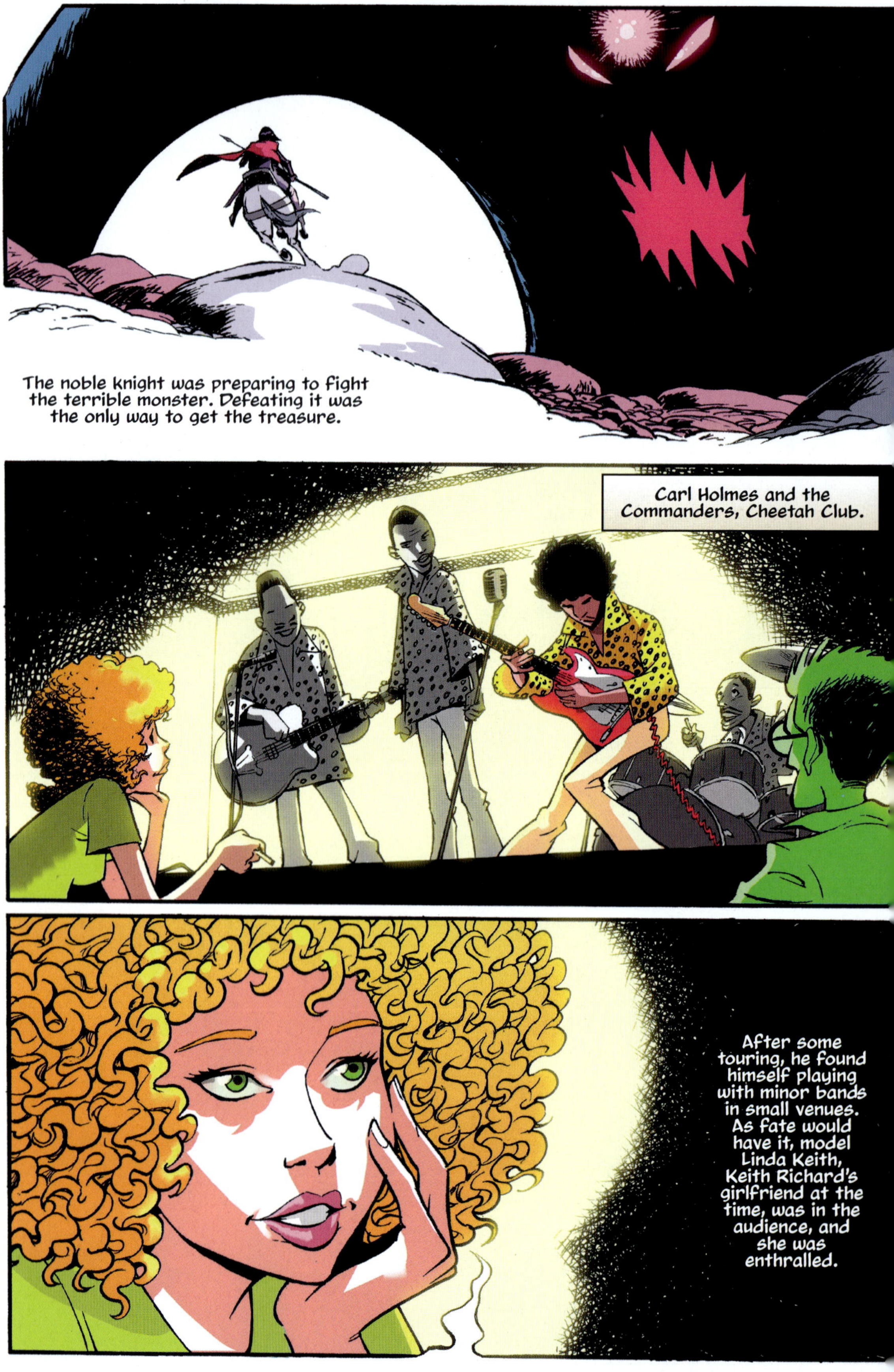
The noble knight was preparing to fight the terrible monster. Defeating it was the only way to get the treasure.
Carl Holmes and the Commanders, Cheetah Club.
After some touring, he found himself playing with minor bands in small venues. As fate would have it, model Linda Keith, Keith Richard's girlfriend at the time, was in the audience, and she was enthralled.

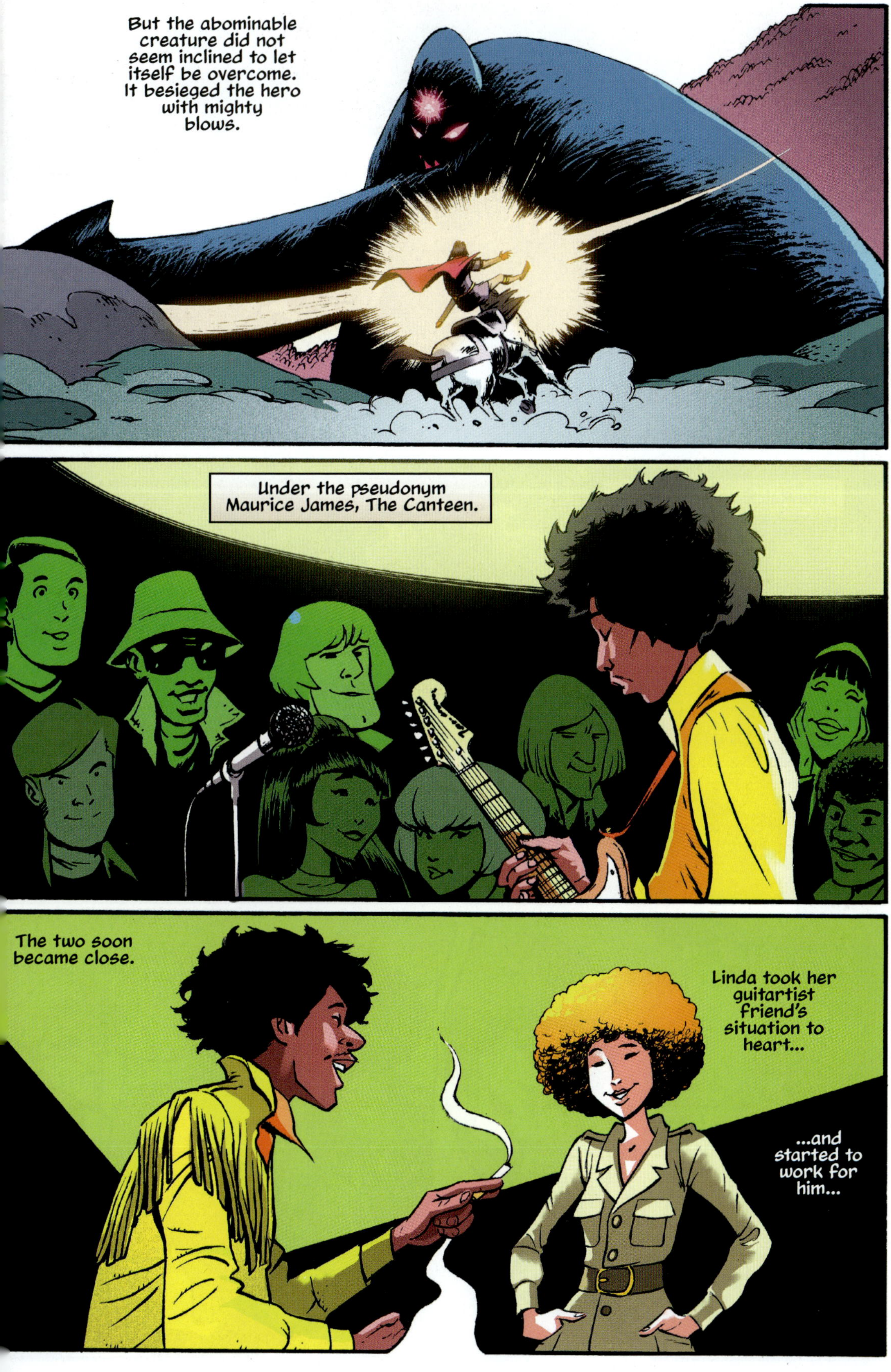
But the abominable creature did not seem inclined to let itself be overcome. It besieged the hero with mighty blows.
Under the pseudonym Maurice James, The Canteen.
The two soon became close.
Linda took her guitartist friend's situation to heart...
...and started to work for him...

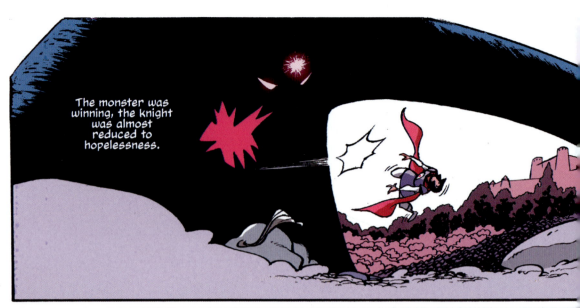

The monster was winning, the knight was almost reduced to hopelessness.

The Rainflowers, 6B6's.

She introduced him to famous managers and producers...

...like Andrew Loog Oldham and Seymour Stein...

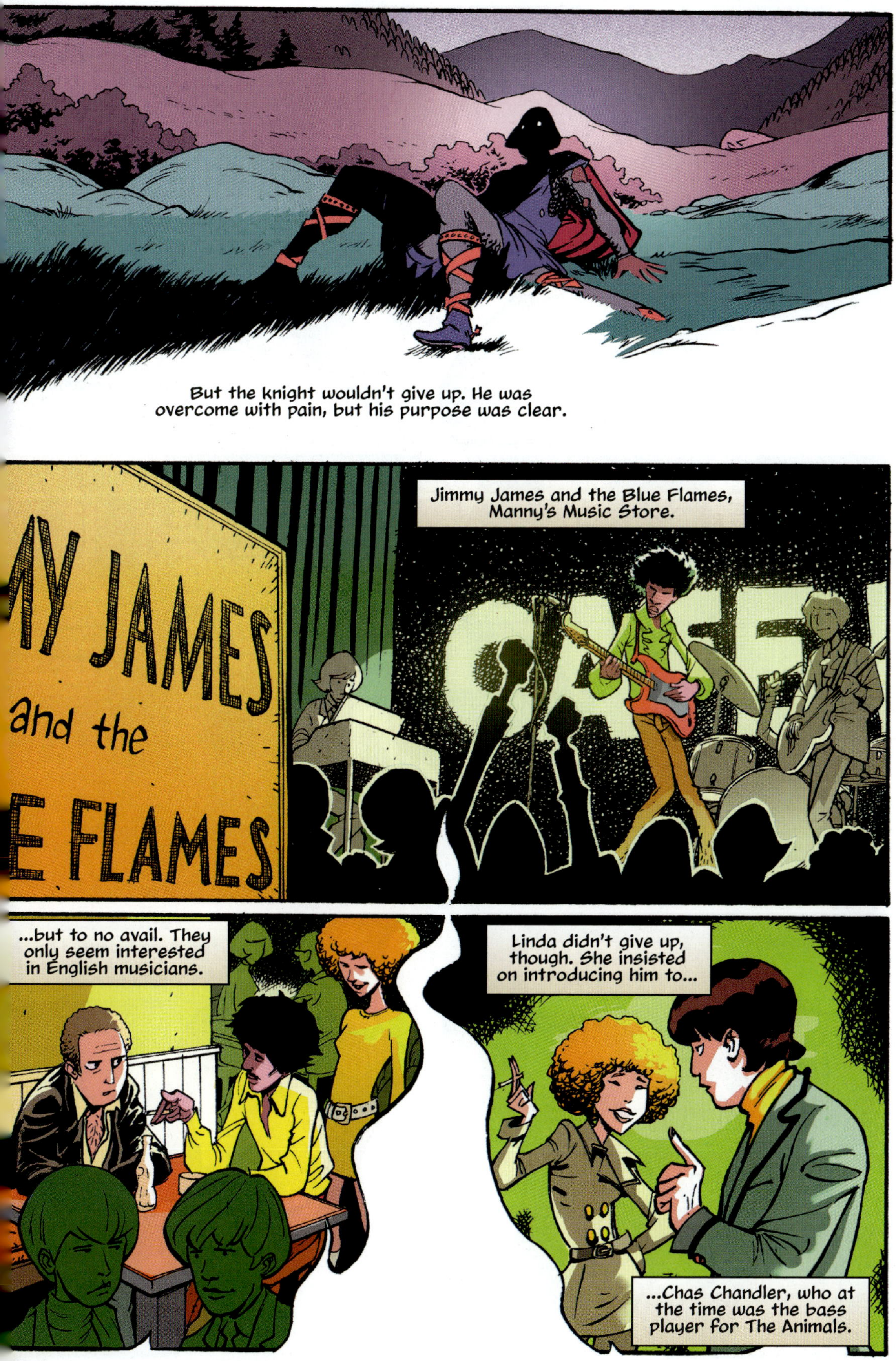
But the knight wouldn't give up. He was overcome with pain, but his purpose was clear.
MY JAMES
and the
E FLAMES
Jimmy James and the Blue Flames, Manny's Music Store.
...but to no avail. They only seem interested in English musicians.
Linda didn't give up, though. She insisted on introducing him to...
...Chas Chandler, who at the time was the bass player for The Animals.

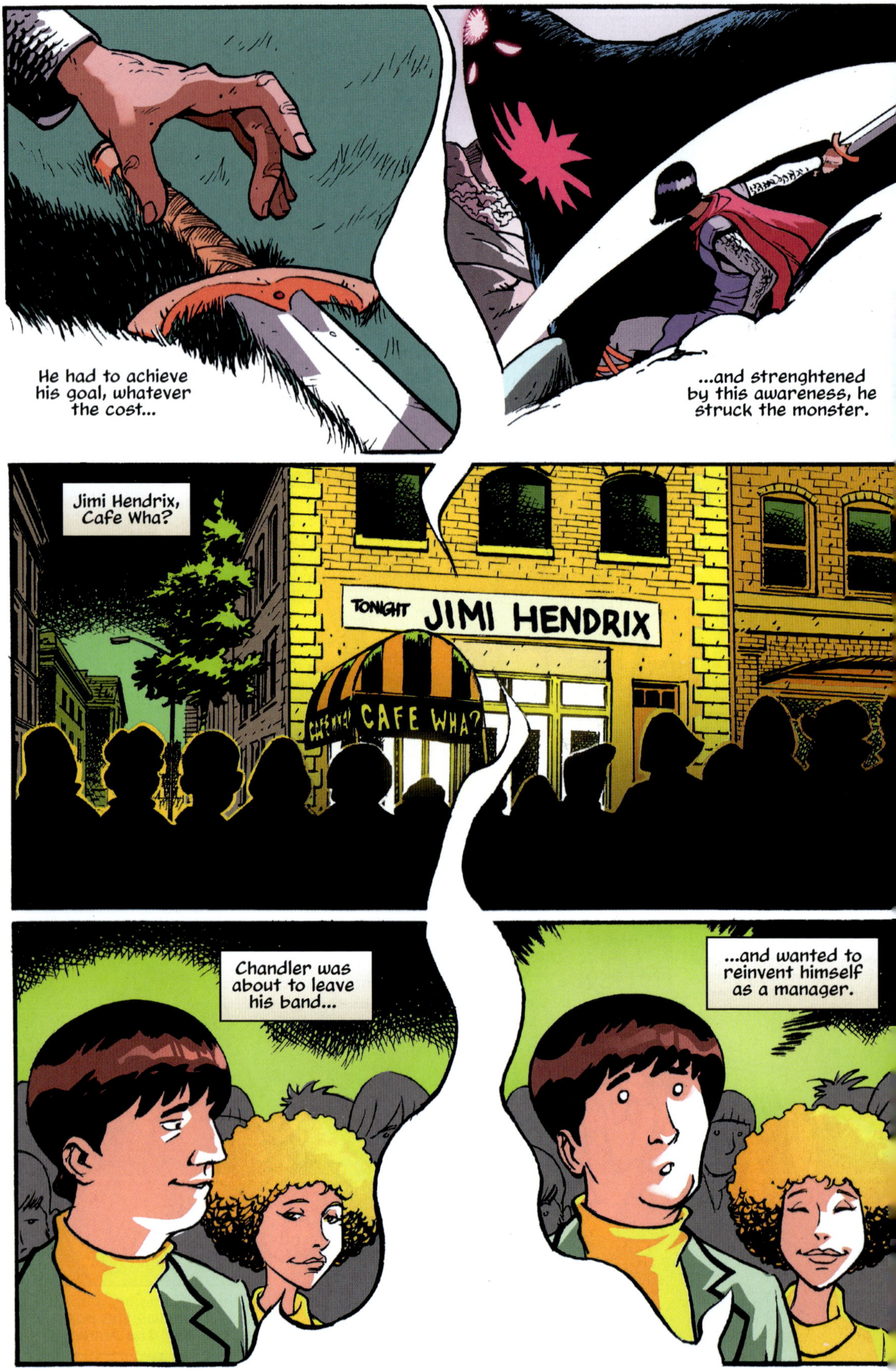
He had to achieve his goal, whatever the cost...
...and strenghtened by this awareness, he struck the monster.
Jimi Hendrix, Cafe Wha?
TONIGHT JIMI HENDRIX
CAFE WHA?
Chandler was about to leave his band...
...and wanted to reinvent himself as a manager.

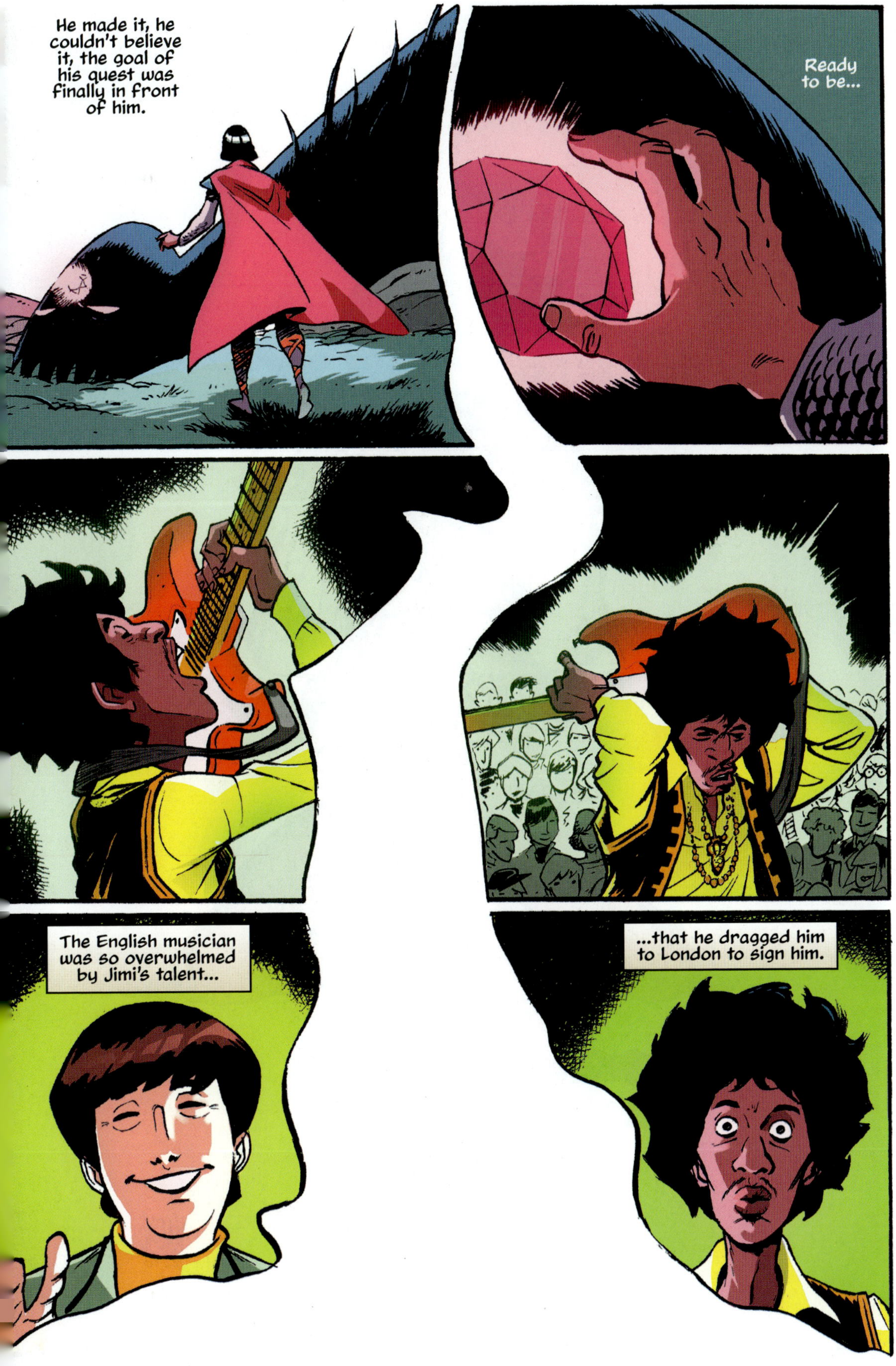
He made it, he couldn't believe it, the goal of his quest was finally in front of him.
Ready to be...
The English musician was so overwhelmed by Jimi's talent...
...that he dragged him to London to sign him.

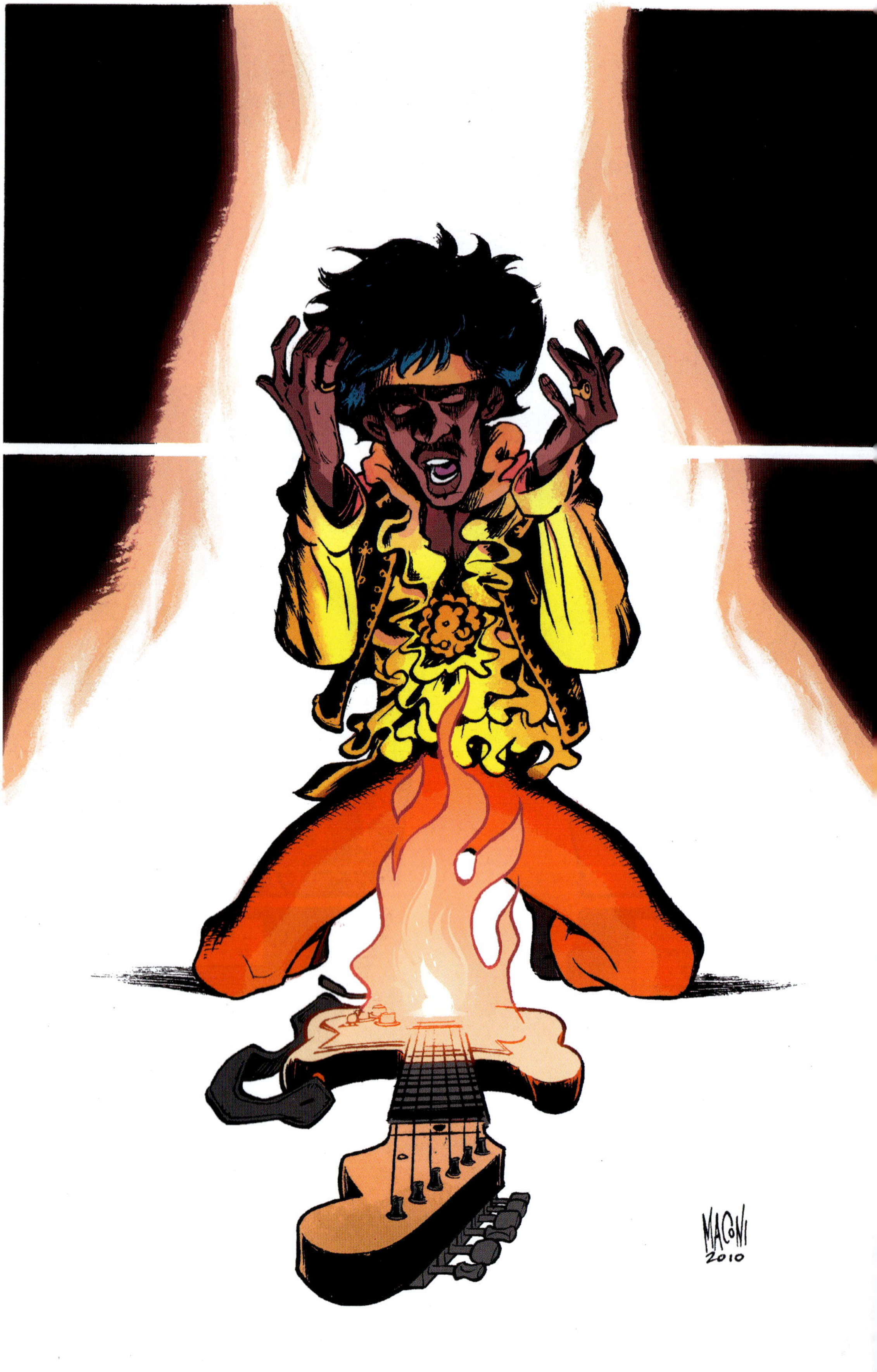
MACONI
2010

# 04.

# CASTLE MADE of SAND

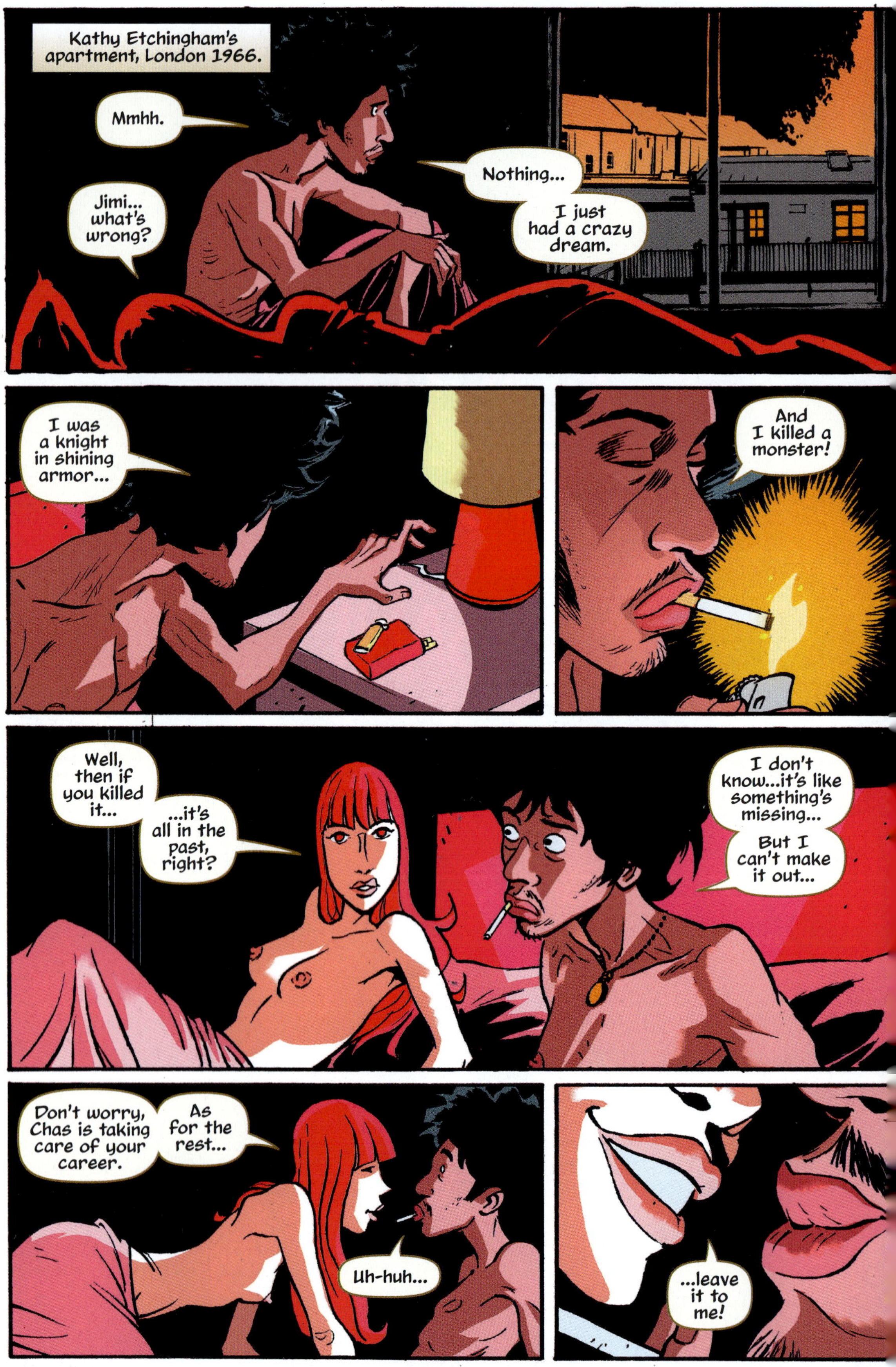
Kathy Etchingham's apartment, London 1966.
Mmhh.
Jimi... what's wrong?
Nothing...
I just had a crazy dream.
I was a knight in shining armor...
And I killed a monster!
Well, then if you killed it...
...it's all in the past, right?
I don't know...it's like something's missing...
But I can't make it out...
Don't worry, Chas is taking care of your career.
As for the rest...
Uh-huh...
...leave it to me!

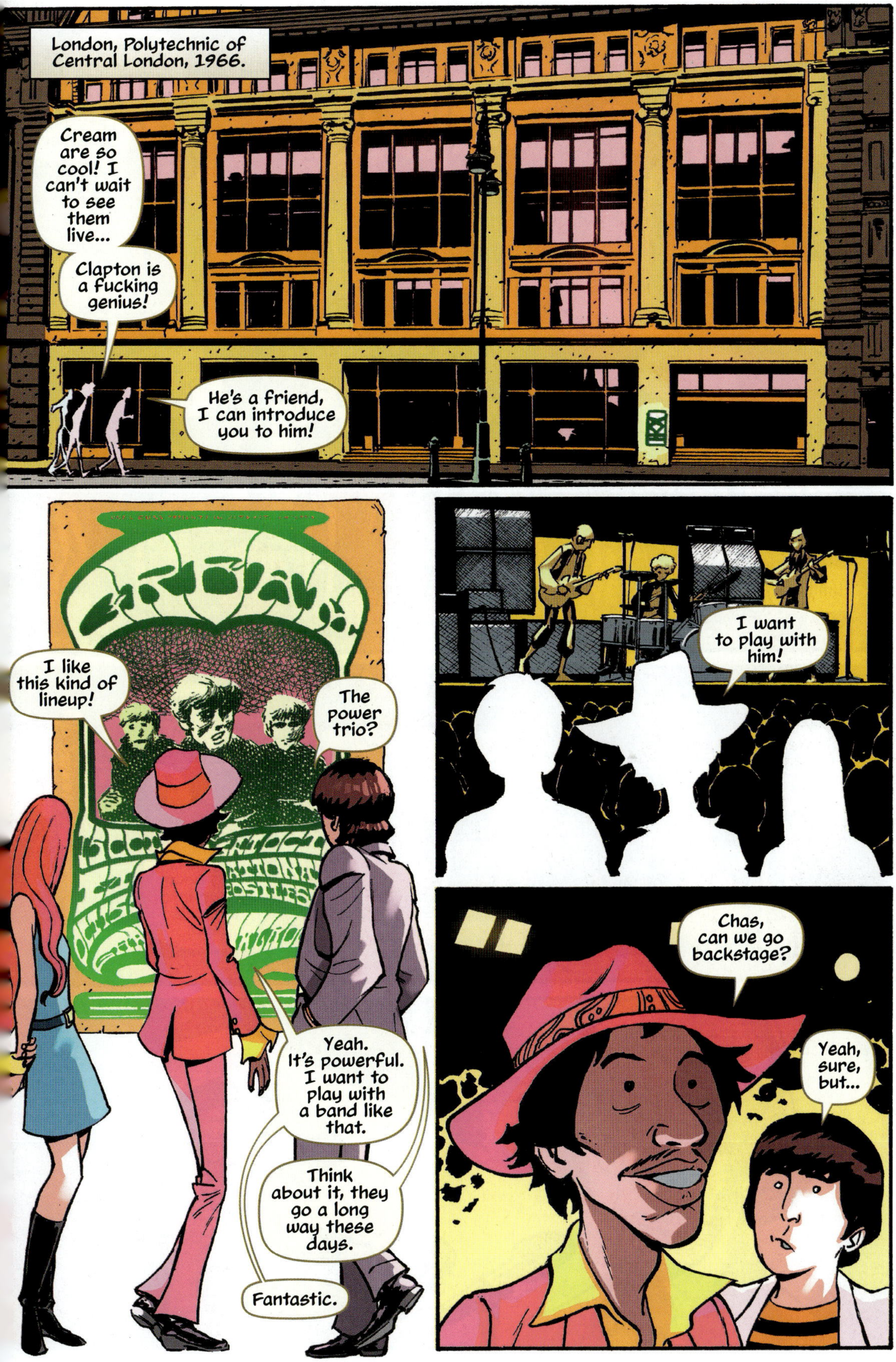

London, Polytechnic of Central London, 1966.
Cream are so cool! I can't wait to see them live...
Clapton is a fucking genius!
He's a friend, I can introduce you to him!
I like this kind of lineup!
The power trio?
Yeah. It's powerful. I want to play with a band like that.
Think about it, they go a long way these days.
Fantastic.
I want to play with him!
Chas, can we go backstage?
Yeah, sure, but...

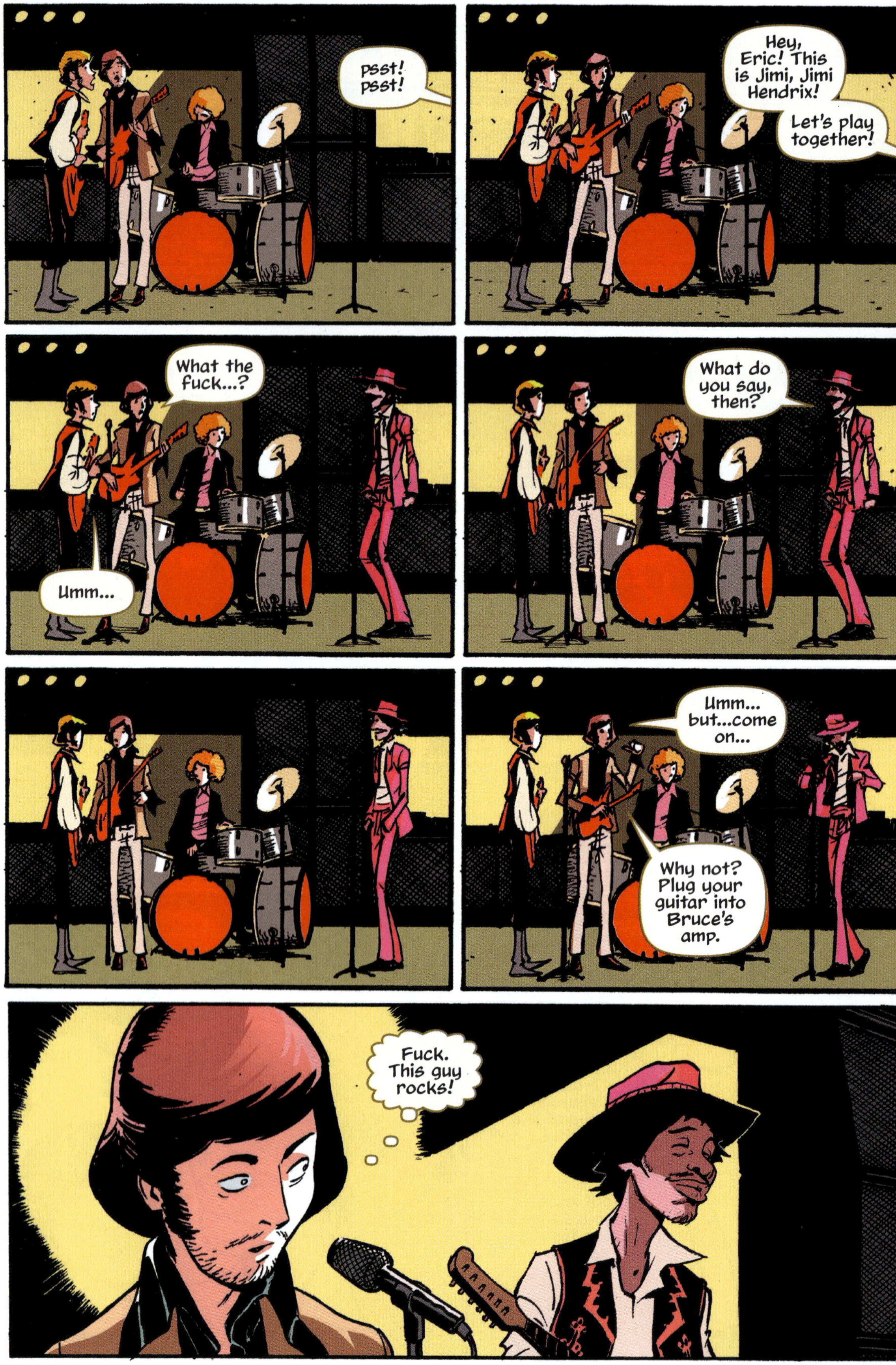
psst! psst!
Hey, Eric! This is Jimi, Jimi Hendrix!
Let's play together!
What the fuck...?
Umm...
What do you say, then?
Umm... but...come on...
Why not? Plug your guitar into Bruce's amp.
Fuck. This guy rocks!

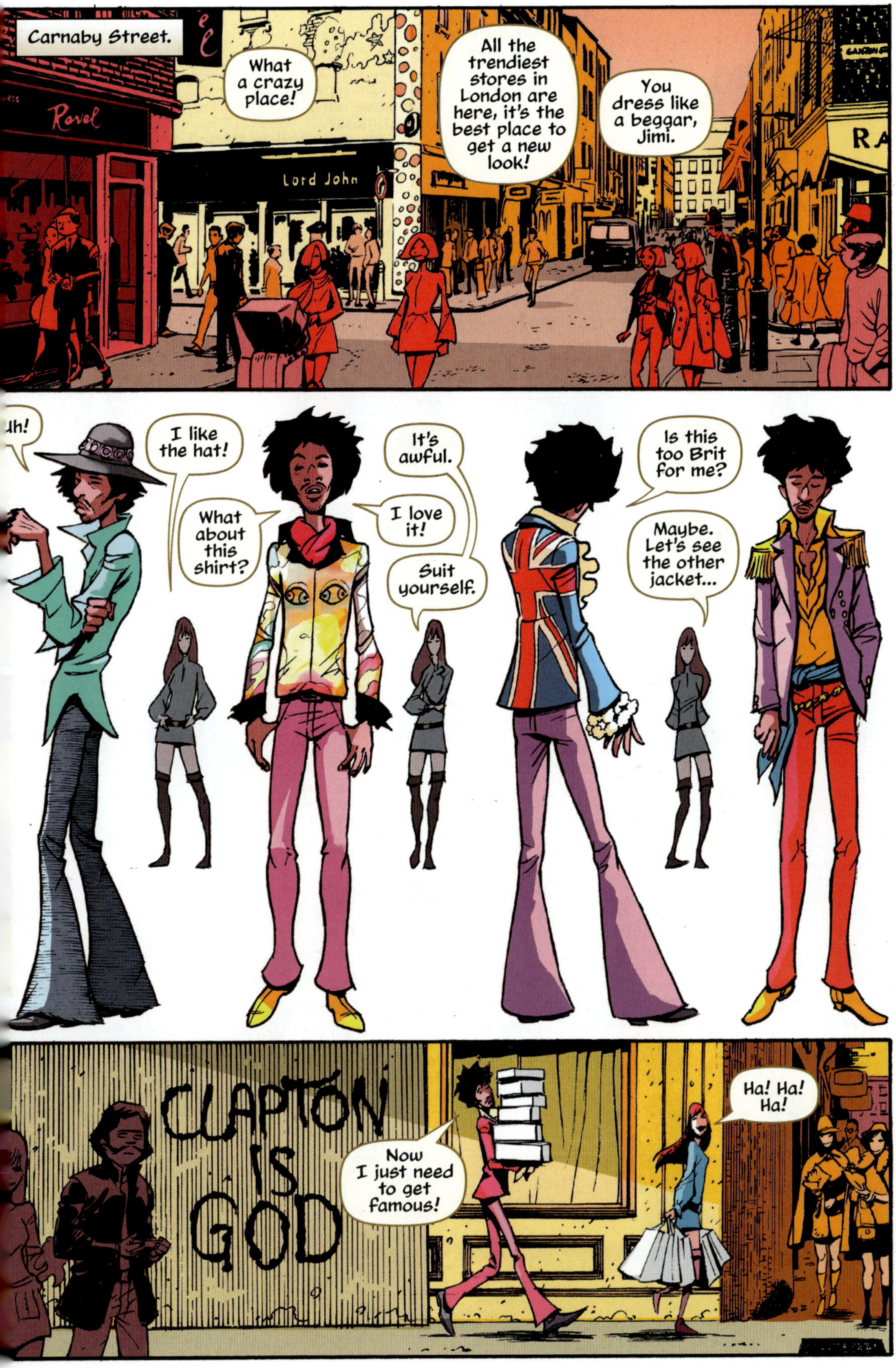
Carnaby Street.
What a crazy place!
All the trendiest stores in London are here, it's the best place to get a new look!
You dress like a beggar, Jimi.
Lord John
uh!
I like the hat!
What about this shirt?
It's awful.
I love it!
Suit yourself.
Is this too Brit for me?
Maybe. Let's see the other jacket...
CLAPTON IS GOD
Now I just need to get famous!
Ha! Ha! Ha!

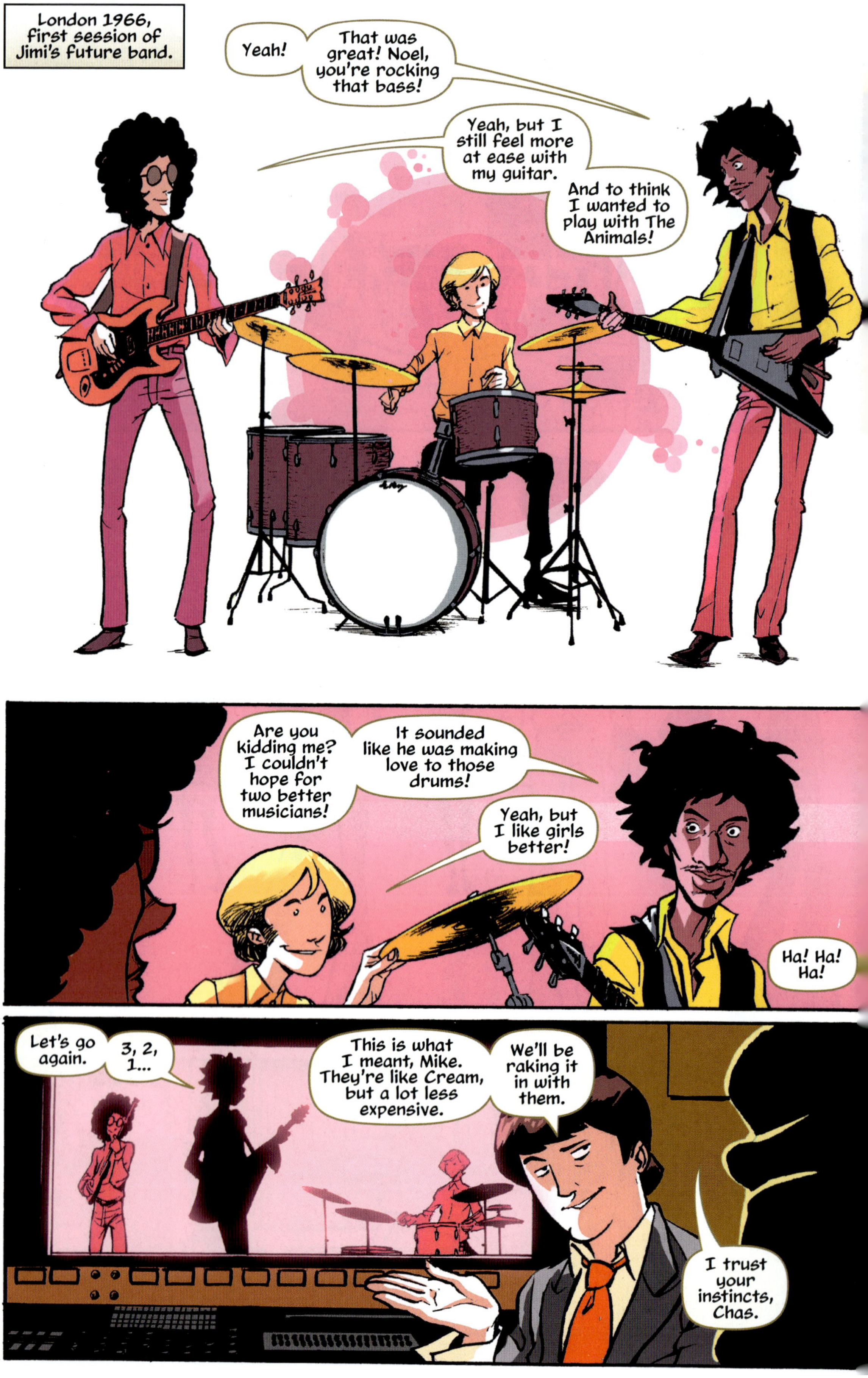
London 1966, first session of Jimi's future band.
Yeah!
That was great! Noel, you're rocking that bass!
Yeah, but I still feel more at ease with my guitar.
And to think I wanted to play with The Animals!
Are you kidding me? I couldn't hope for two better musicians!
It sounded like he was making love to those drums!
Yeah, but I like girls better!
Ha! Ha! Ha!
Let's go again.
3, 2, 1...
This is what I meant, Mike. They're like Cream, but a lot less expensive.
We'll be raking it in with them.
I trust your instincts, Chas.

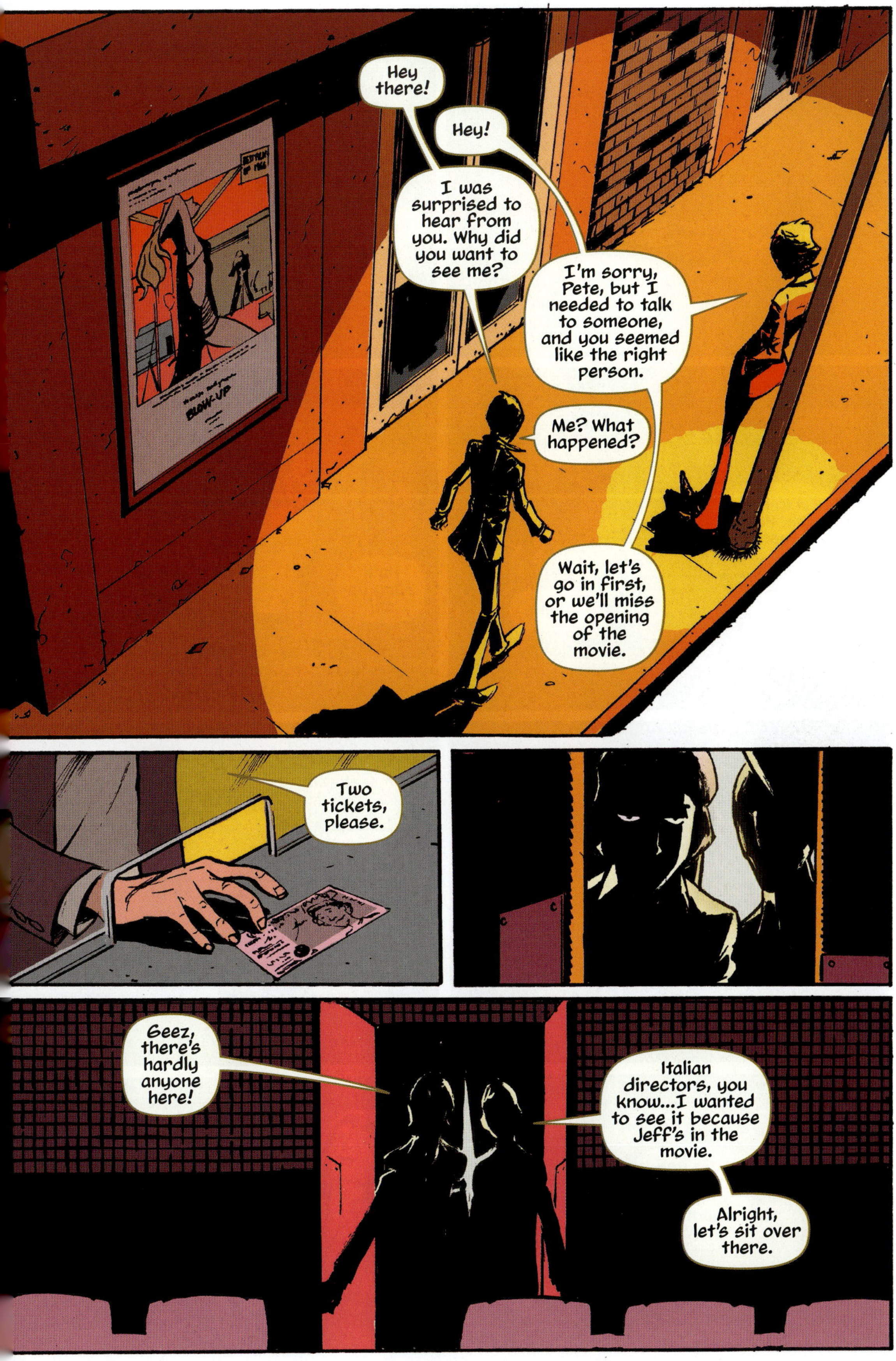

Hey there!
Hey!
I was surprised to hear from you. Why did you want to see me?
I'm sorry, Pete, but I needed to talk to someone, and you seemed like the right person.
Me? What happened?
Wait, let's go in first, or we'll miss the opening of the movie.
BLOW-UP
Two tickets, please.
Geez, there's hardly anyone here!
Italian directors, you know...I wanted to see it because Jeff's in the movie.
Alright, let's sit over there.

So! What's eating you?

Hendrix.

I heard of him. Is he really that good?

Fuck, man, yeah. He's a monster.

Hmm.

He'll bury us all!

So, it's actually possible for someone to scare the great Eric Clapton? Ha! Ha! Ha!

There's nothing to laugh at. He'll eat you and The Who up, too!

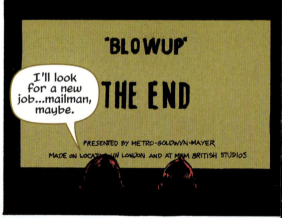

I'll look for a new job...mailman, maybe.

"BLOWUP"

THE END

PRESENTED BY METRO-GOLDWYN-MAYER

MADE ON LOCATION IN LONDON AND AT MGM BRITISH STUDIOS

Did you understand anything about this movie?

Me?

Nope!

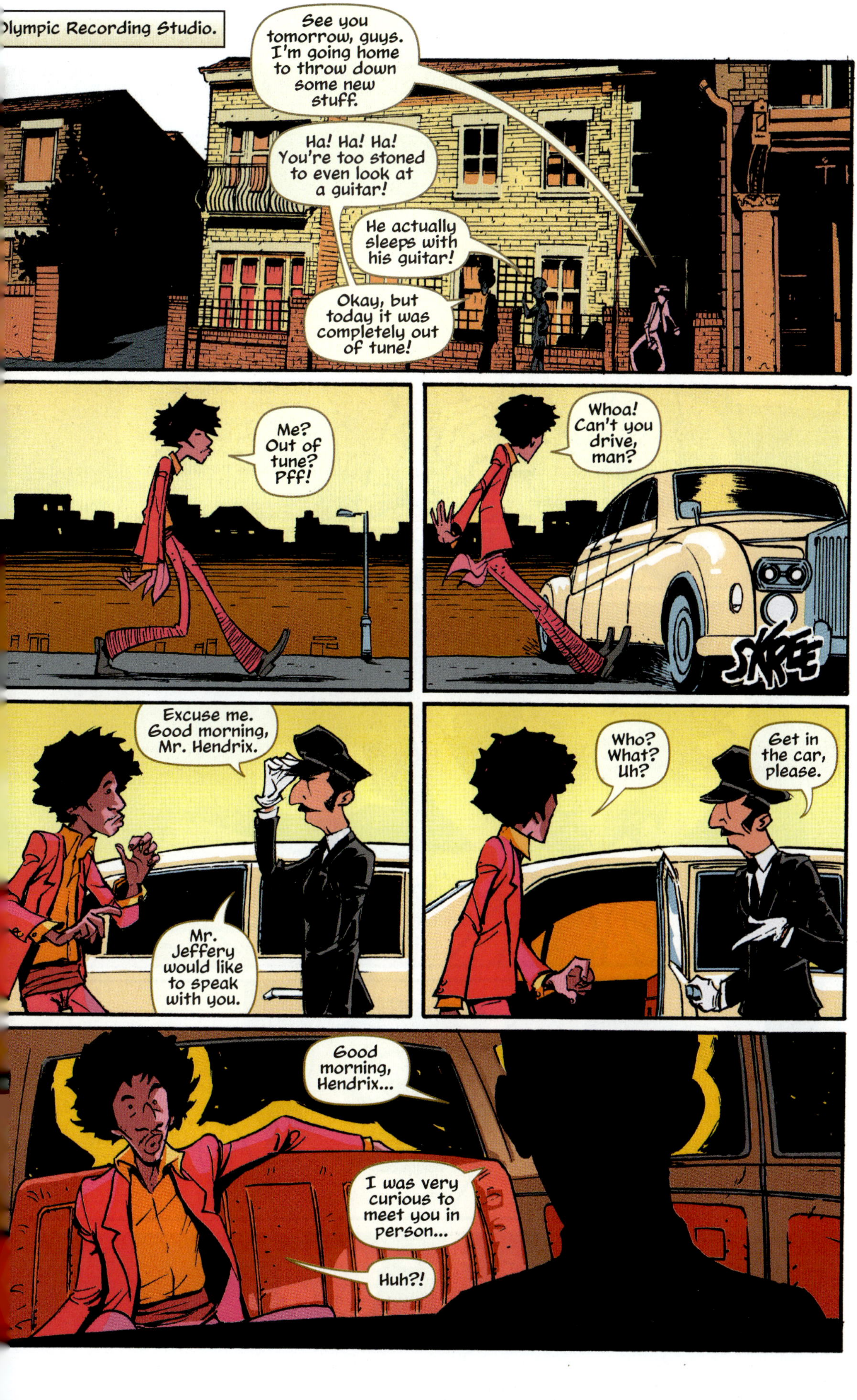
Olympic Recording Studio.
See you tomorrow, guys. I'm going home to throw down some new stuff.
Ha! Ha! Ha! You're too stoned to even look at a guitar!
He actually sleeps with his guitar!
Okay, but today it was completely out of tune!
Me? Out of tune? Pff!
Whoa! Can't you drive, man?
SKREE
Excuse me. Good morning, Mr. Hendrix.
Mr. Jeffery would like to speak with you.
Who? What? Uh?
Get in the car, please.
Good morning, Hendrix...
I was very curious to meet you in person...
Huh?!

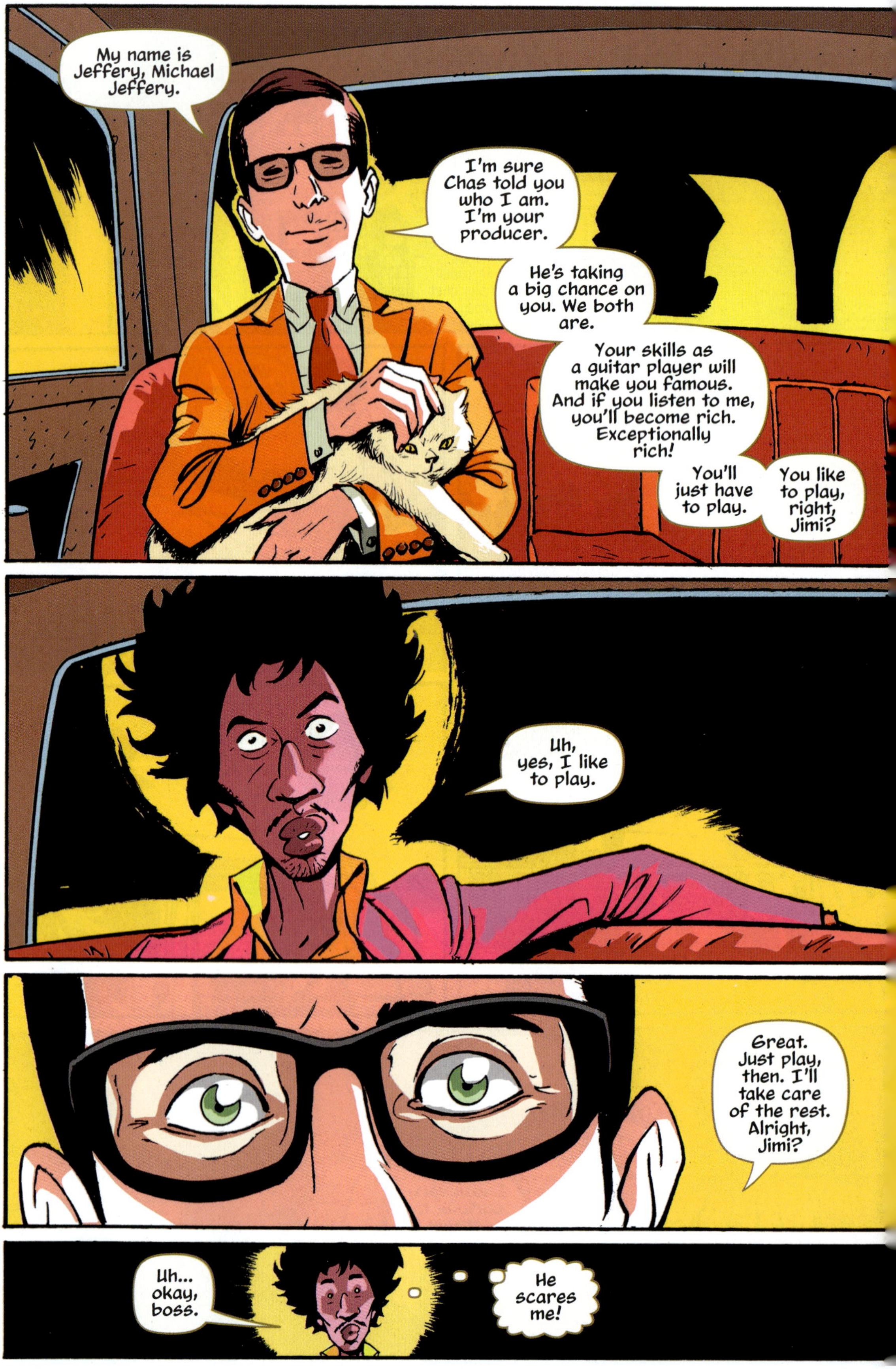

My name is Jeffery, Michael Jeffery.
I'm sure Chas told you who I am. I'm your producer.
He's taking a big chance on you. We both are.
Your skills as a guitar player will make you famous. And if you listen to me, you'll become rich. Exceptionally rich!
You'll just have to play.
You like to play, right, Jimi?
Uh, yes, I like to play.
Great. Just play, then. I'll take care of the rest. Alright, Jimi?
Uh... okay, boss.
He scares me!

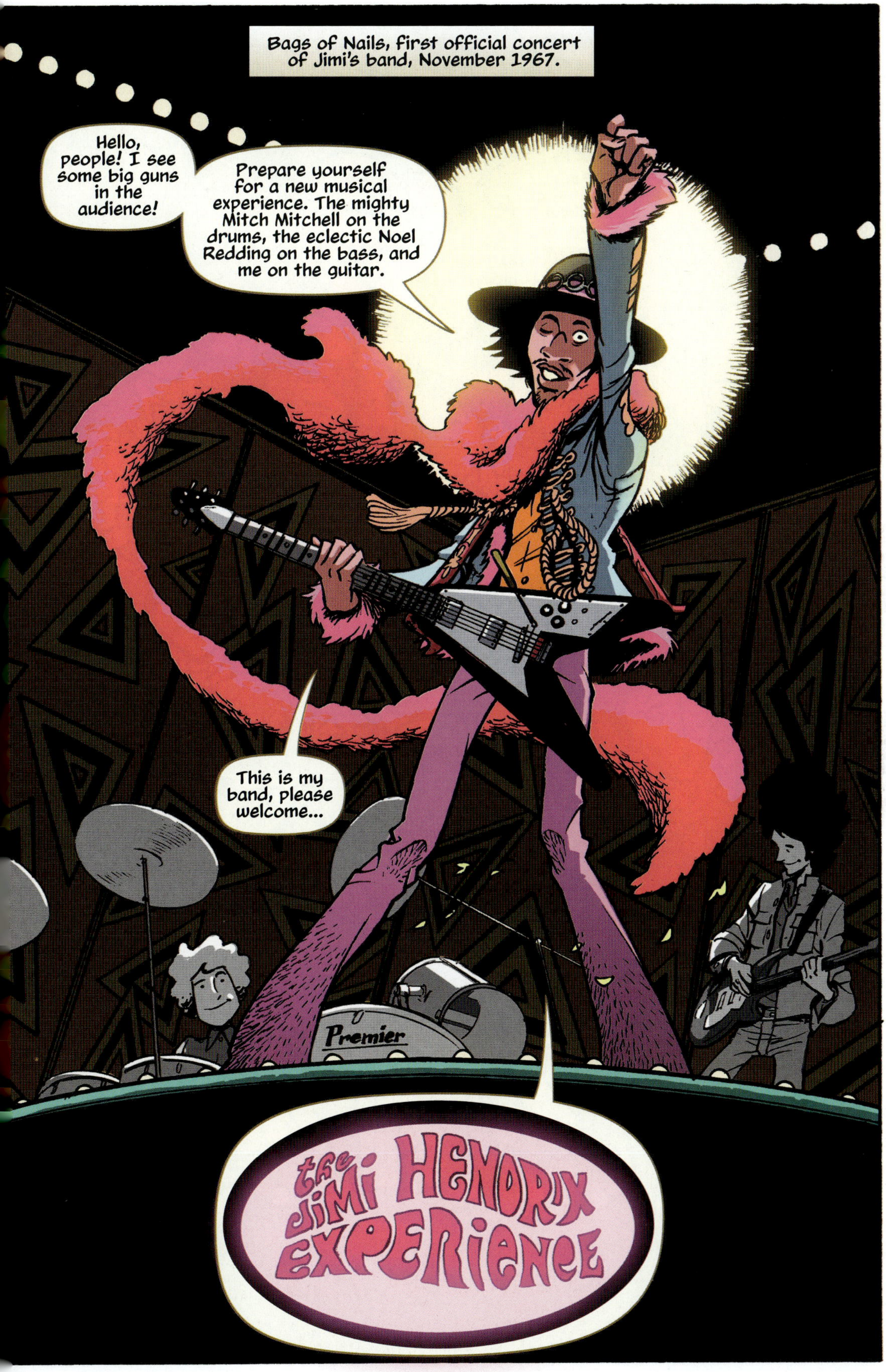

Bags of Nails, first official concert of Jimi's band, November 1967.
Hello, people! I see some big guns in the audience!
Prepare yourself for a new musical experience. The mighty Mitch Mitchell on the drums, the eclectic Noel Redding on the bass, and me on the guitar.
This is my band, please welcome...
the Jimi Hendrix Experience
Premier

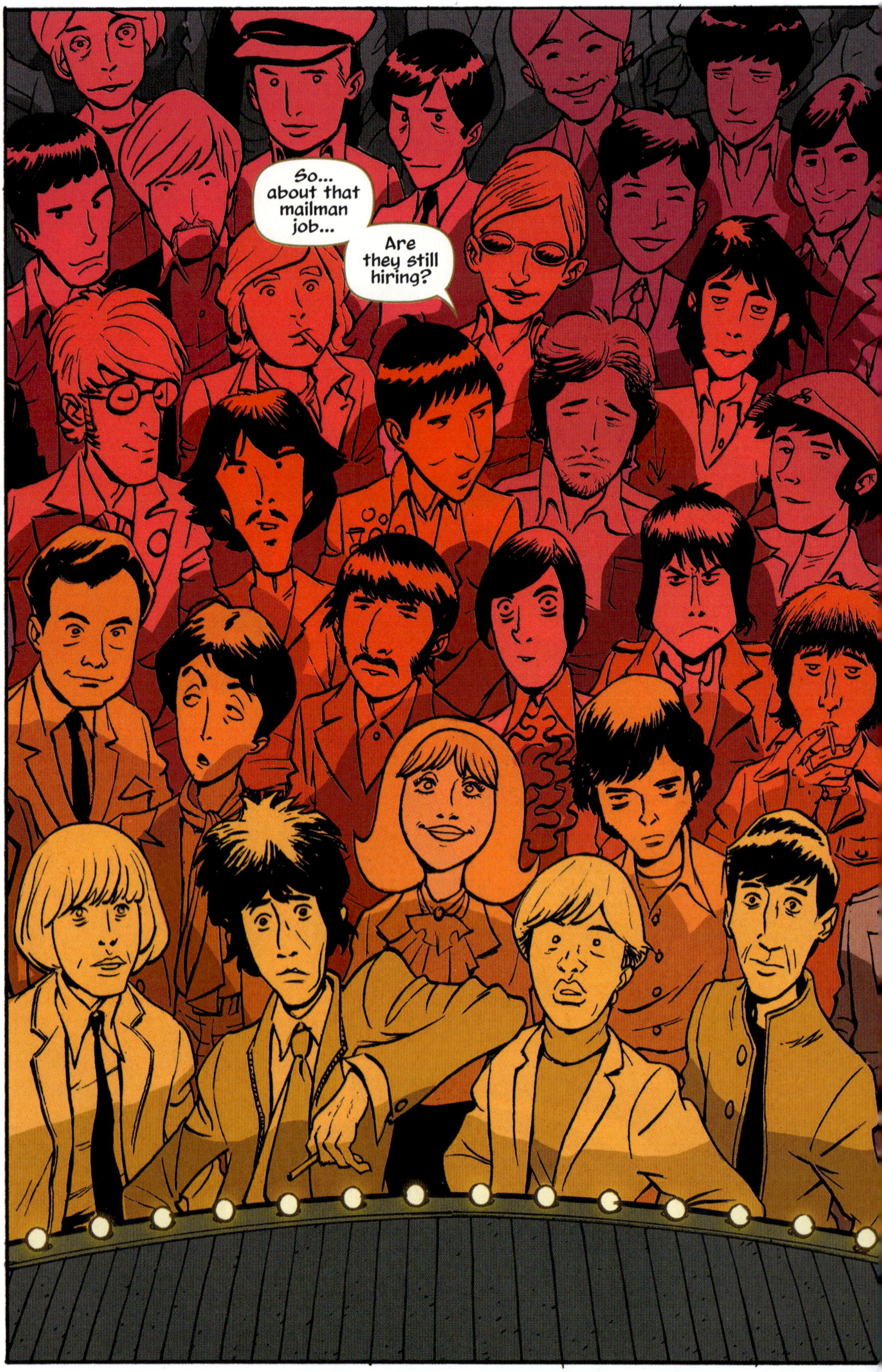
So... about that mailman job...
Are they still hiring?

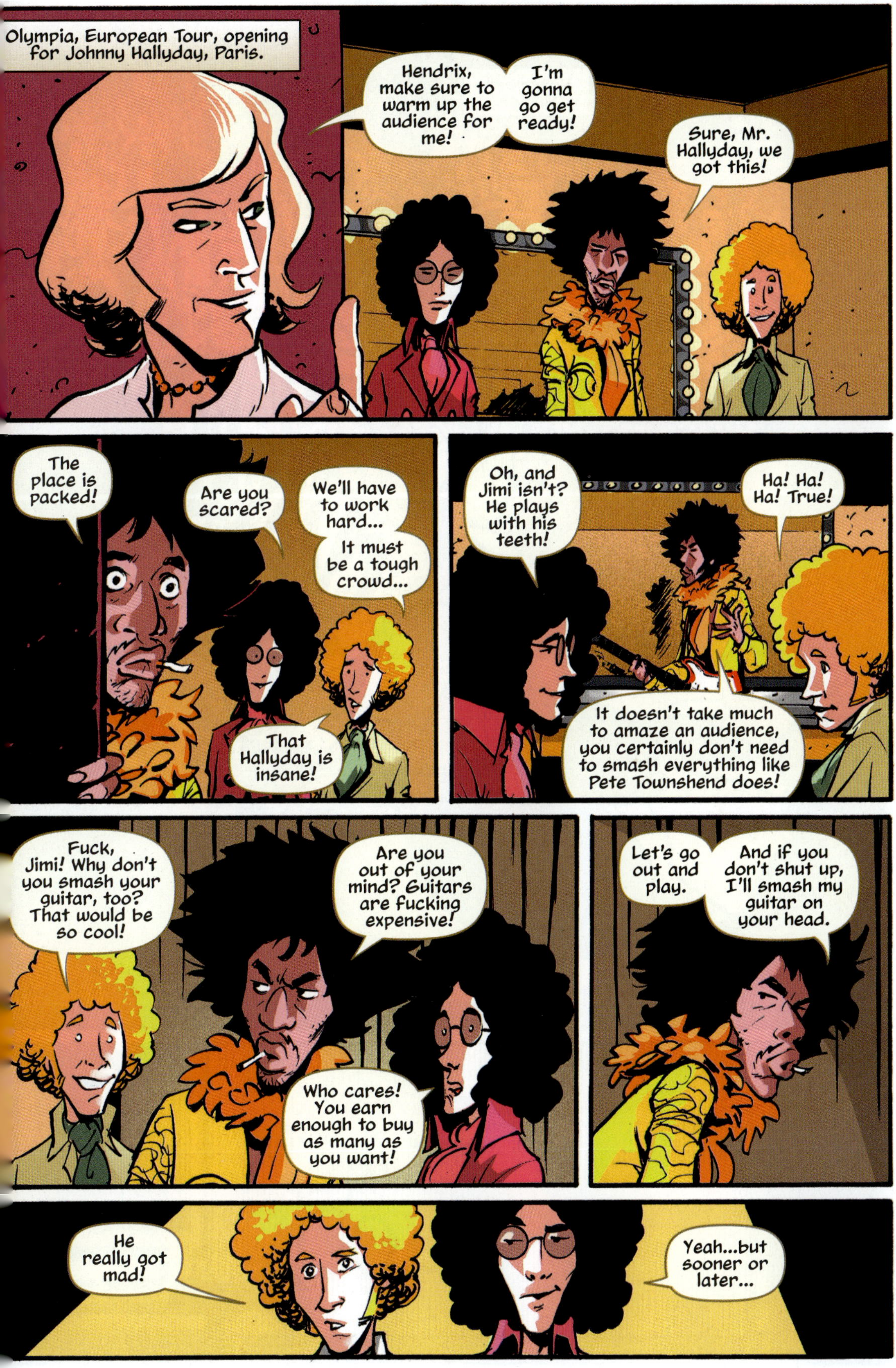
Olympia, European Tour, opening for Johnny Hallyday, Paris.
Hendrix, make sure to warm up the audience for me!
I'm gonna go get ready!
Sure, Mr. Hallyday, we got this!
The place is packed!
Are you scared?
We'll have to work hard...
It must be a tough crowd...
That Hallyday is insane!
Oh, and Jimi isn't? He plays with his teeth!
Ha! Ha! Ha! True!
It doesn't take much to amaze an audience, you certainly don't need to smash everything like Pete Townshend does!
Fuck, Jimi! Why don't you smash your guitar, too? That would be so cool!
Are you out of your mind? Guitars are fucking expensive!
Who cares! You earn enough to buy as many as you want!
Let's go out and play.
And if you don't shut up, I'll smash my guitar on your head.
He really got mad!
Yeah...but sooner or later...

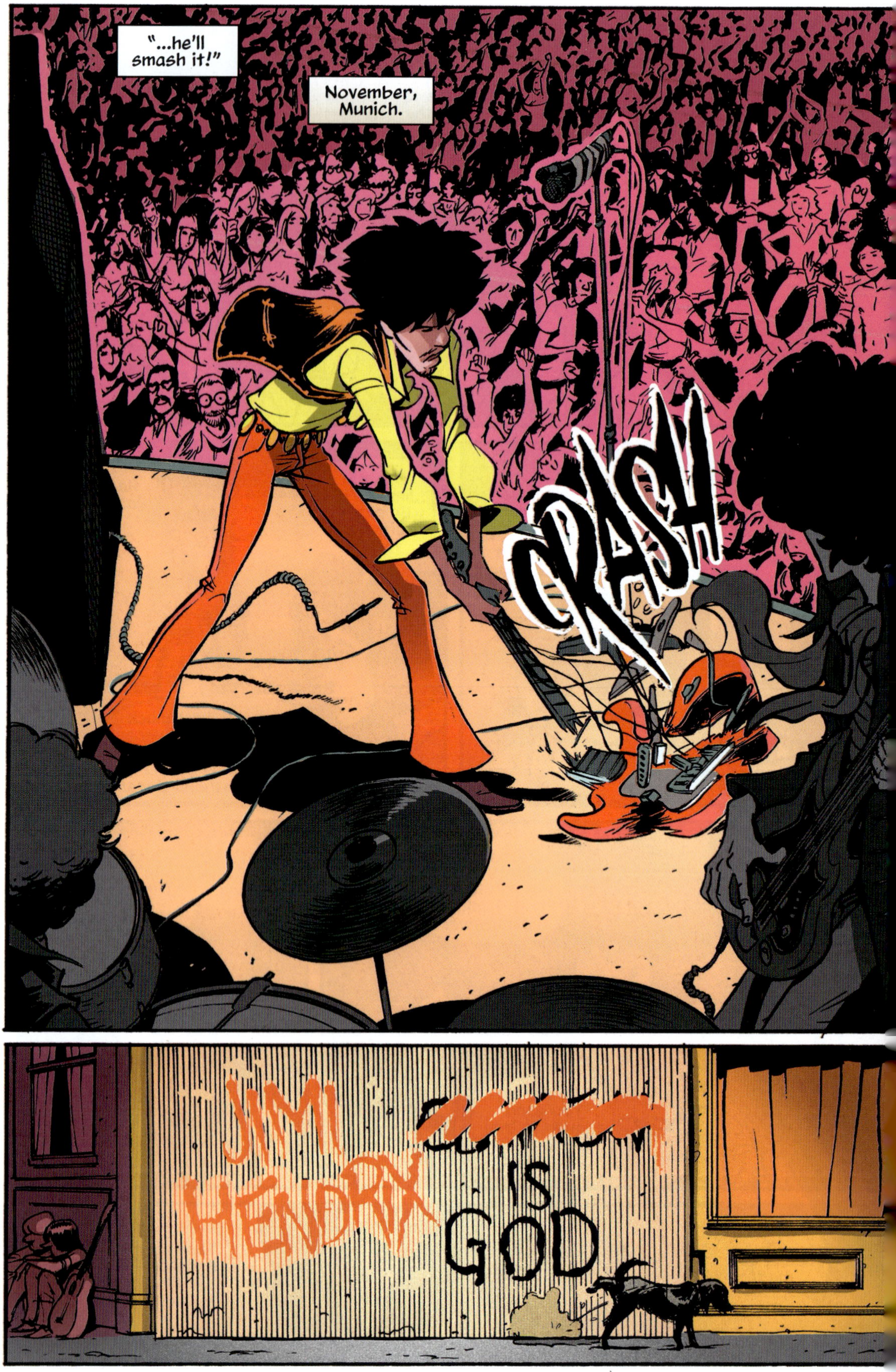
"...he'll smash it!"
November, Munich.
CRASH
JIMI HENDRIX
IS GOD

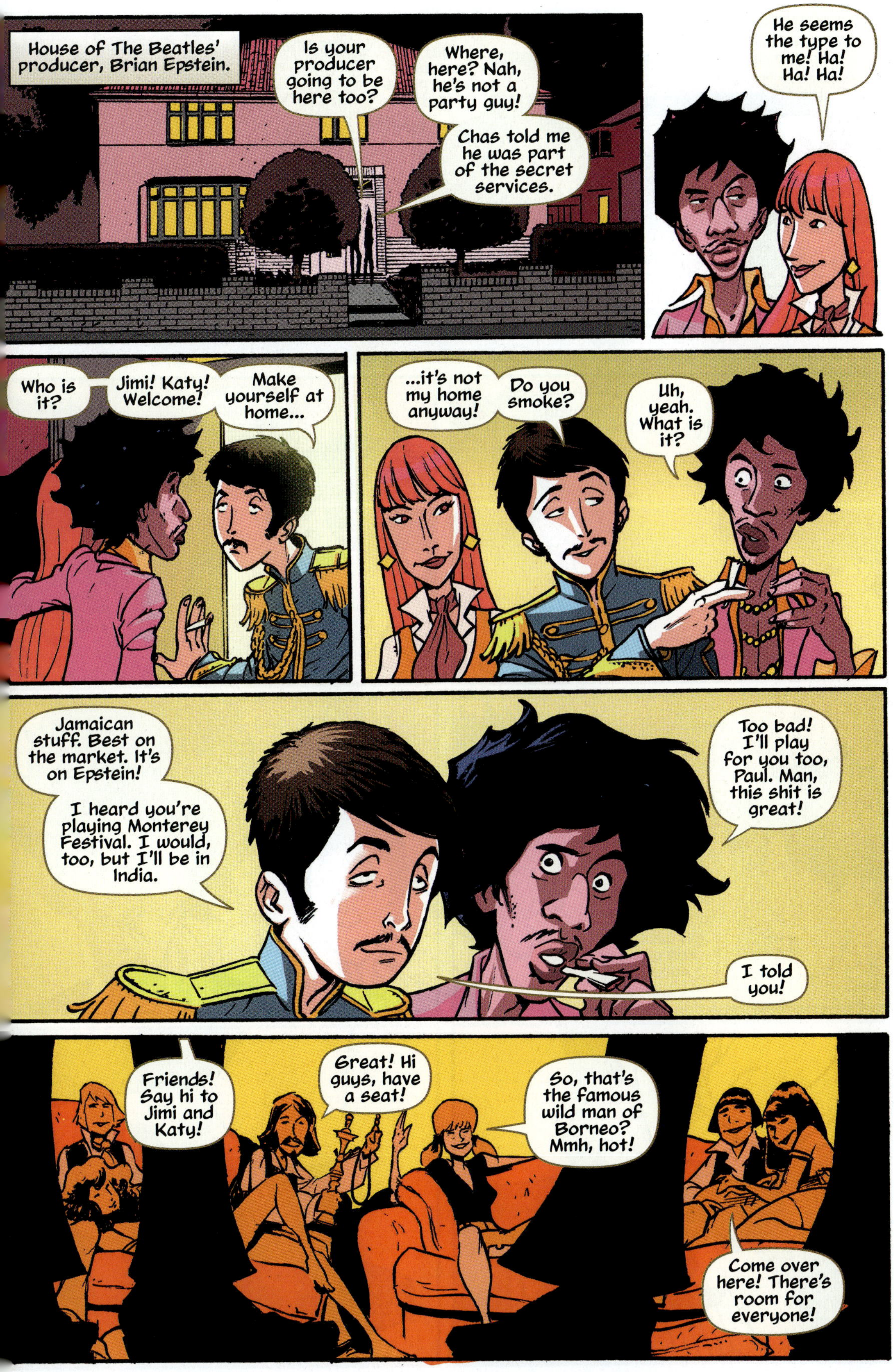
House of The Beatles' producer, Brian Epstein.
Is your producer going to be here too?
Where, here? Nah, he's not a party guy!
Chas told me he was part of the secret services.
He seems the type to me! Ha! Ha! Ha!
Who is it?
Jimi! Katy! Welcome!
Make yourself at home...
...it's not my home anyway!
Do you smoke?
Uh, yeah. What is it?
Jamaican stuff. Best on the market. It's on Epstein!
I heard you're playing Monterey Festival. I would, too, but I'll be in India.
Too bad! I'll play for you too, Paul. Man, this shit is great!
I told you!
Friends! Say hi to Jimi and Katy!
Great! Hi guys, have a seat!
So, that's the famous wild man of Borneo? Mmh, hot!
Come over here! There's room for everyone!

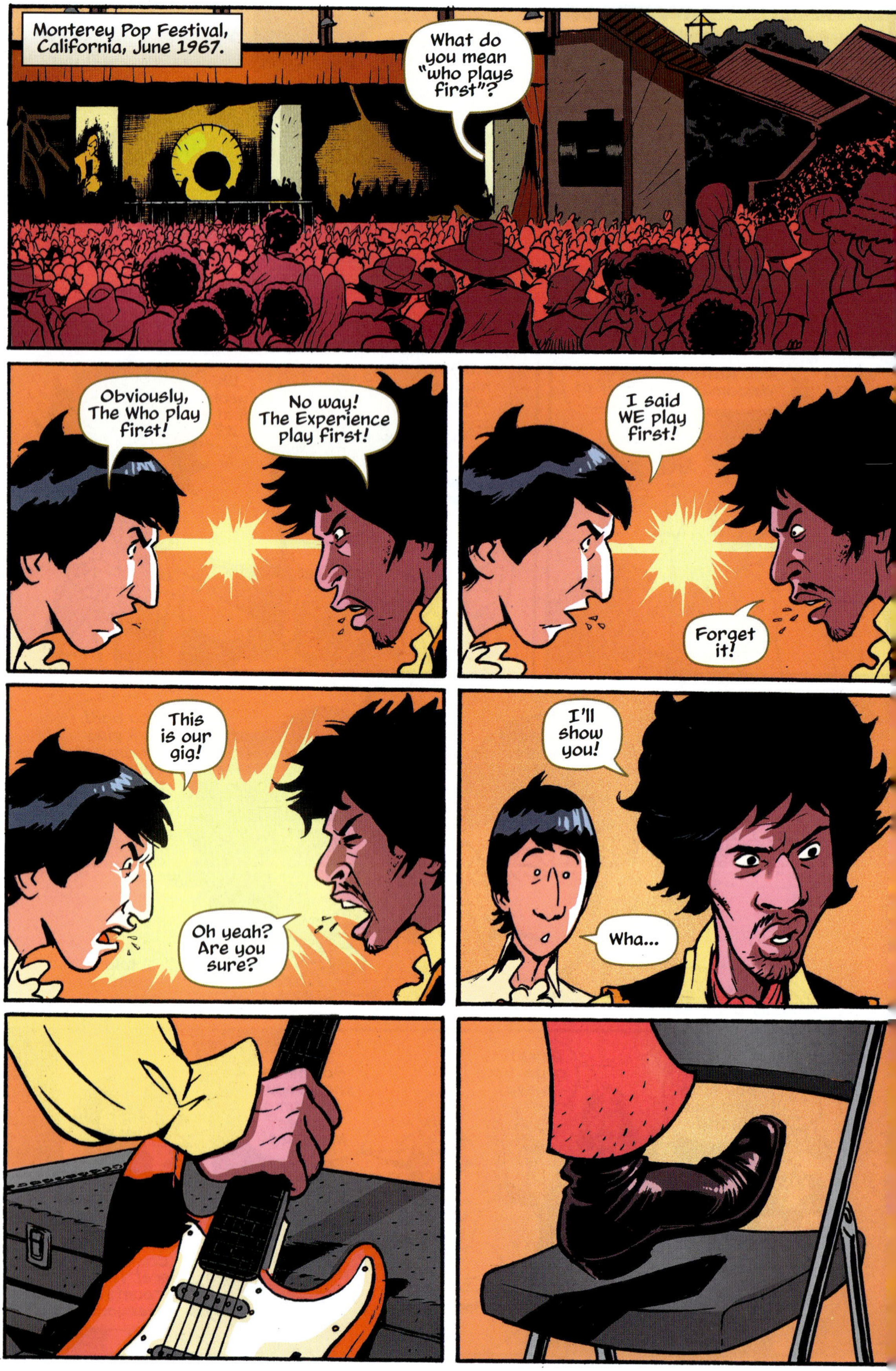
Monterey Pop Festival, California, June 1967.
What do you mean "who plays first"?
Obviously, The Who play first!
No way! The Experience play first!
I said WE play first!
Forget it!
This is our gig!
Oh yeah? Are you sure?
I'll show you!
Wha...

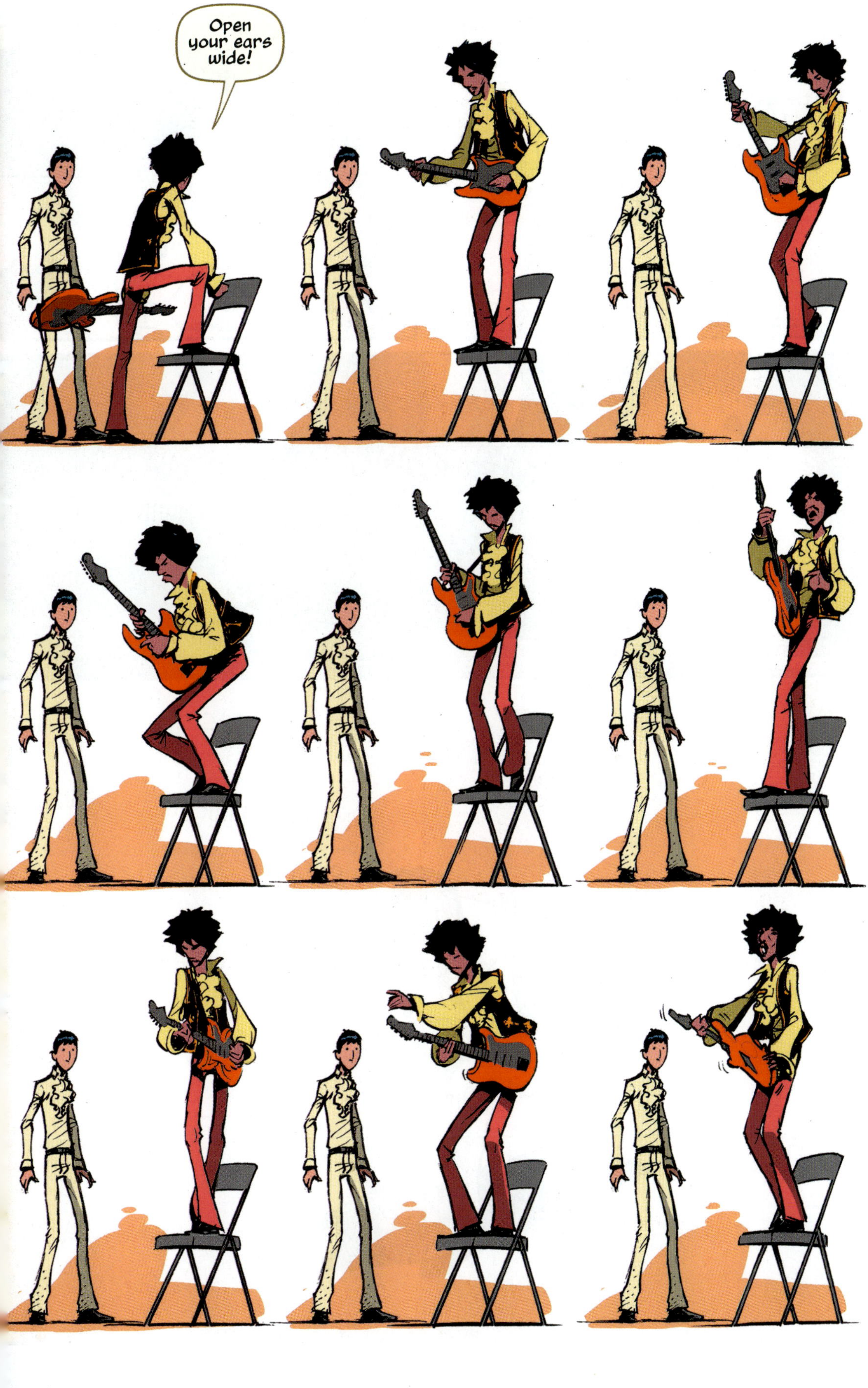
Open your ears wide!

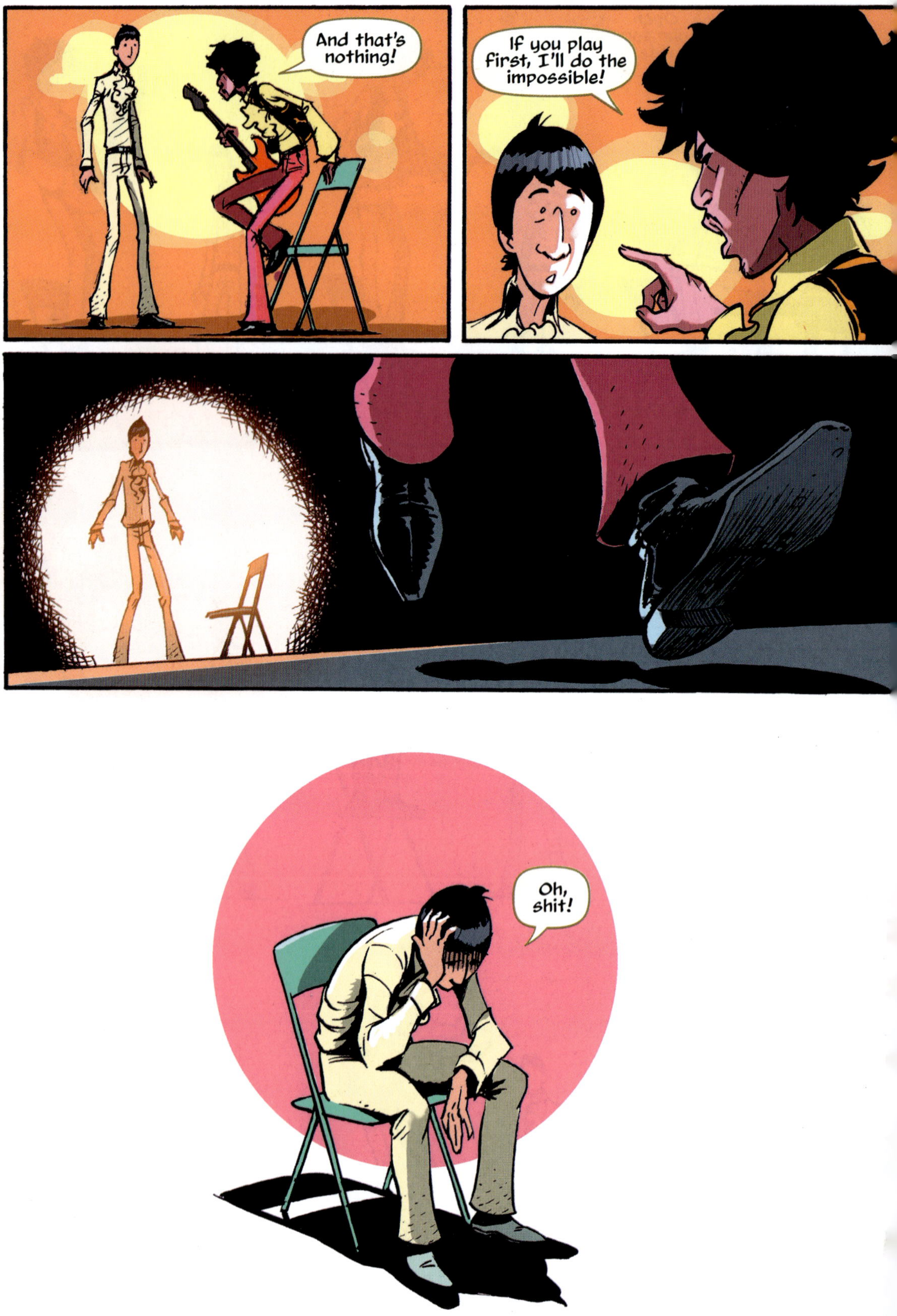
And that's nothing!
If you play first, I'll do the impossible!
Oh, shit!

# 05.

# FIRE

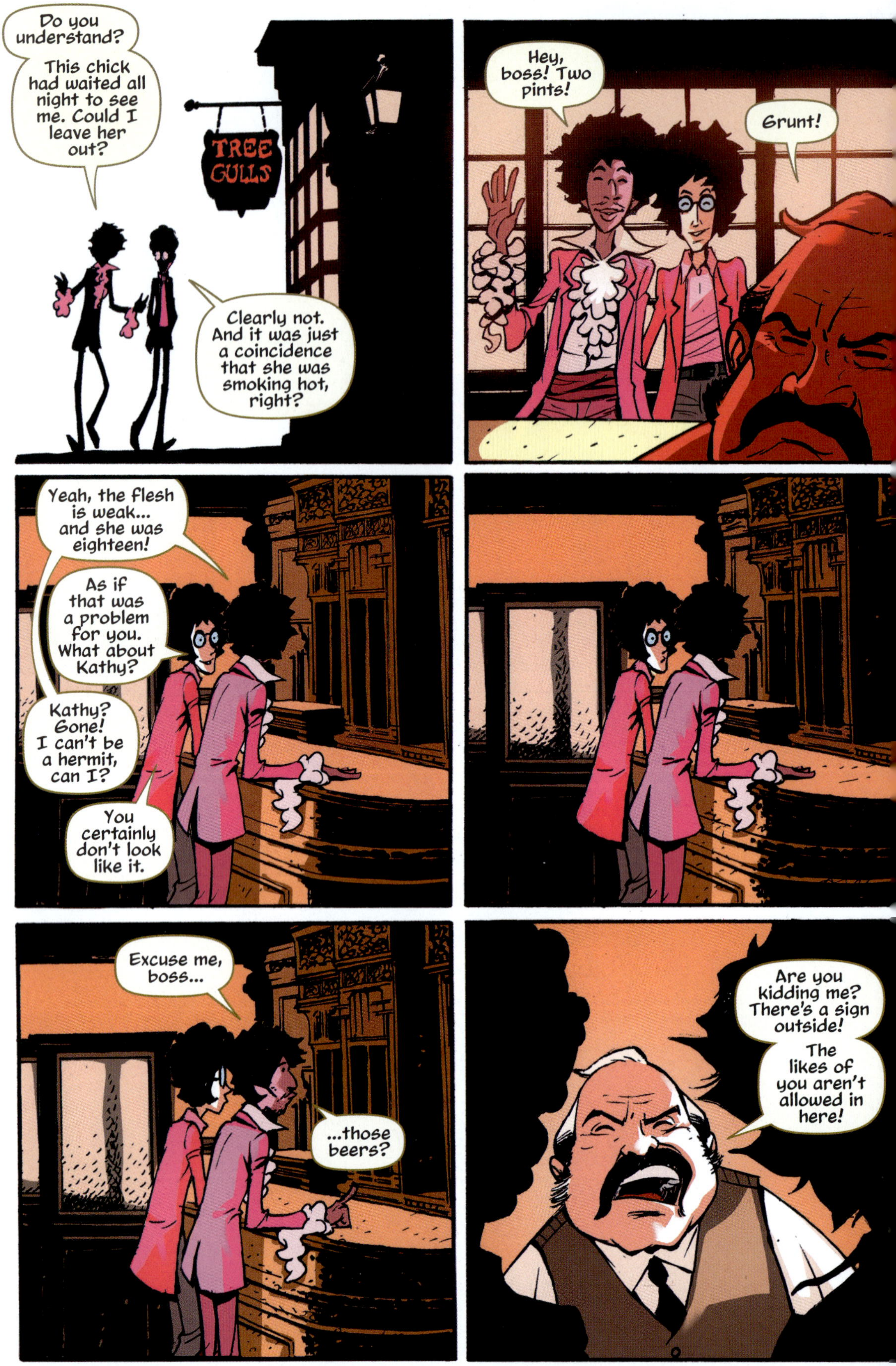
Do you understand?
This chick had waited all night to see me. Could I leave her out?
TREE GULLS
Clearly not. And it was just a coincidence that she was smoking hot, right?
Hey, boss! Two pints!
Grunt!
Yeah, the flesh is weak... and she was eighteen!
As if that was a problem for you. What about Kathy?
Kathy? Gone! I can't be a hermit, can I?
You certainly don't look like it.
Excuse me, boss...
...those beers?
Are you kidding me? There's a sign outside!
The likes of you aren't allowed in here!

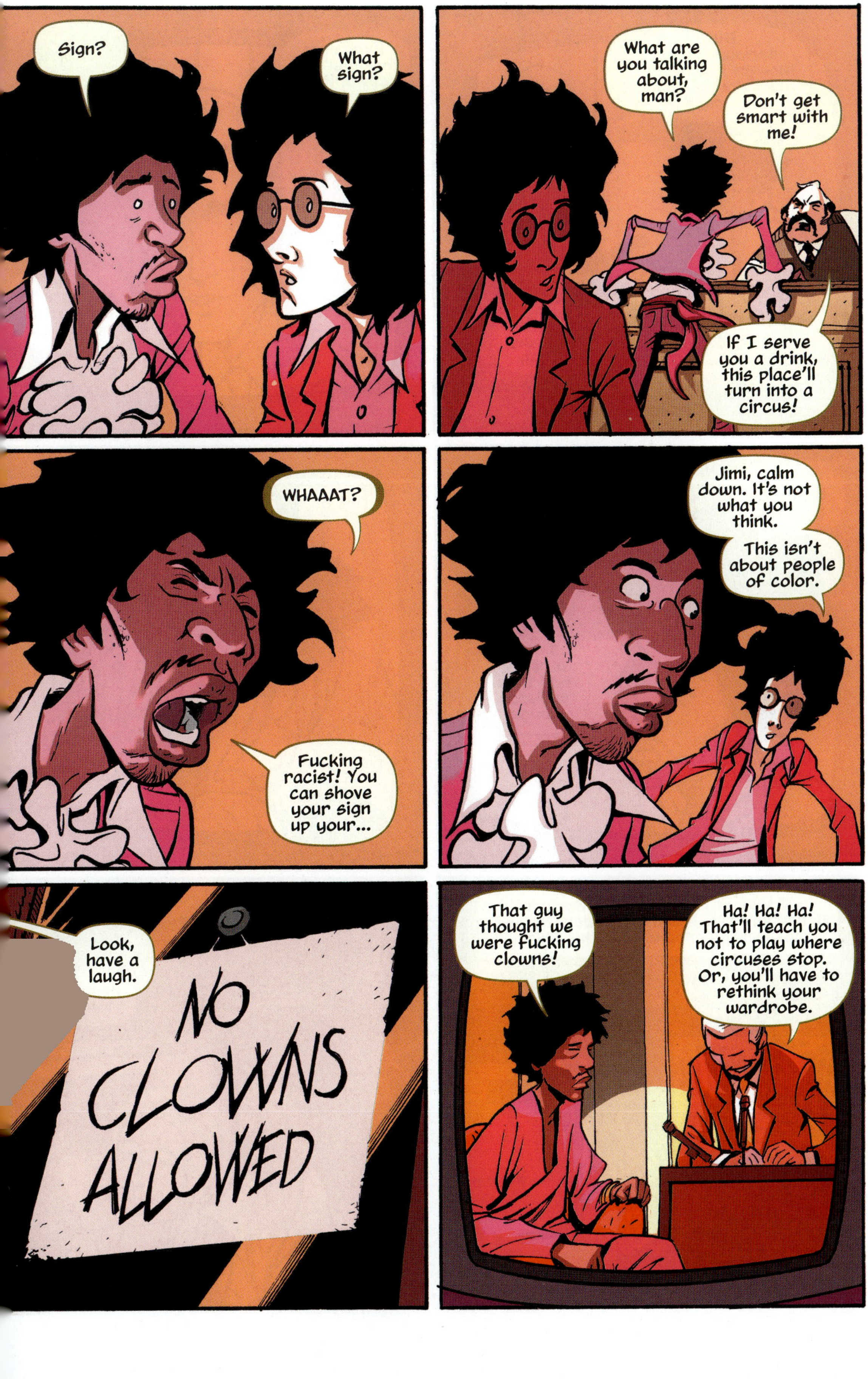
Sign?
What sign?
What are you talking about, man?
Don't get smart with me!
If I serve you a drink, this place'll turn into a circus!
WHAAAT?
Fucking racist! You can shove your sign up your...
Jimi, calm down. It's not what you think.
This isn't about people of color.
Look, have a laugh.
NO CLOWNS ALLOWED
That guy thought we were fucking clowns!
Ha! Ha! Ha! That'll teach you not to play where circuses stop. Or, you'll have to rethink your wardrobe.

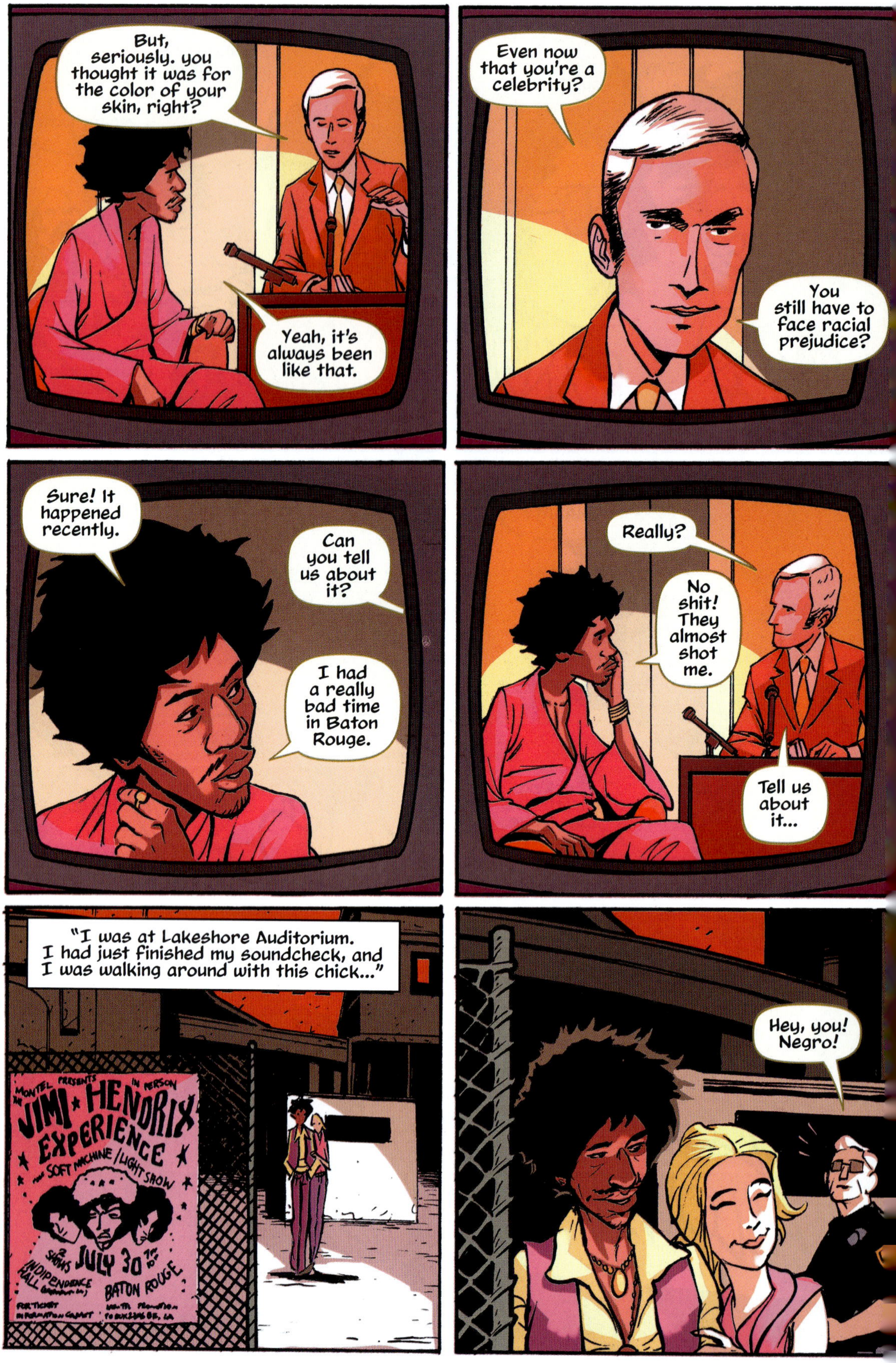
But, seriously. you thought it was for the color of your skin, right?
Yeah, it's always been like that.
Even now that you're a celebrity?
You still have to face racial prejudice?
Sure! It happened recently.
Can you tell us about it?
I had a really bad time in Baton Rouge.
Really?
No shit! They almost shot me.
Tell us about it...
"I was at Lakeshore Auditorium. I had just finished my soundcheck, and I was walking around with this chick..."
PRESENTS IN PERSON
JIMI HENDRIX EXPERIENCE
SOFT MACHINE / LIGHT SHOW
2 SHOWS JULY 30
INDEPENDENCE HALL
BATON ROUGE
Hey, you! Negro!

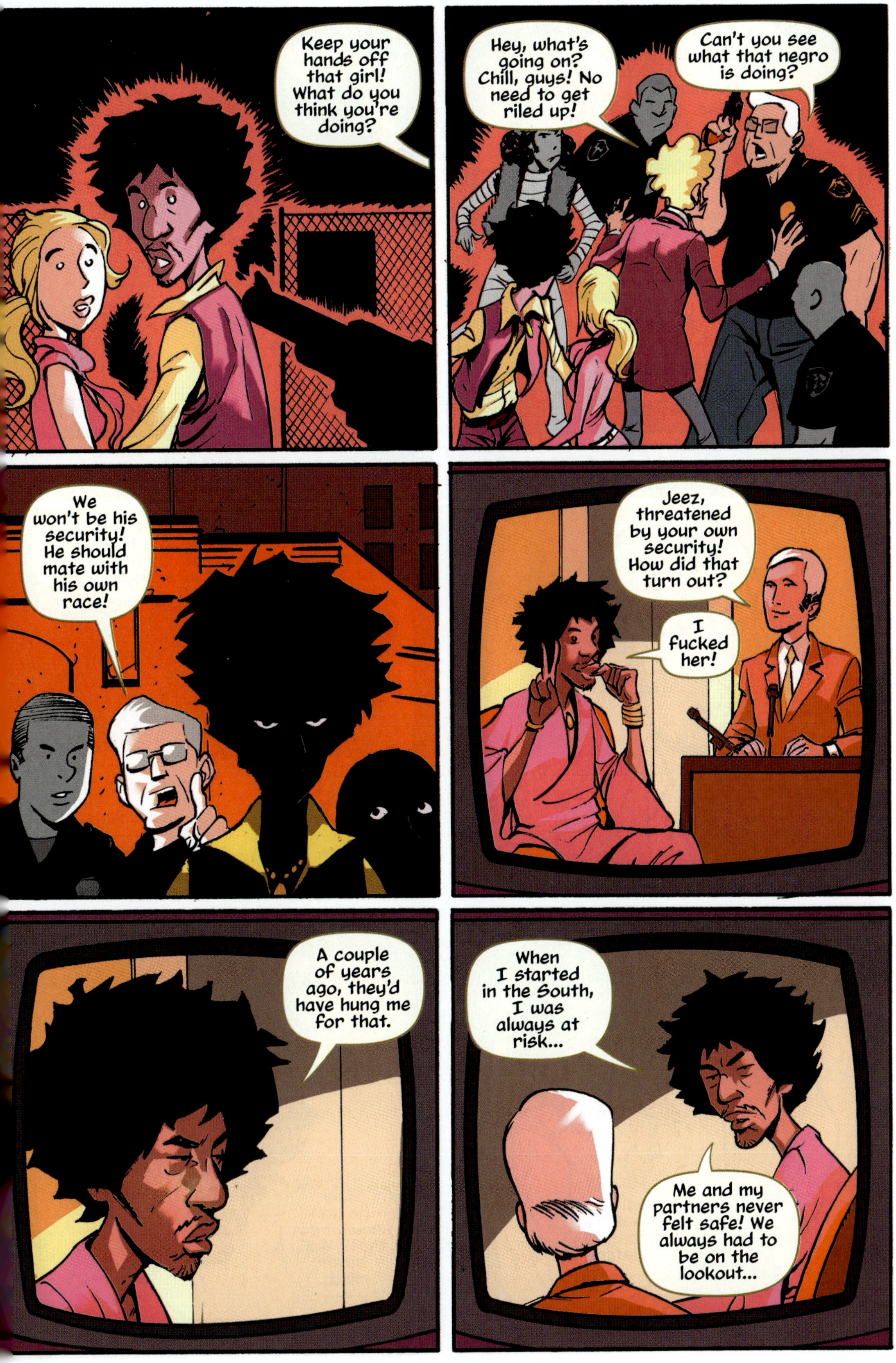
Keep your hands off that girl! What do you think you're doing?
Hey, what's going on? Chill, guys! No need to get riled up!
Can't you see what that negro is doing?
We won't be his security! He should mate with his own race!
Jeez, threatened by your own security! How did that turn out?
I fucked her!
A couple of years ago, they'd have hung me for that.
When I started in the South, I was always at risk...
Me and my partners never felt safe! We always had to be on the lookout...

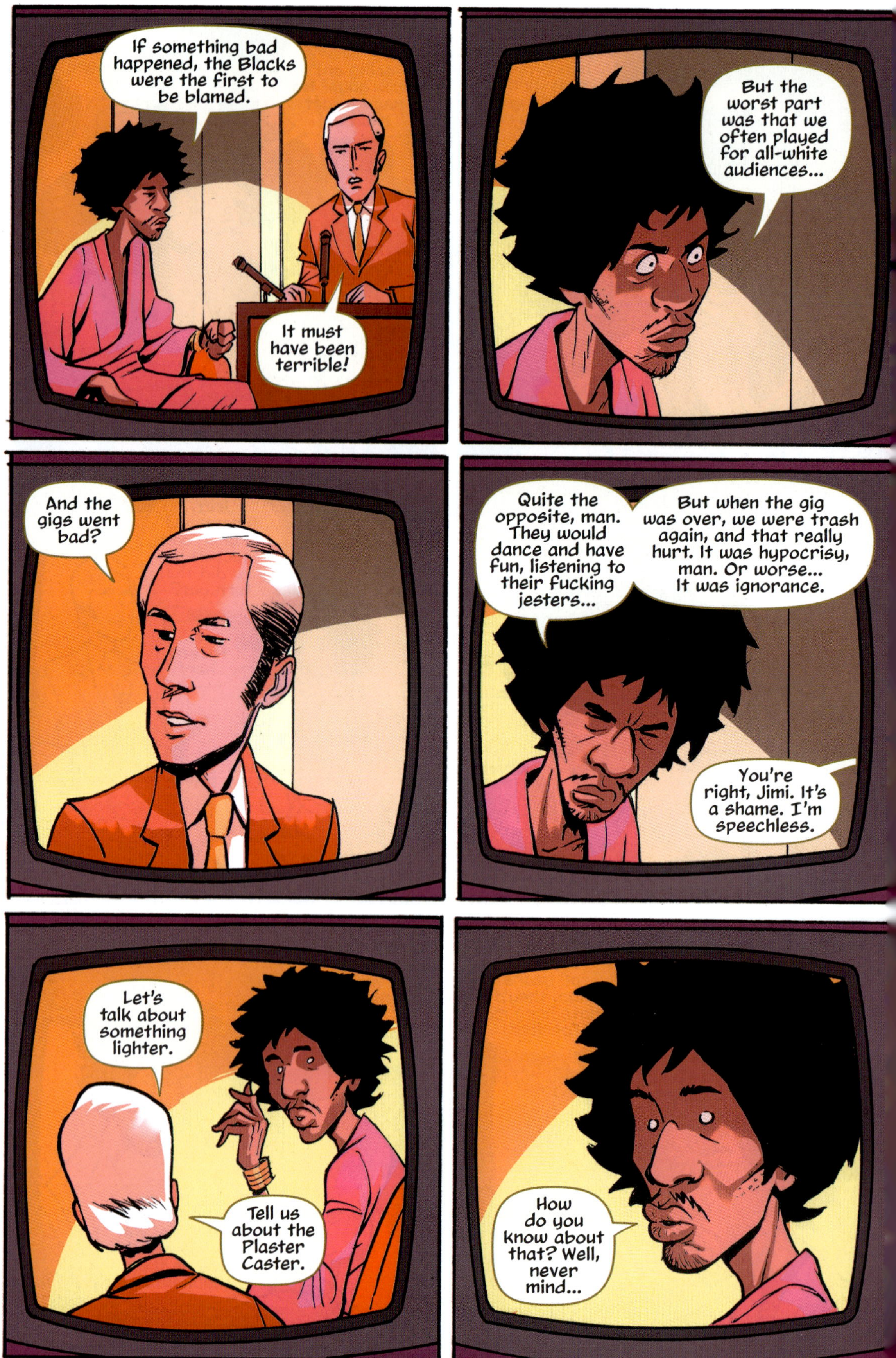
If something bad happened, the Blacks were the first to be blamed.
It must have been terrible!
But the worst part was that we often played for all-white audiences...
And the gigs went bad?
Quite the opposite, man. They would dance and have fun, listening to their fucking jesters...
But when the gig was over, we were trash again, and that really hurt. It was hypocrisy, man. Or worse... It was ignorance.
You're right, Jimi. It's a shame. I'm speechless.
Let's talk about something lighter.
Tell us about the Plaster Caster.
How do you know about that? Well, never mind...

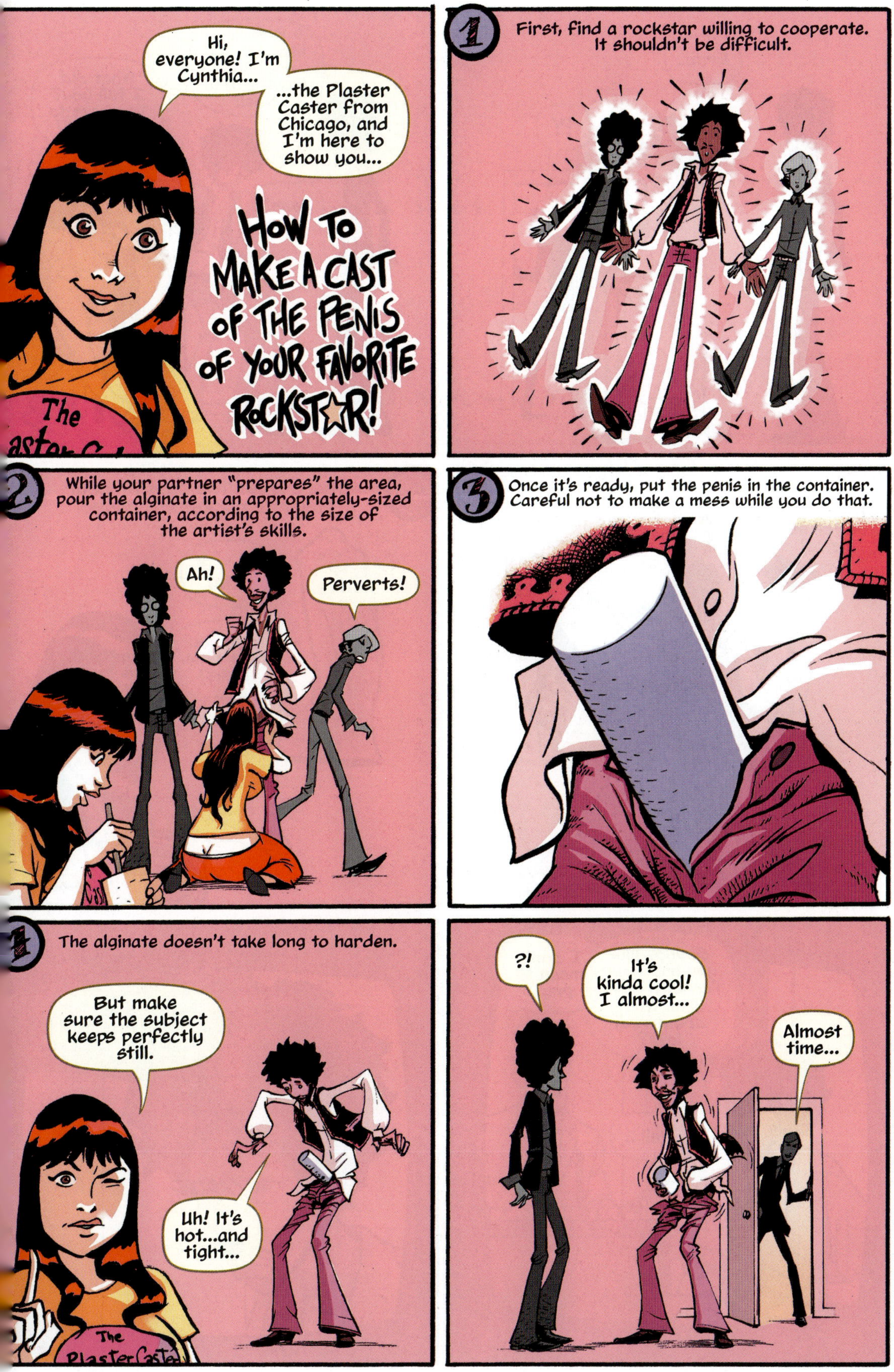

Hi, everyone! I'm Cynthia...
...the Plaster Caster from Chicago, and I'm here to show you...
HOW TO MAKE A CAST OF THE PENIS OF YOUR FAVORITE ROCKSTAR!
1
First, find a rockstar willing to cooperate. It shouldn't be difficult.
2
While your partner "prepares" the area, pour the alginate in an appropriately-sized container, according to the size of the artist's skills.
Ah!
Perverts!
3
Once it's ready, put the penis in the container. Careful not to make a mess while you do that.
The alginate doesn't take long to harden.
But make sure the subject keeps perfectly still.
Uh! It's hot...and tight...
?!
It's kinda cool! I almost...
Almost time...

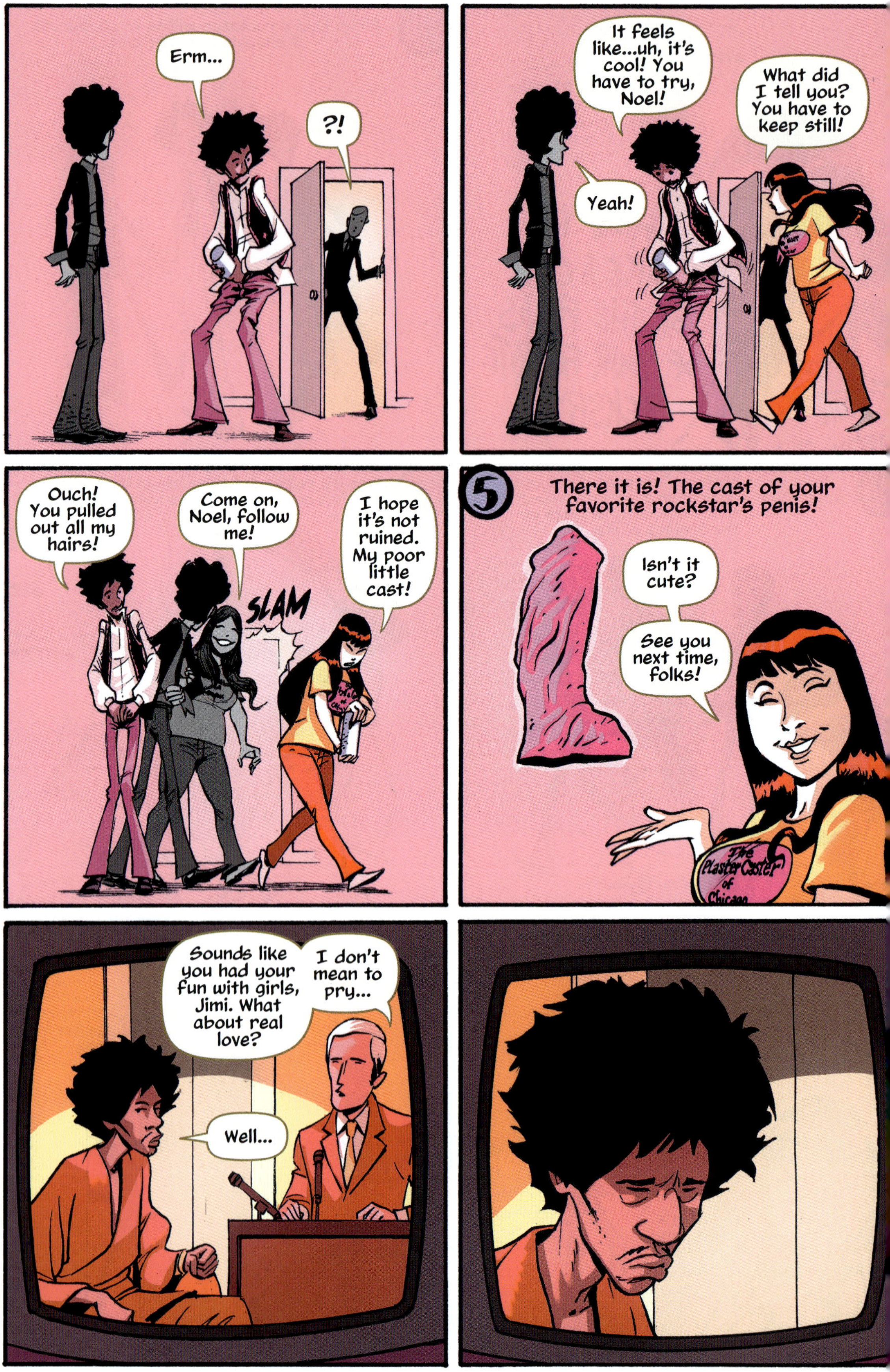
Erm...
?!
It feels like...uh, it's cool! You have to try, Noel!
Yeah!
What did I tell you? You have to keep still!
Ouch! You pulled out all my hairs!
Come on, Noel, follow me!
SLAM
I hope it's not ruined. My poor little cast!
5
There it is! The cast of your favorite rockstar's penis!
Isn't it cute?
See you next time, folks!
The Plaster Caster of
Sounds like you had your fun with girls, Jimi. What about real love?
I don't mean to pry...
Well...

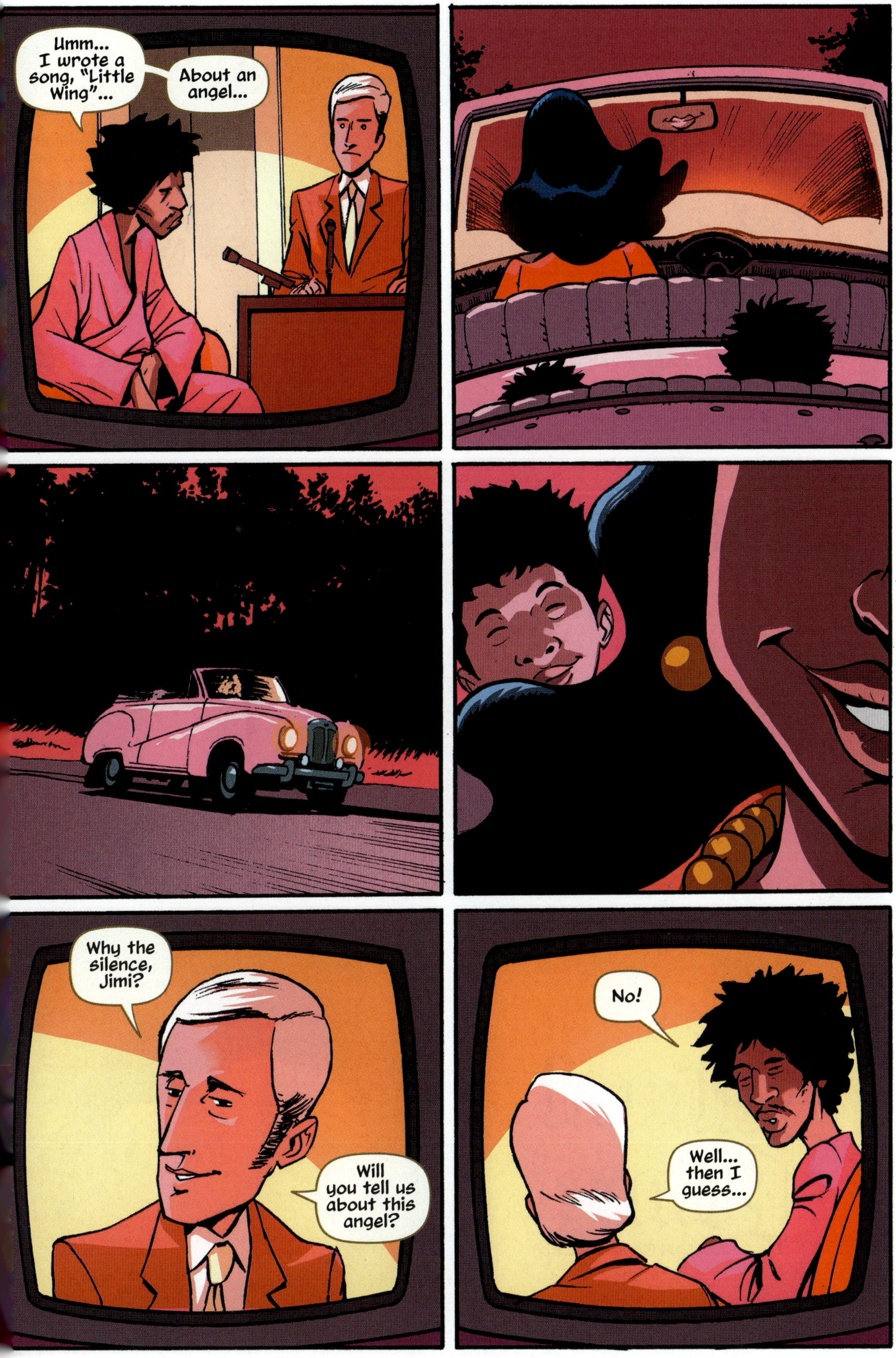
Umm... I wrote a song, "Little Wing"...
About an angel...
Why the silence, Jimi?
Will you tell us about this angel?
No!
Well... then I guess...

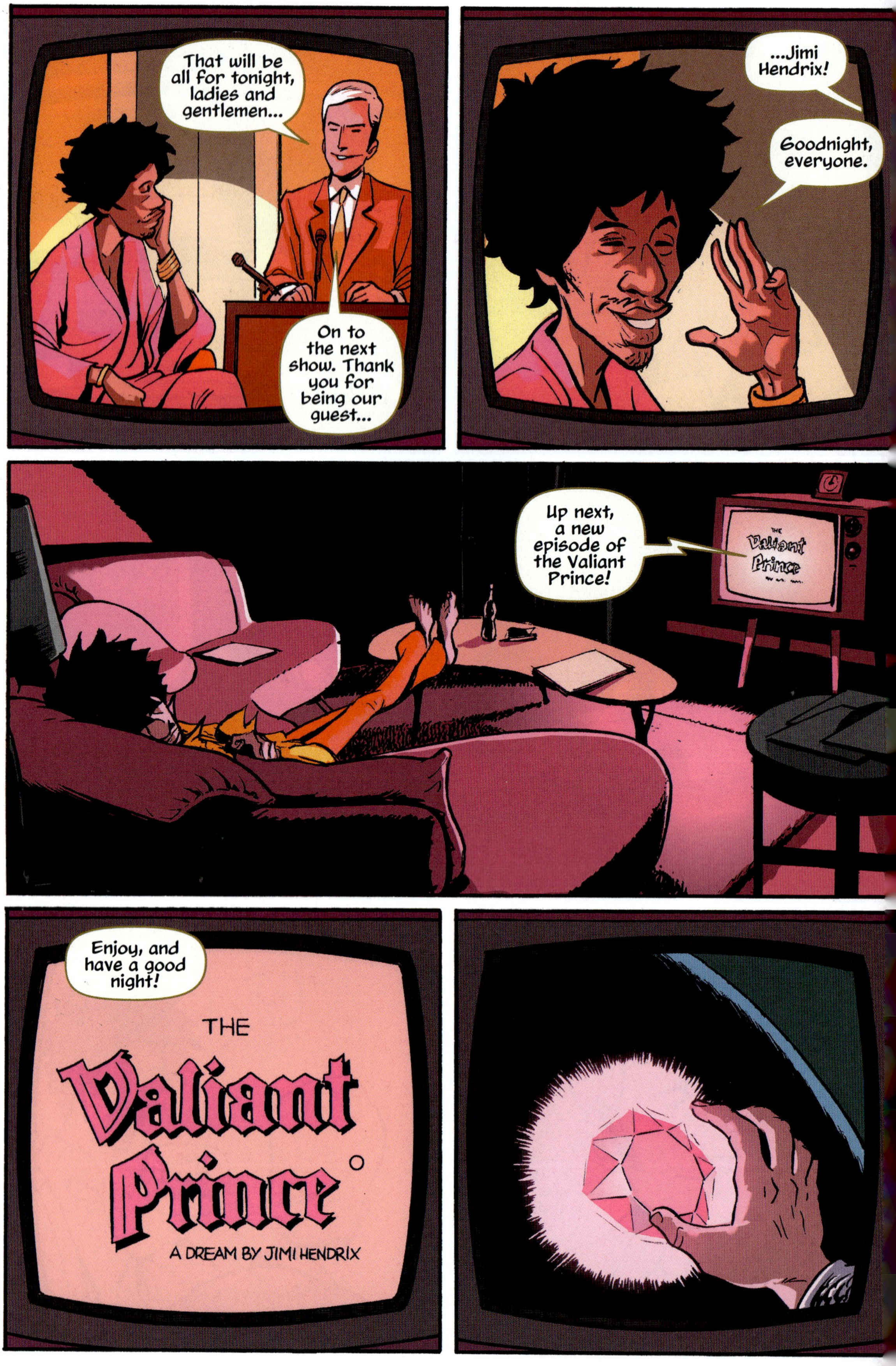
That will be all for tonight, ladies and gentlemen...
On to the next show. Thank you for being our guest...
...Jimi Hendrix!
Goodnight, everyone.
Up next, a new episode of the Valiant Prince!
Enjoy, and have a good night!
THE
Valiant Prince
A DREAM BY JIMI HENDRIX

# 06.

# ALL ALONG the WATCHTOWER

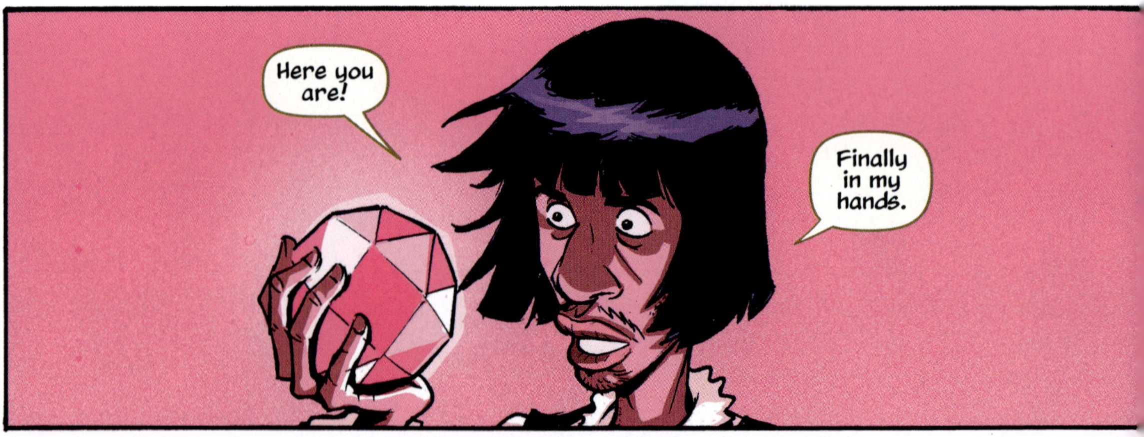
Here you are!
Finally in my hands.

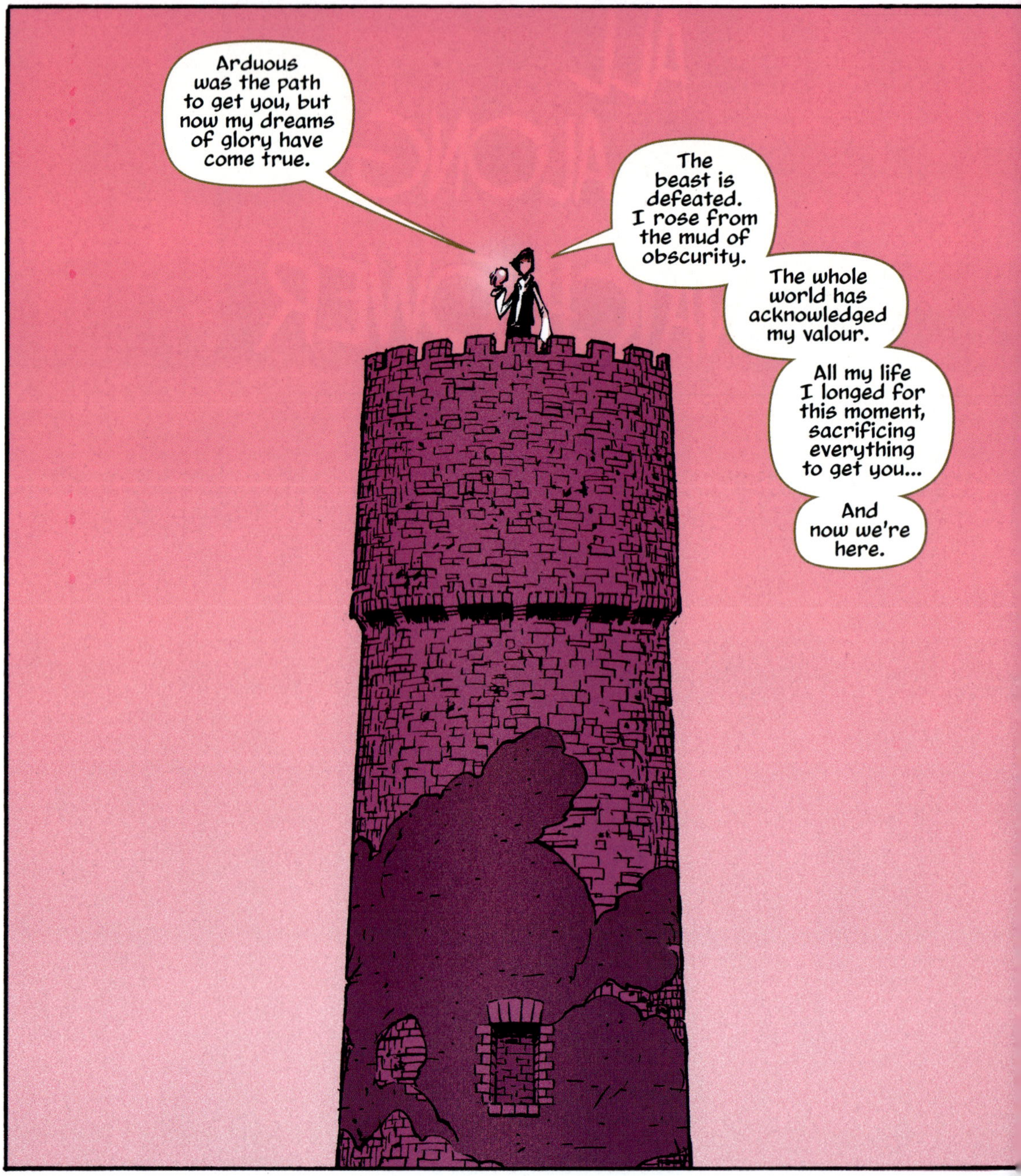
Arduous was the path to get you, but now my dreams of glory have come true.
The beast is defeated. I rose from the mud of obscurity.
The whole world has acknowledged my valour.
All my life I longed for this moment, sacrificing everything to get you...
And now we're here.

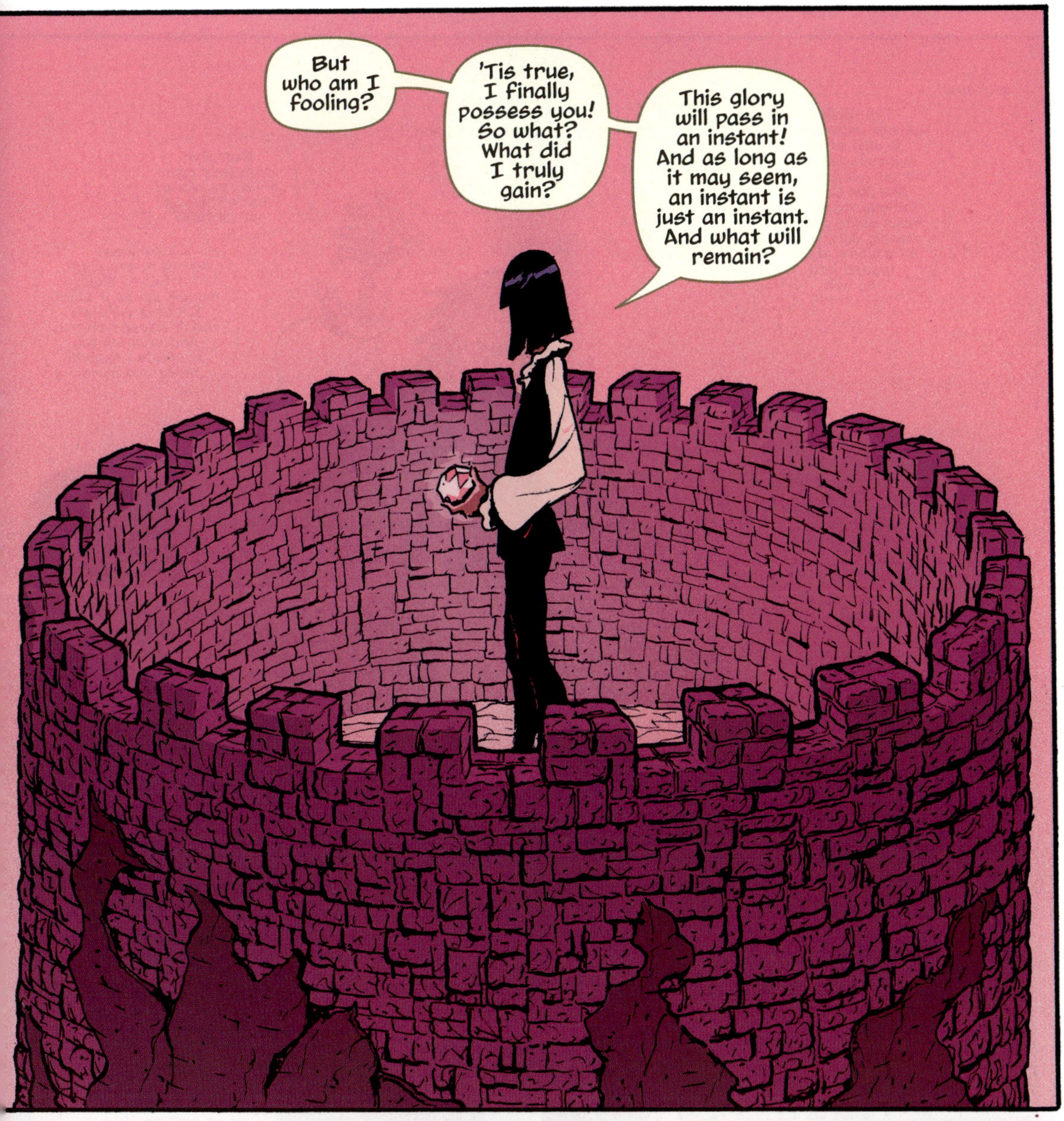
But who am I fooling?
'Tis true, I finally possess you! So what? What did I truly gain?
This glory will pass in an instant! And as long as it may seem, an instant is just an instant. And what will remain?

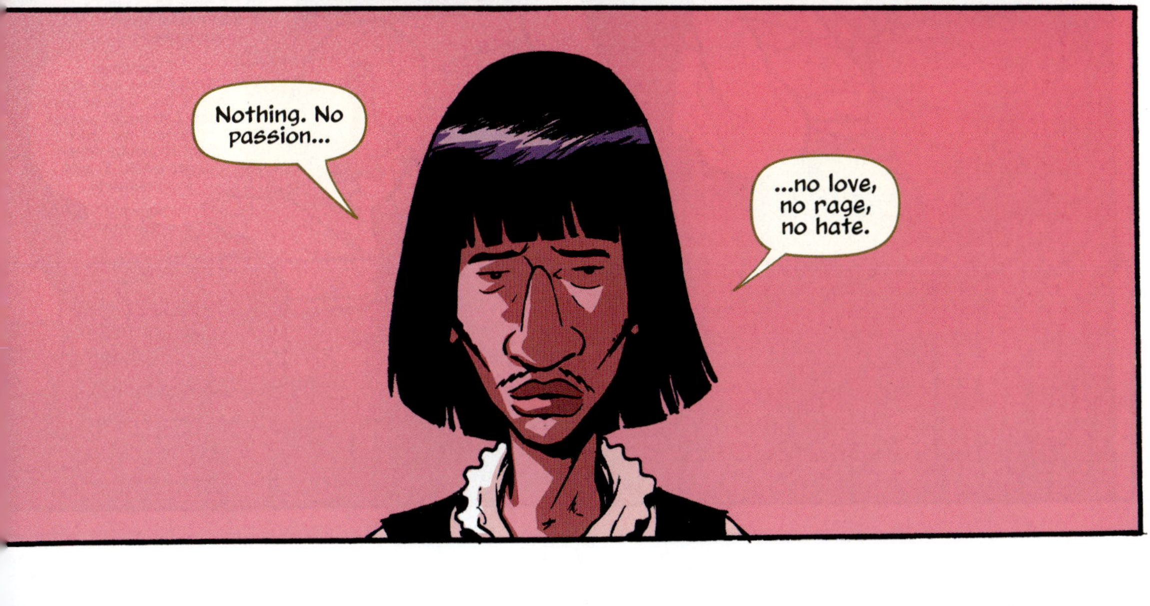
Nothing. No passion...
...no love, no rage, no hate.

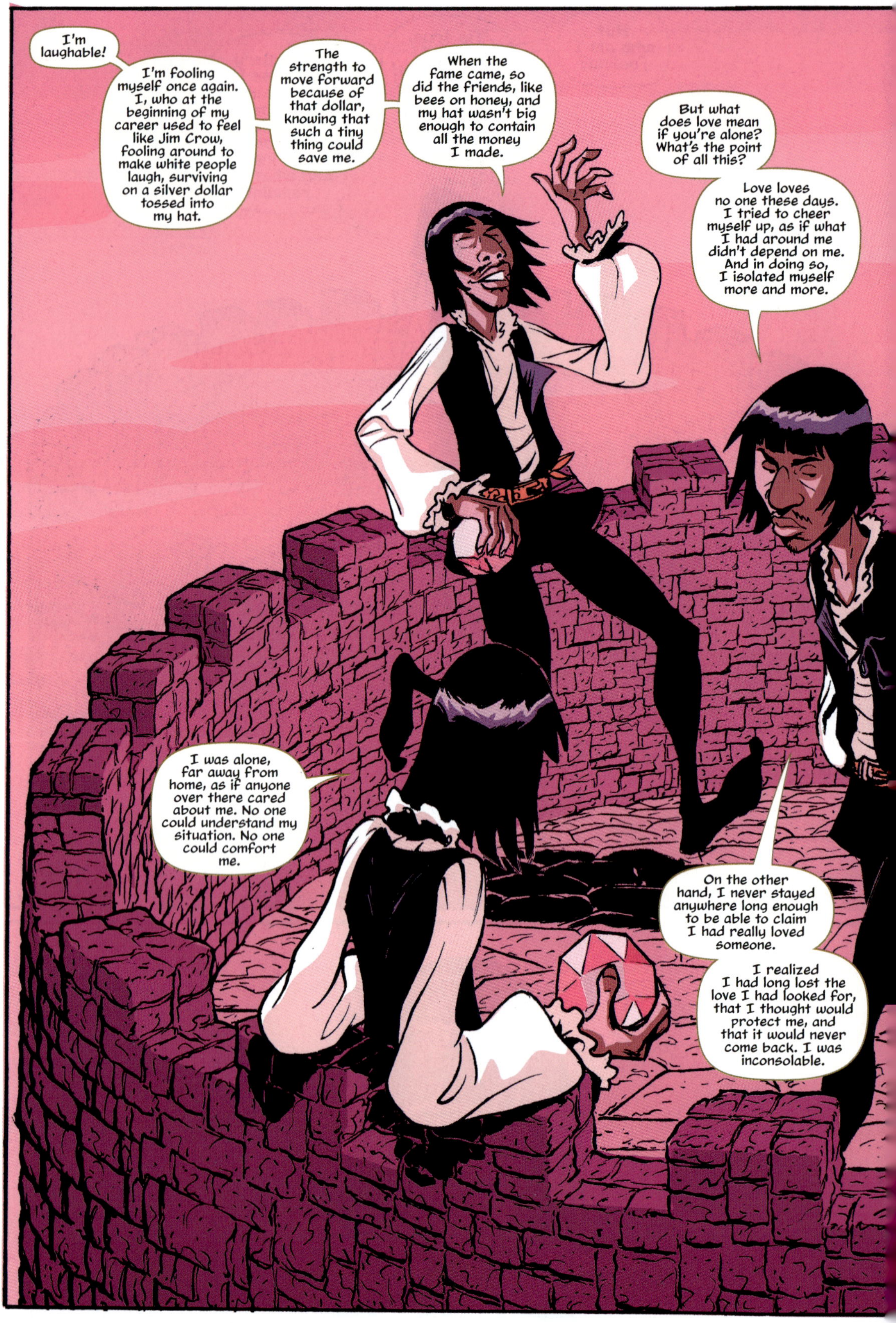
I'm laughable!
I'm fooling myself once again. I, who at the beginning of my career used to feel like Jim Crow, fooling around to make white people laugh, surviving on a silver dollar tossed into my hat.
The strength to move forward because of that dollar, knowing that such a tiny thing could save me.
When the fame came, so did the friends, like bees on honey, and my hat wasn't big enough to contain all the money I made.
But what does love mean if you're alone? What's the point of all this?
Love loves no one these days. I tried to cheer myself up, as if what I had around me didn't depend on me. And in doing so, I isolated myself more and more.
I was alone, far away from home, as if anyone over there cared about me. No one could understand my situation. No one could comfort me.
On the other hand, I never stayed anywhere long enough to be able to claim I had really loved someone.
I realized I had long lost the love I had looked for, that I thought would protect me, and that it would never come back. I was inconsolable.

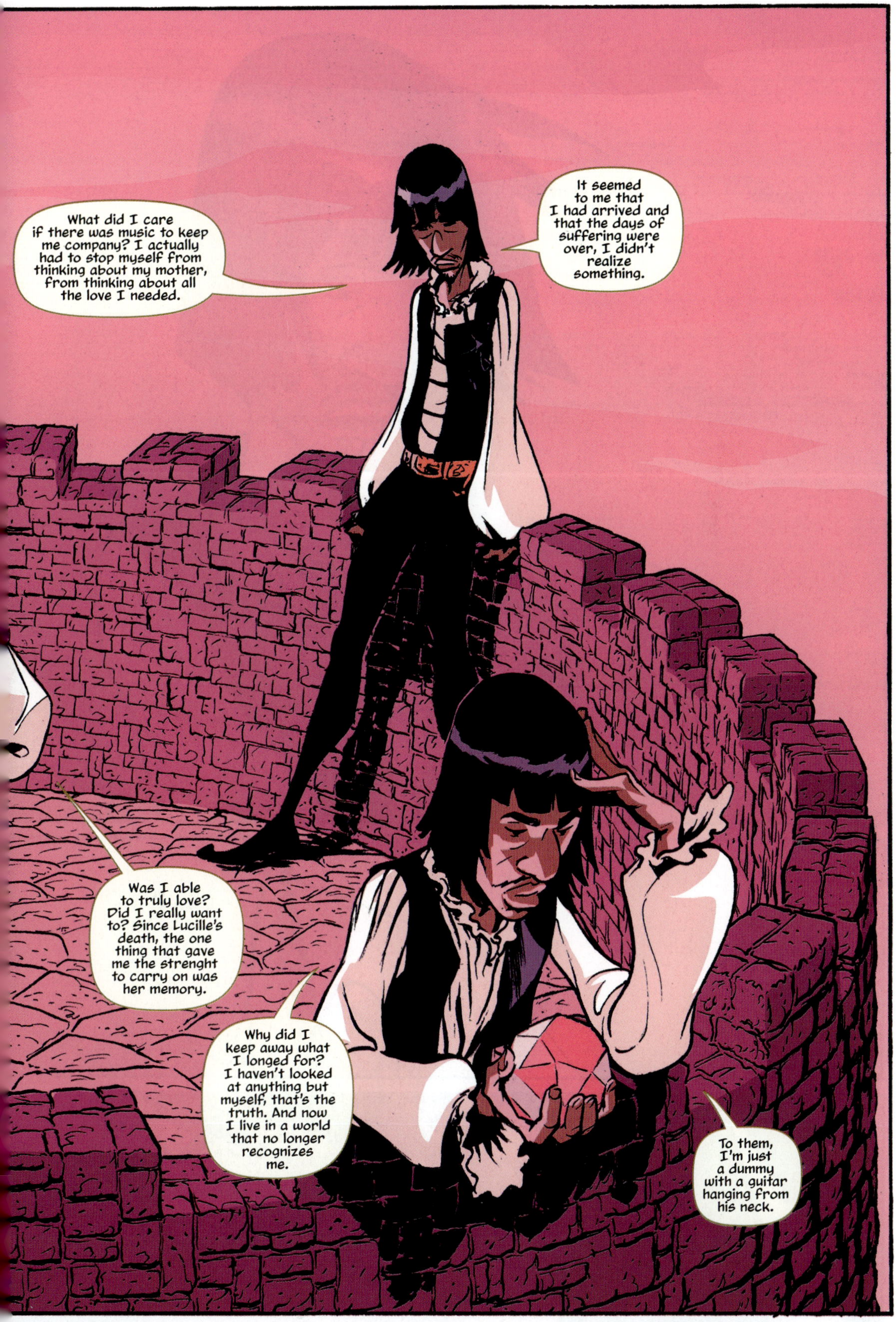
What did I care if there was music to keep me company? I actually had to stop myself from thinking about my mother, from thinking about all the love I needed.
It seemed to me that I had arrived and that the days of suffering were over, I didn't realize something.
Was I able to truly love? Did I really want to? Since Lucille's death, the one thing that gave me the strenght to carry on was her memory.
Why did I keep away what I longed for? I haven't looked at anything but myself, that's the truth. And now I live in a world that no longer recognizes me.
To them, I'm just a dummy with a guitar hanging from his neck.

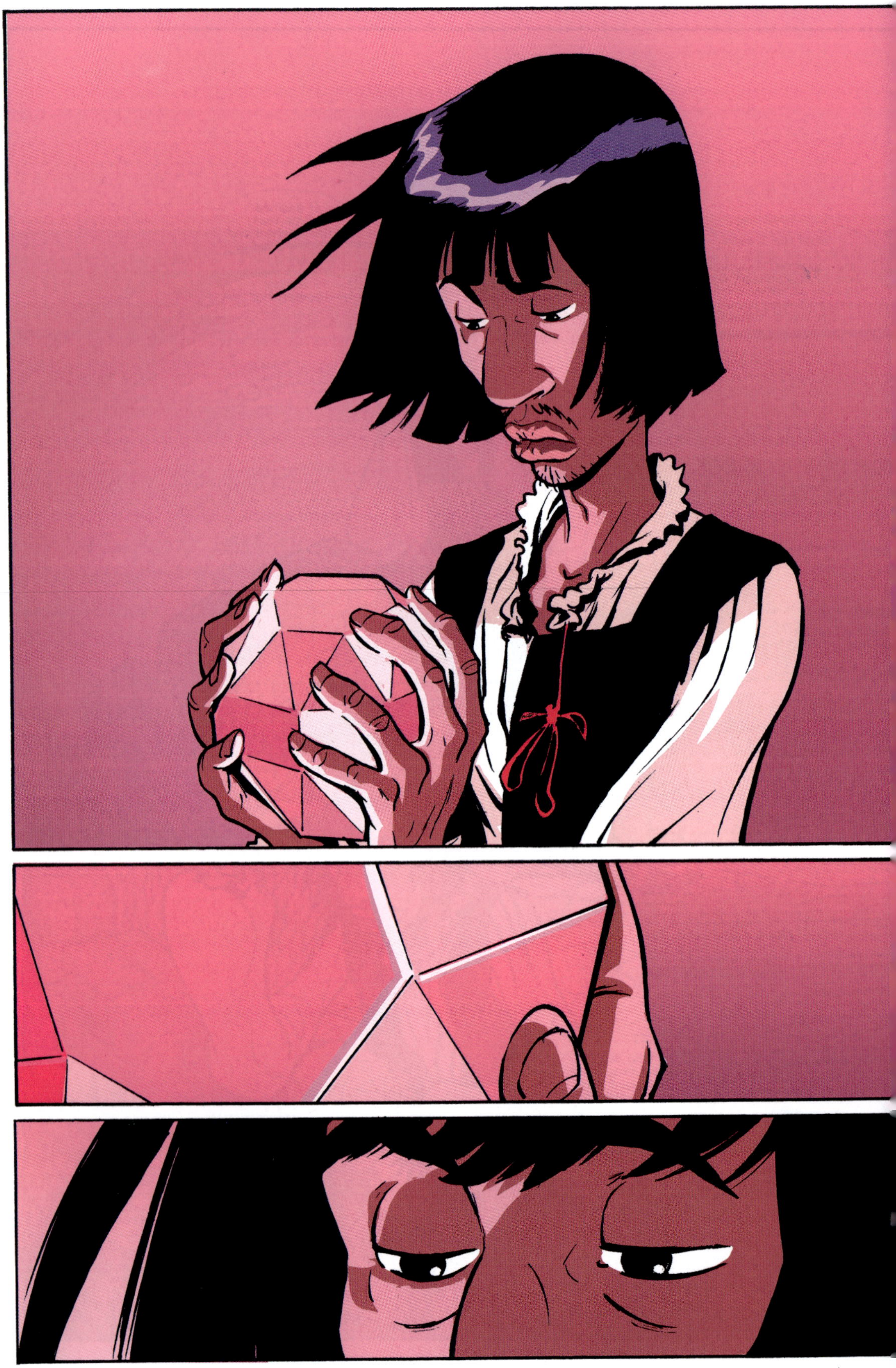

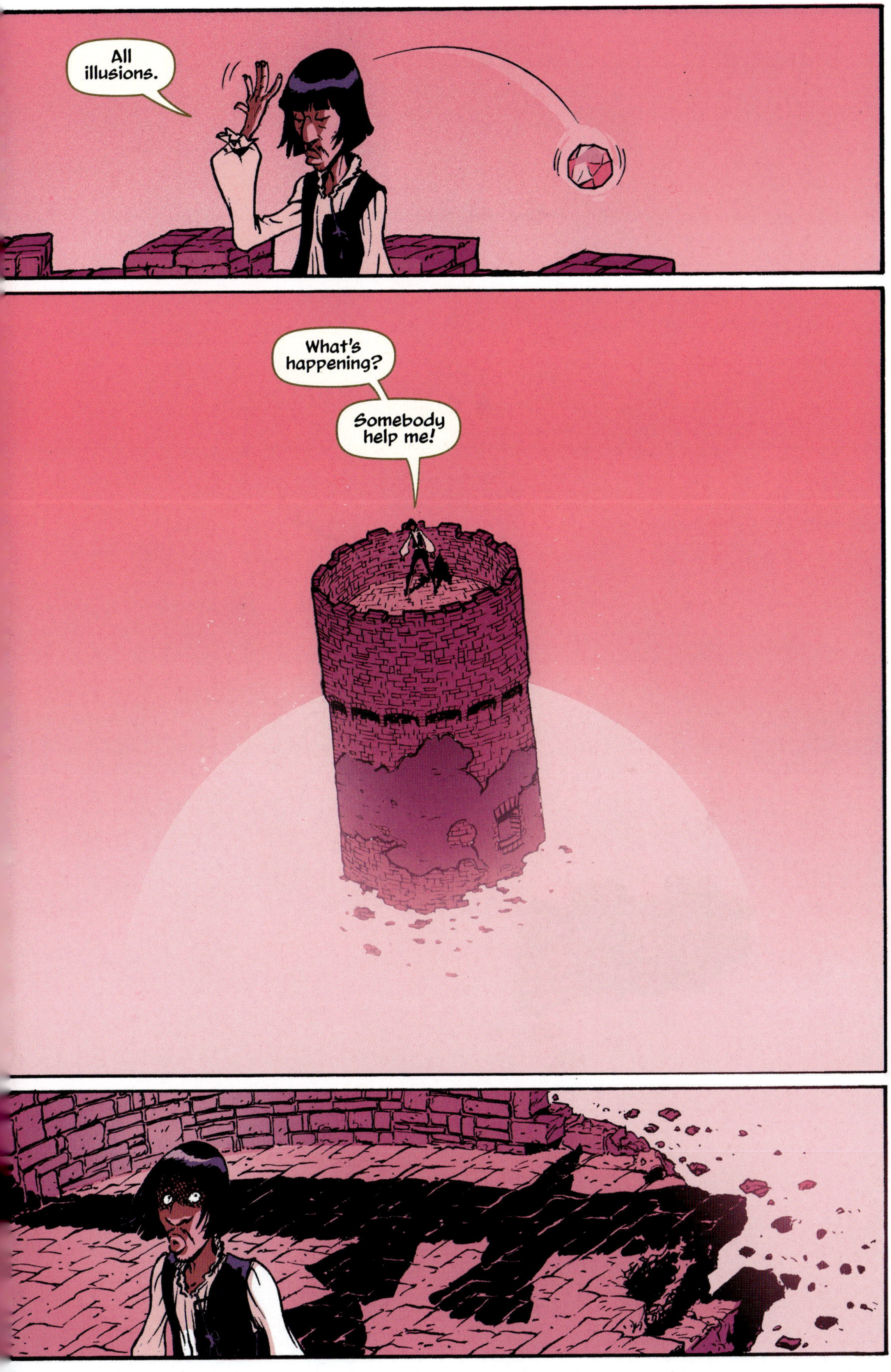
All illusions.
What's happening?
Somebody help me!

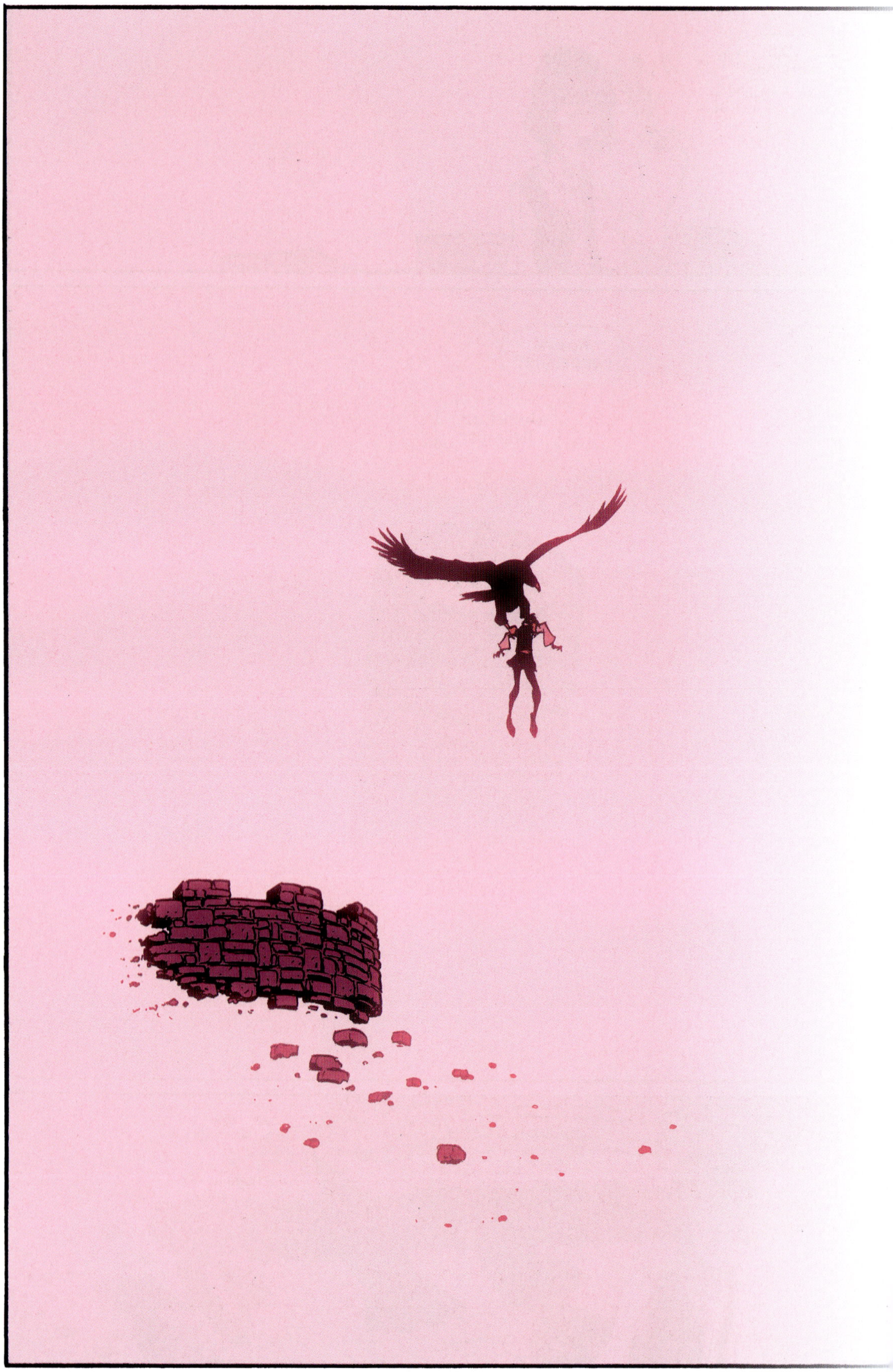

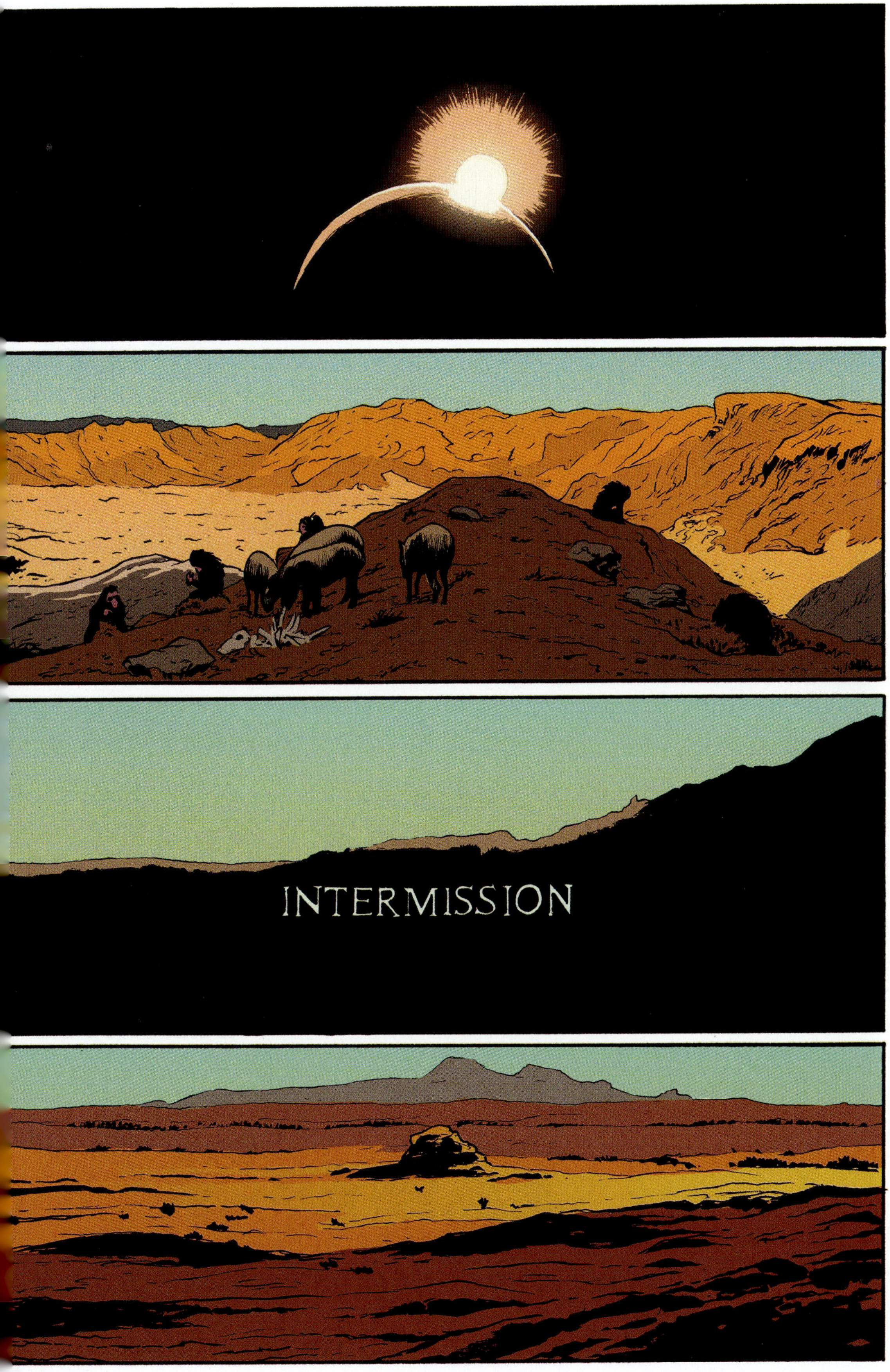
INTERMISSION

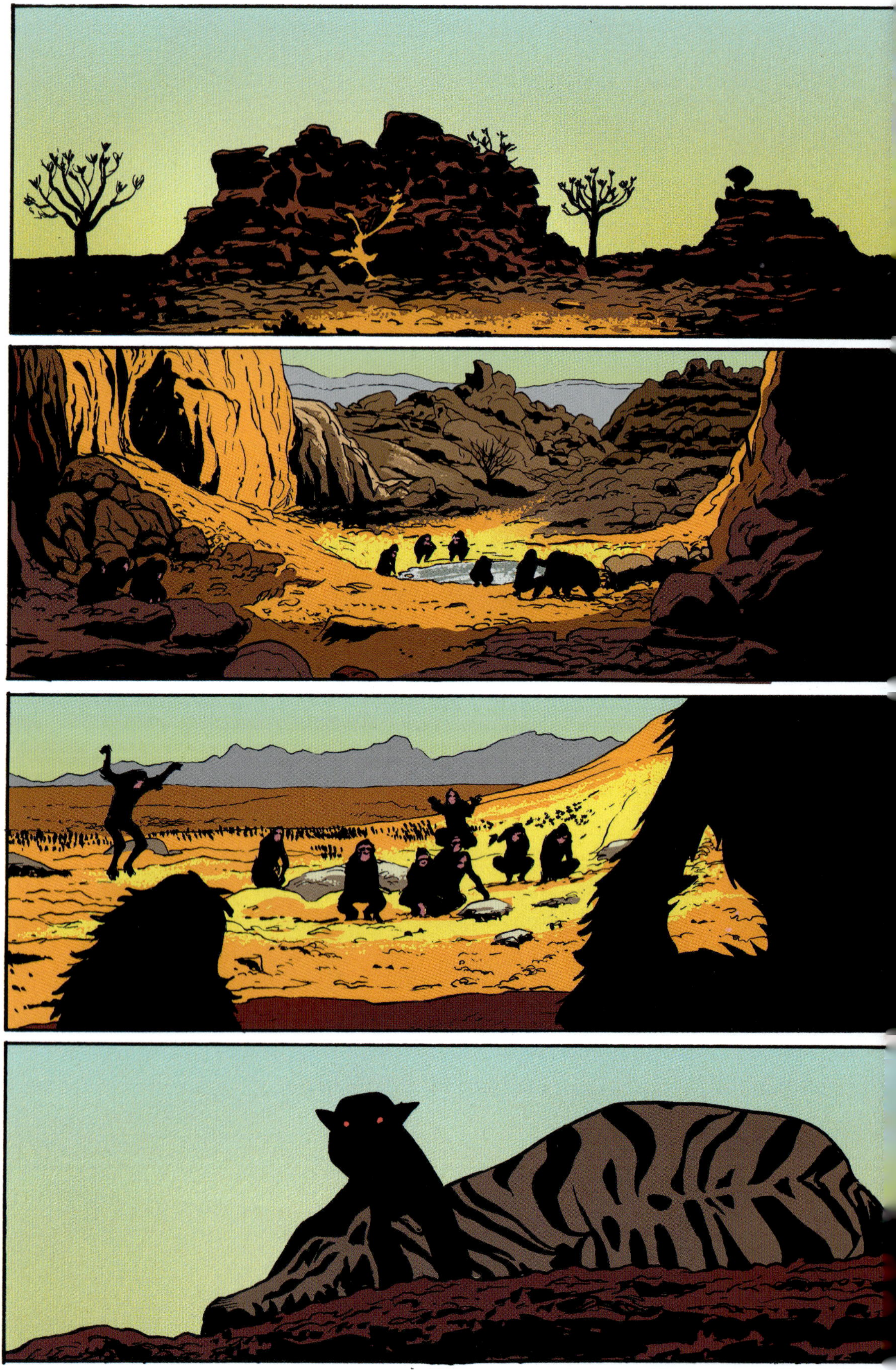

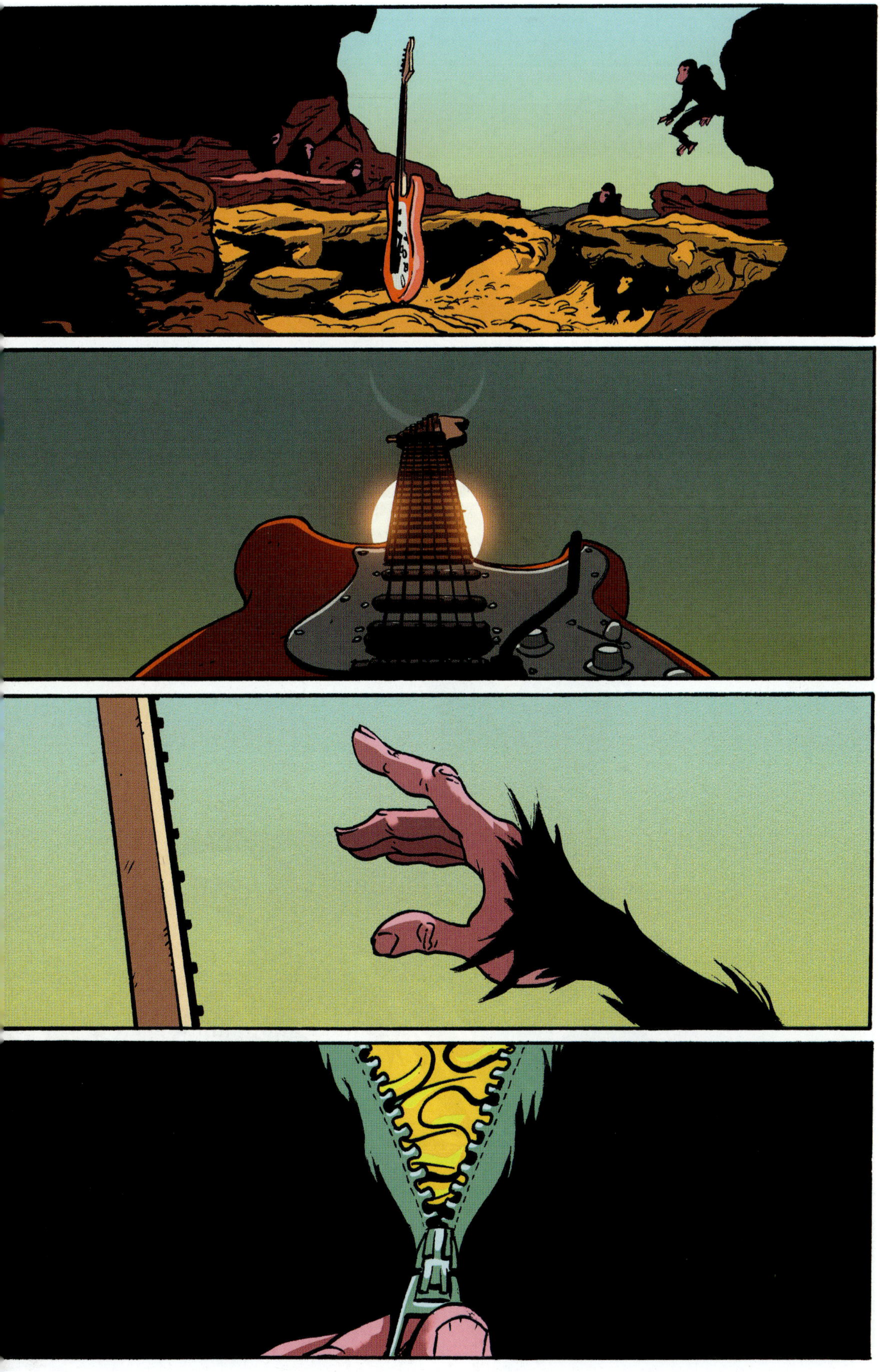

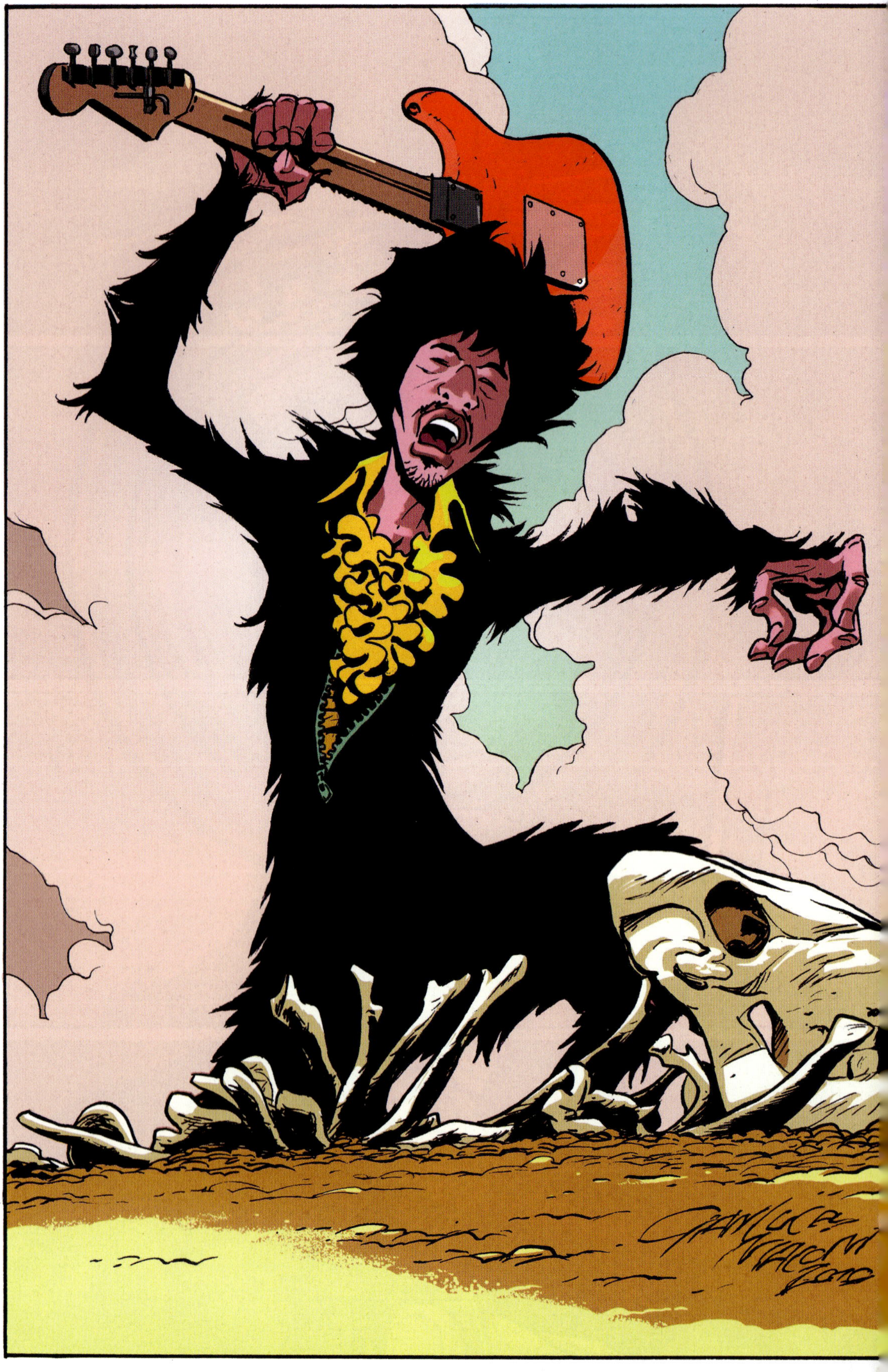

03

# 07.

# MACHINE GUN

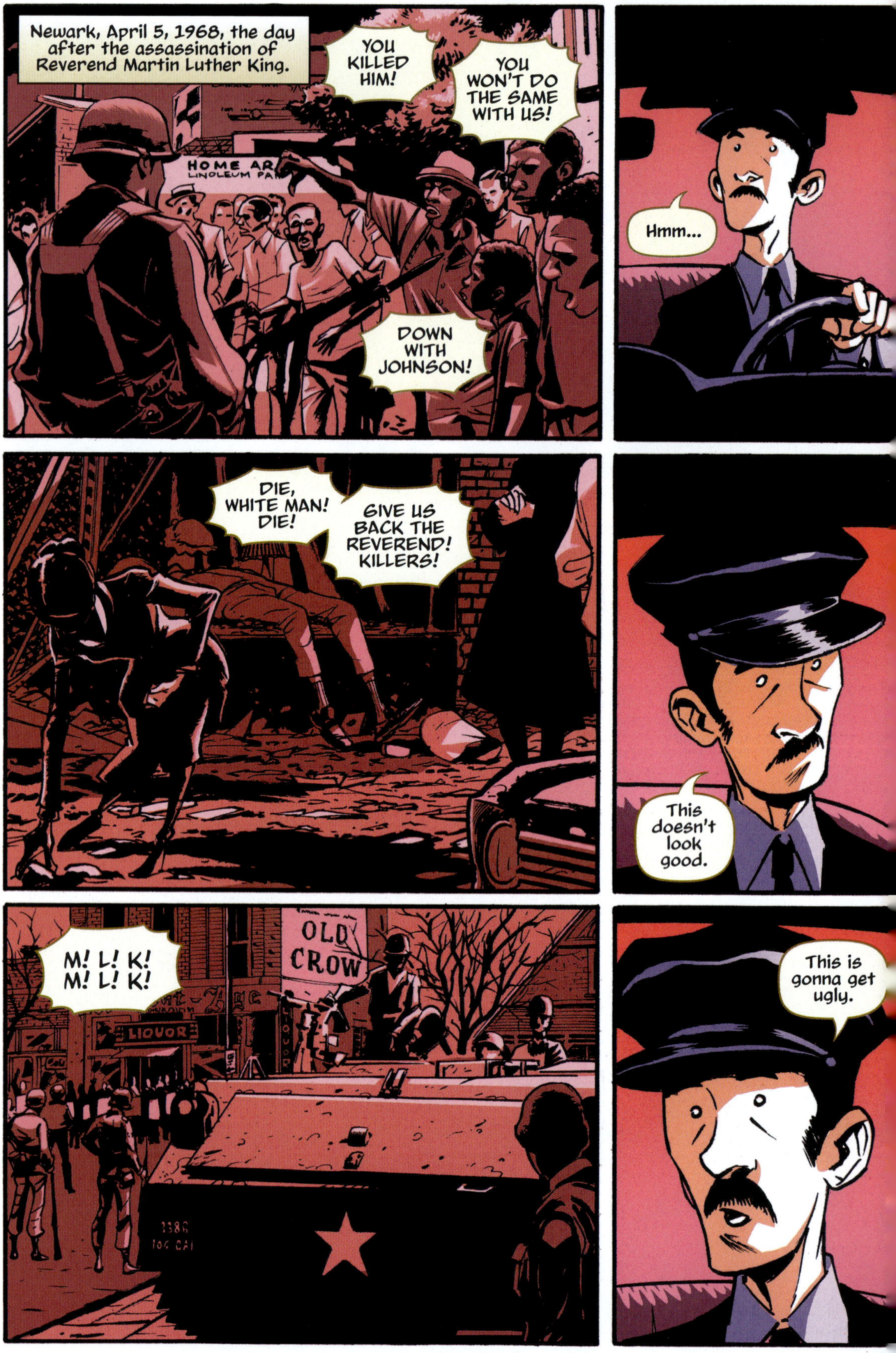
Newark, April 5, 1968, the day after the assassination of Reverend Martin Luther King.
YOU KILLED HIM!
YOU WON'T DO THE SAME WITH US!
DOWN WITH JOHNSON!
Hmm...
DIE, WHITE MAN! DIE!
GIVE US BACK THE REVEREND! KILLERS!
This doesn't look good.
OLD CROW
LIQUOR
M! L! K! M! L! K!
This is gonna get ugly.

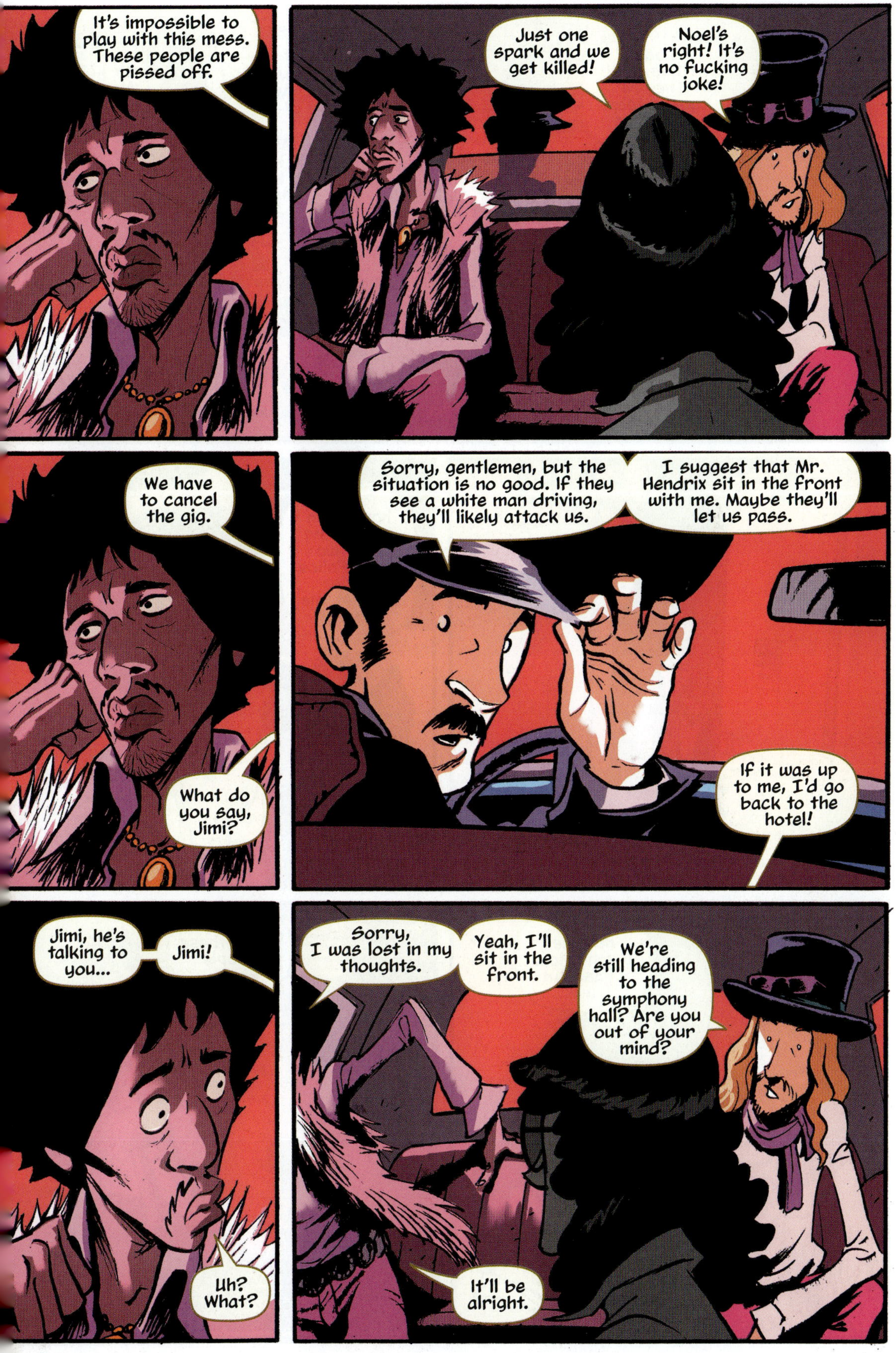
It's impossible to play with this mess. These people are pissed off.
Just one spark and we get killed!
Noel's right! It's no fucking joke!
We have to cancel the gig.
What do you say, Jimi?
Sorry, gentlemen, but the situation is no good. If they see a white man driving, they'll likely attack us.
I suggest that Mr. Hendrix sit in the front with me. Maybe they'll let us pass.
If it was up to me, I'd go back to the hotel!
Jimi, he's talking to you...
Jimi!
Uh? What?
Sorry, I was lost in my thoughts.
Yeah, I'll sit in the front.
We're still heading to the symphony hall? Are you out of your mind?
It'll be alright.

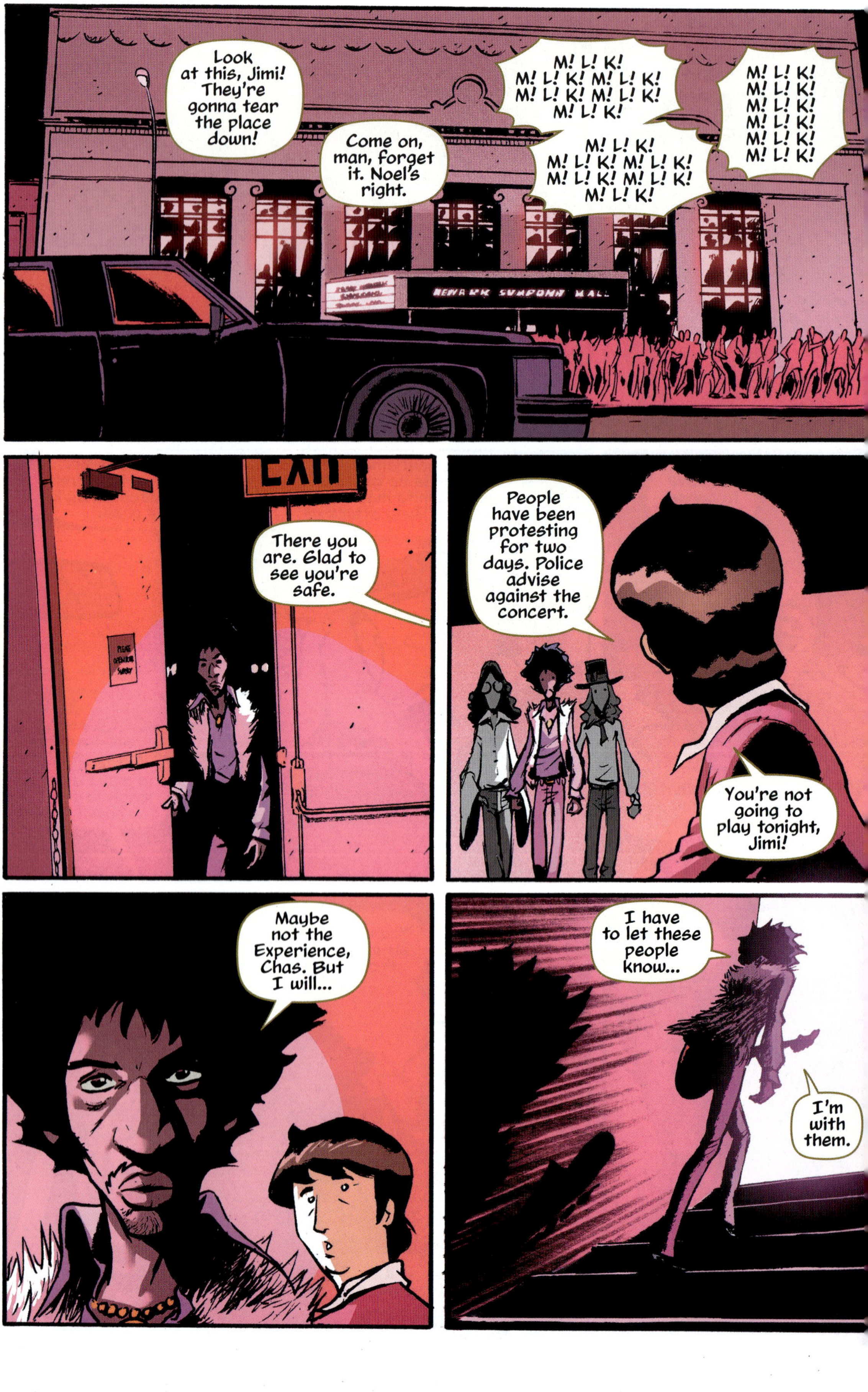
Look at this, Jimi! They're gonna tear the place down!
Come on, man, forget it. Noel's right.
M! L! K! M! L! K! M! L! K! M! L! K! M! L! K! M! L! K!
M! L! K! M! L! K! M! L! K! M! L! K! M! L! K! M! L! K!
M! L! K! M! L! K! M! L! K! M! L! K! M! L! K! M! L! K!
There you are. Glad to see you're safe.
People have been protesting for two days. Police advise against the concert.
You're not going to play tonight, Jimi!
Maybe not the Experience, Chas. But I will...
I have to let these people know...
I'm with them.

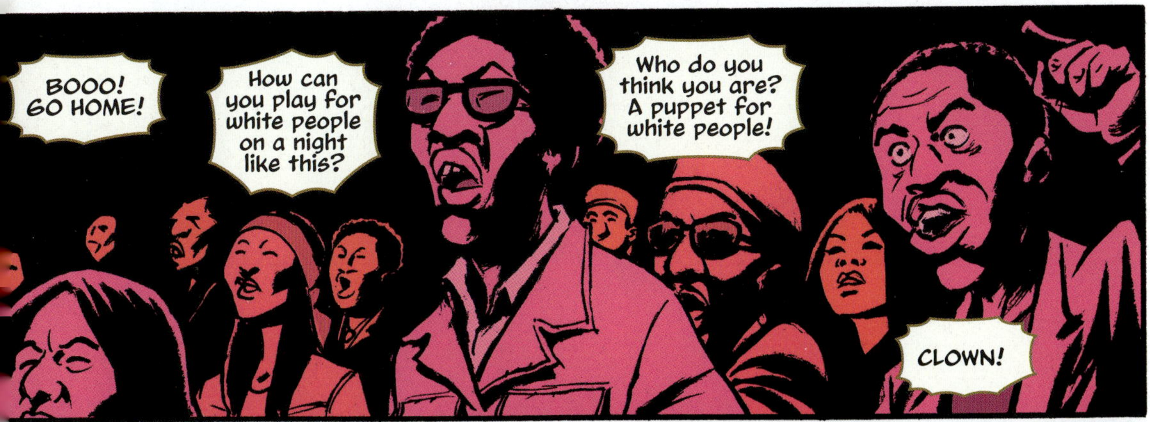
BOOO! GO HOME!
How can you play for white people on a night like this?
Who do you think you are? A puppet for white people!
CLOWN!

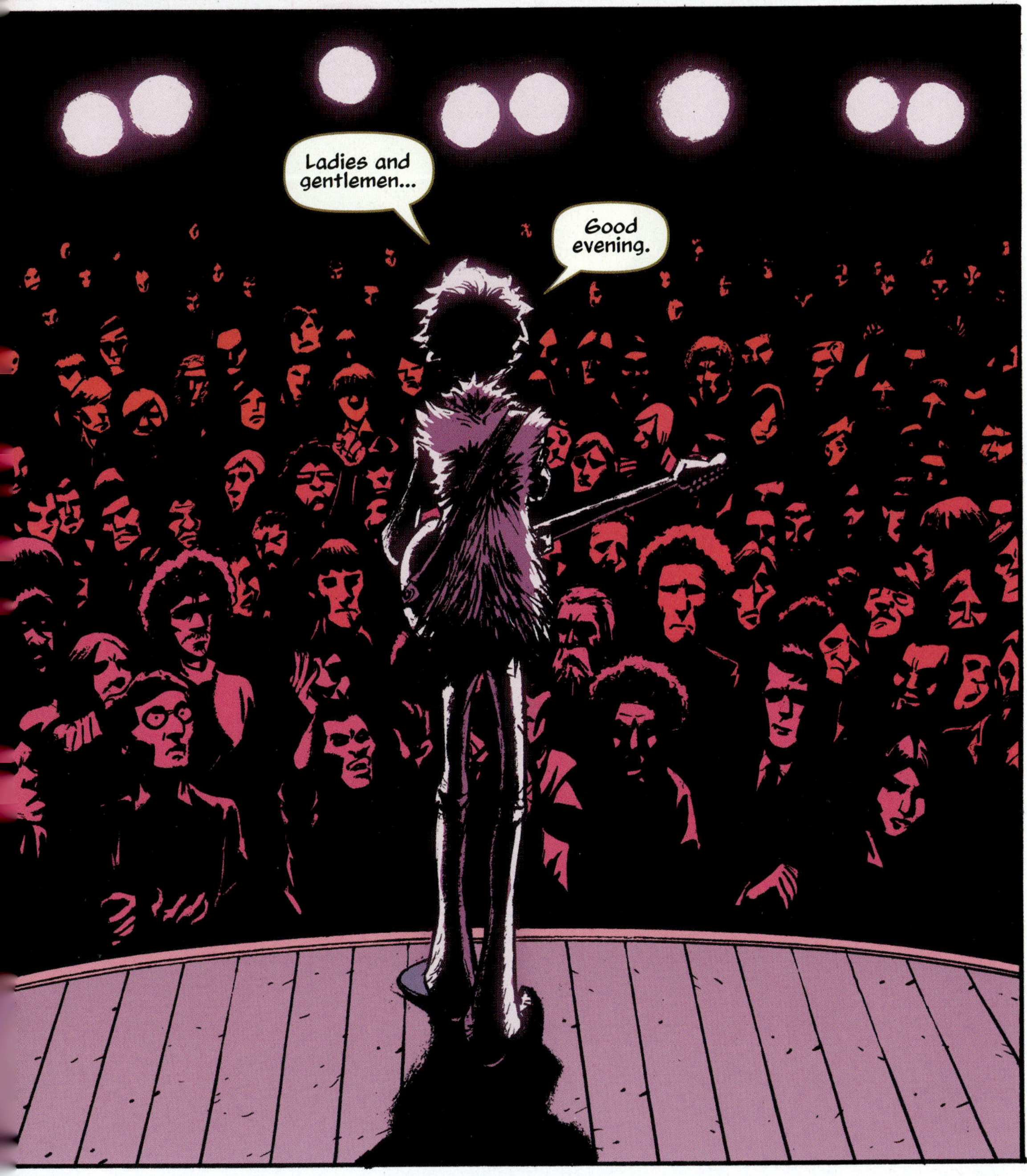
Ladies and gentlemen...
Good evening.

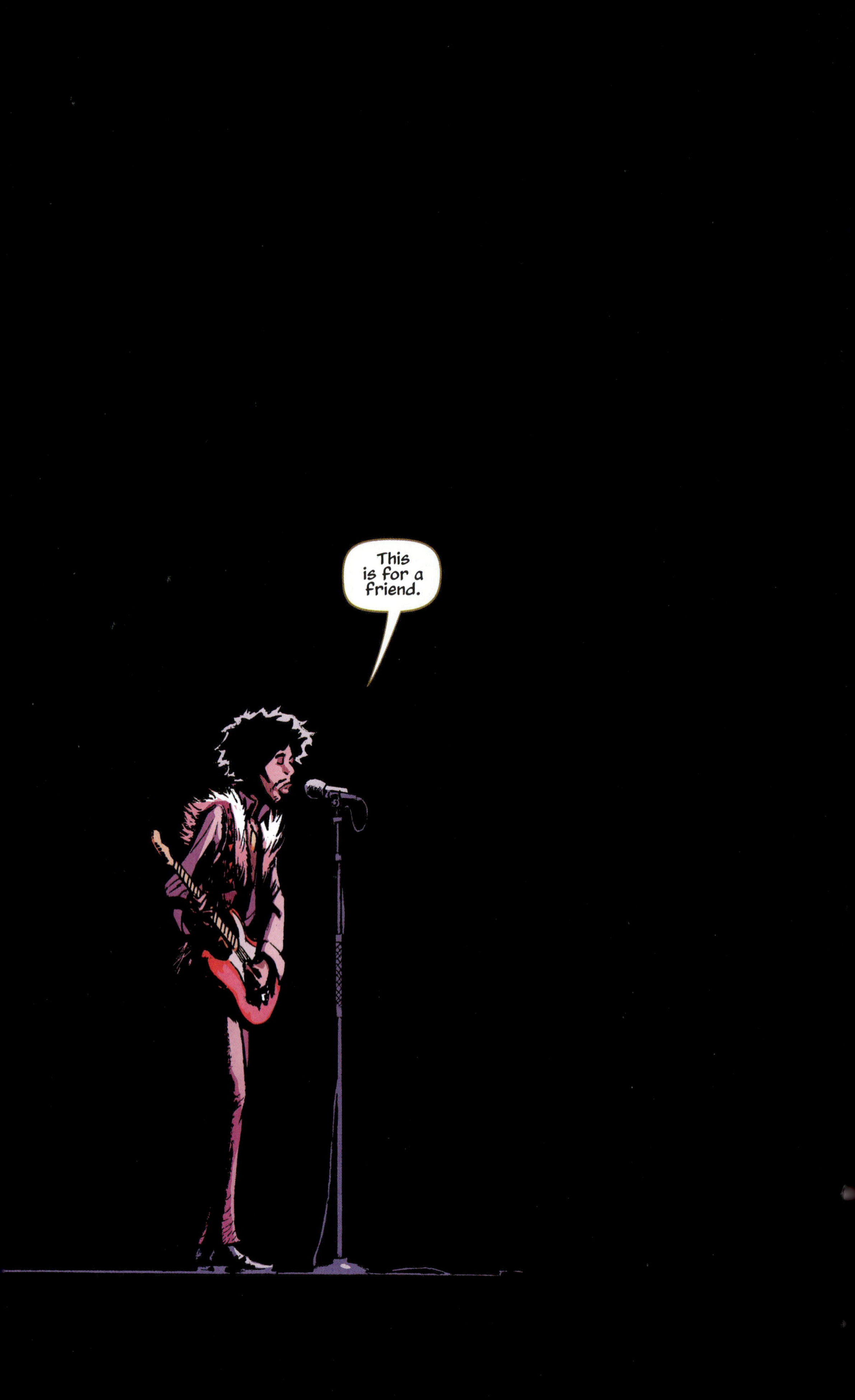
This is for a friend.

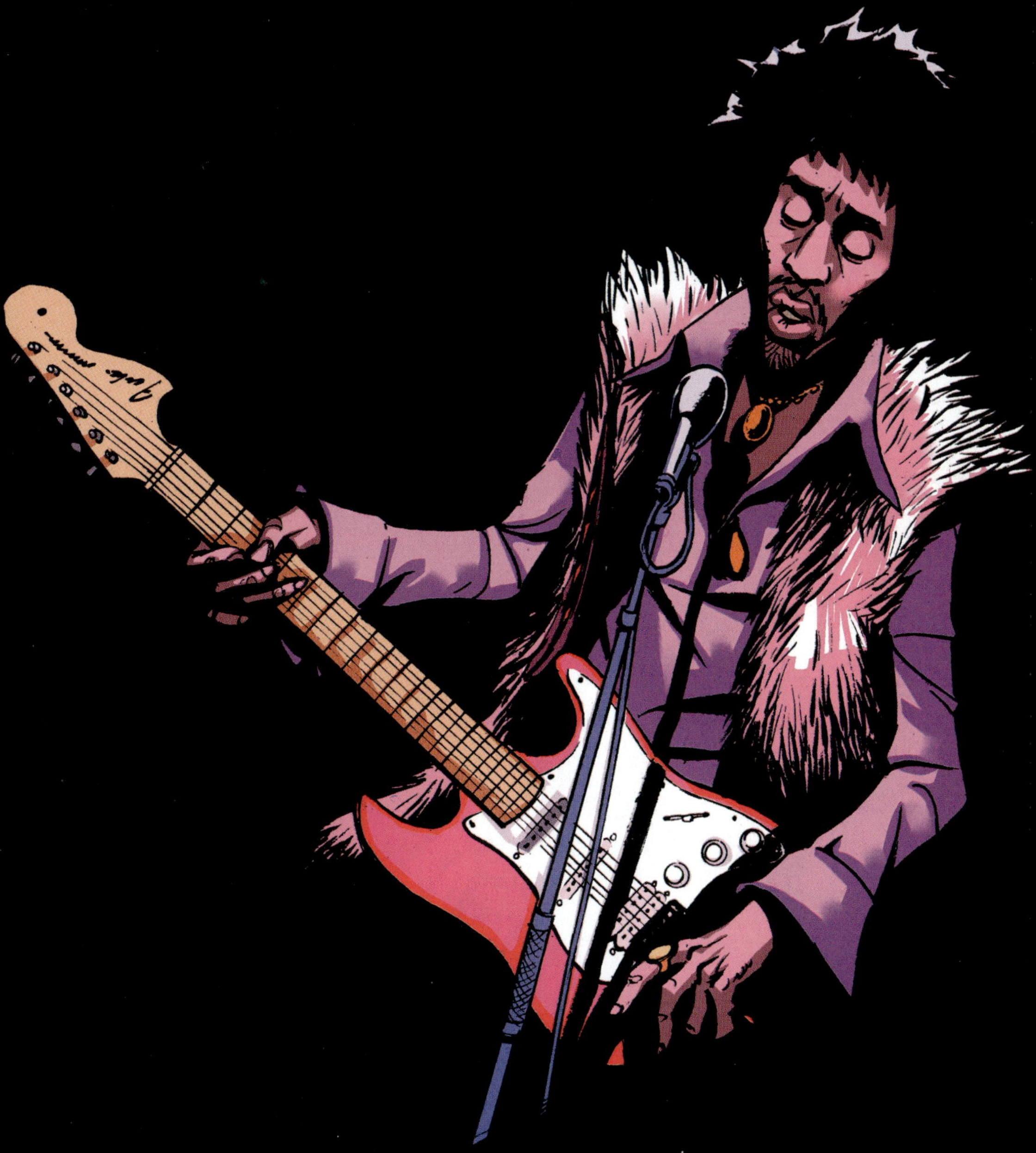

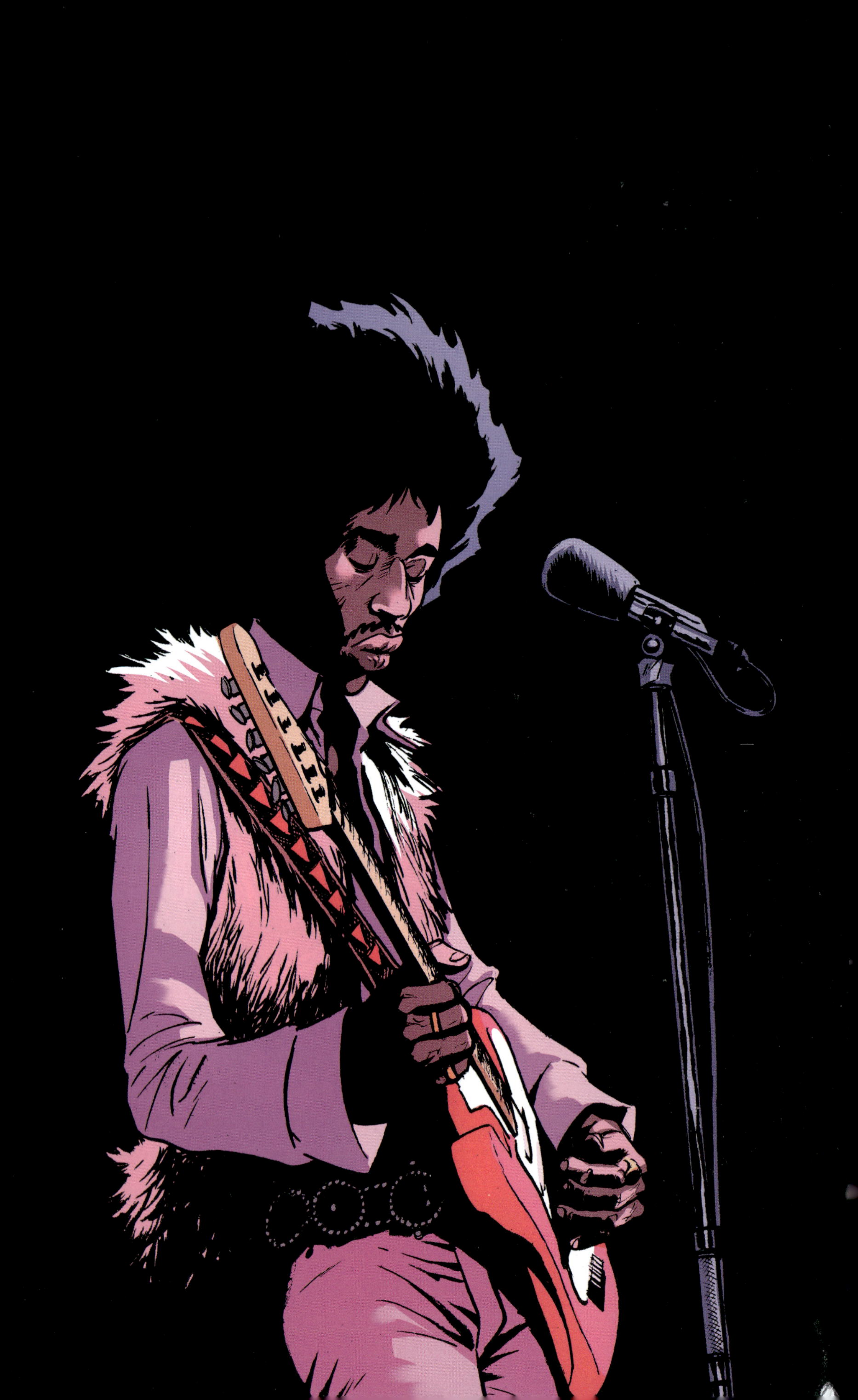

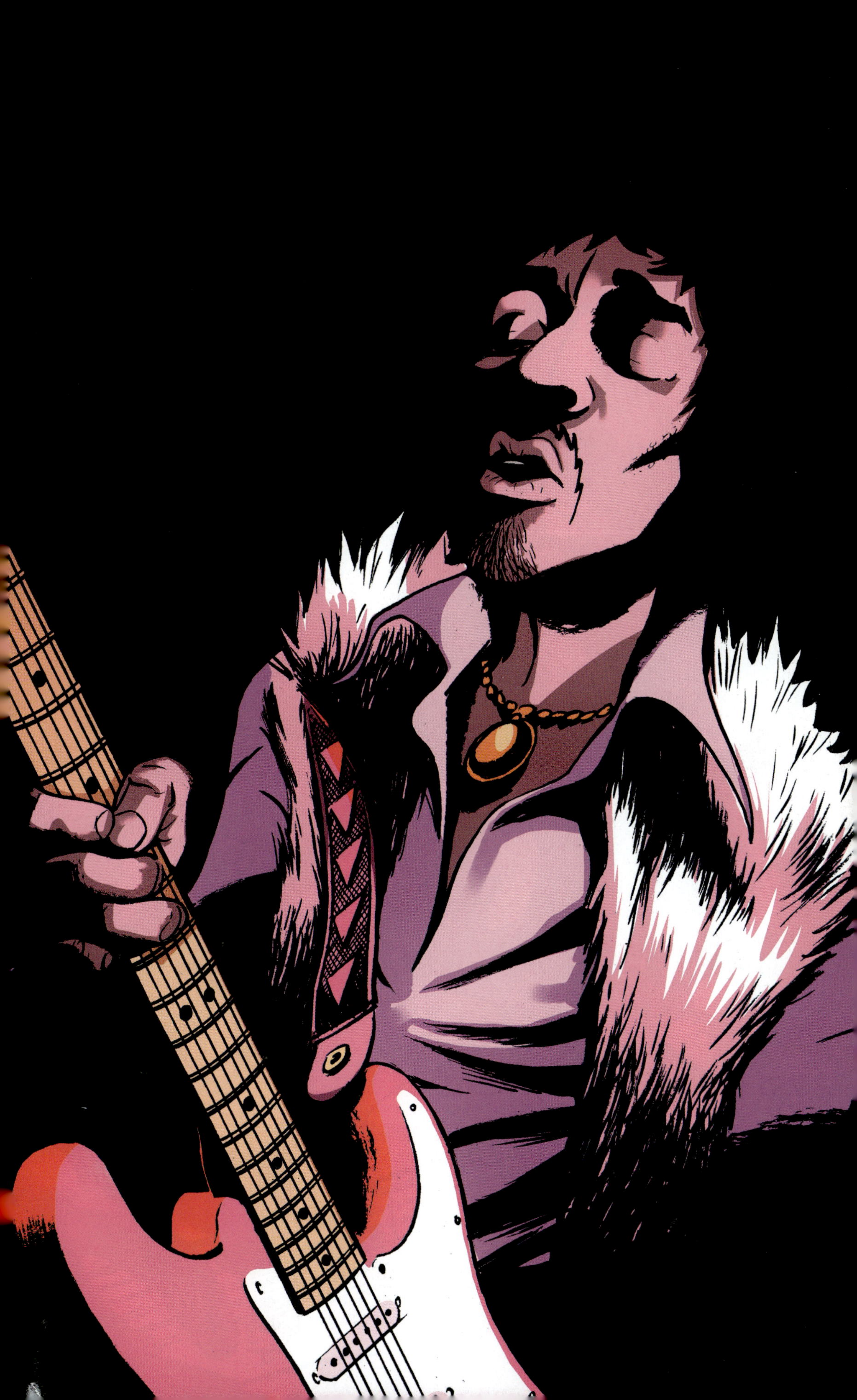

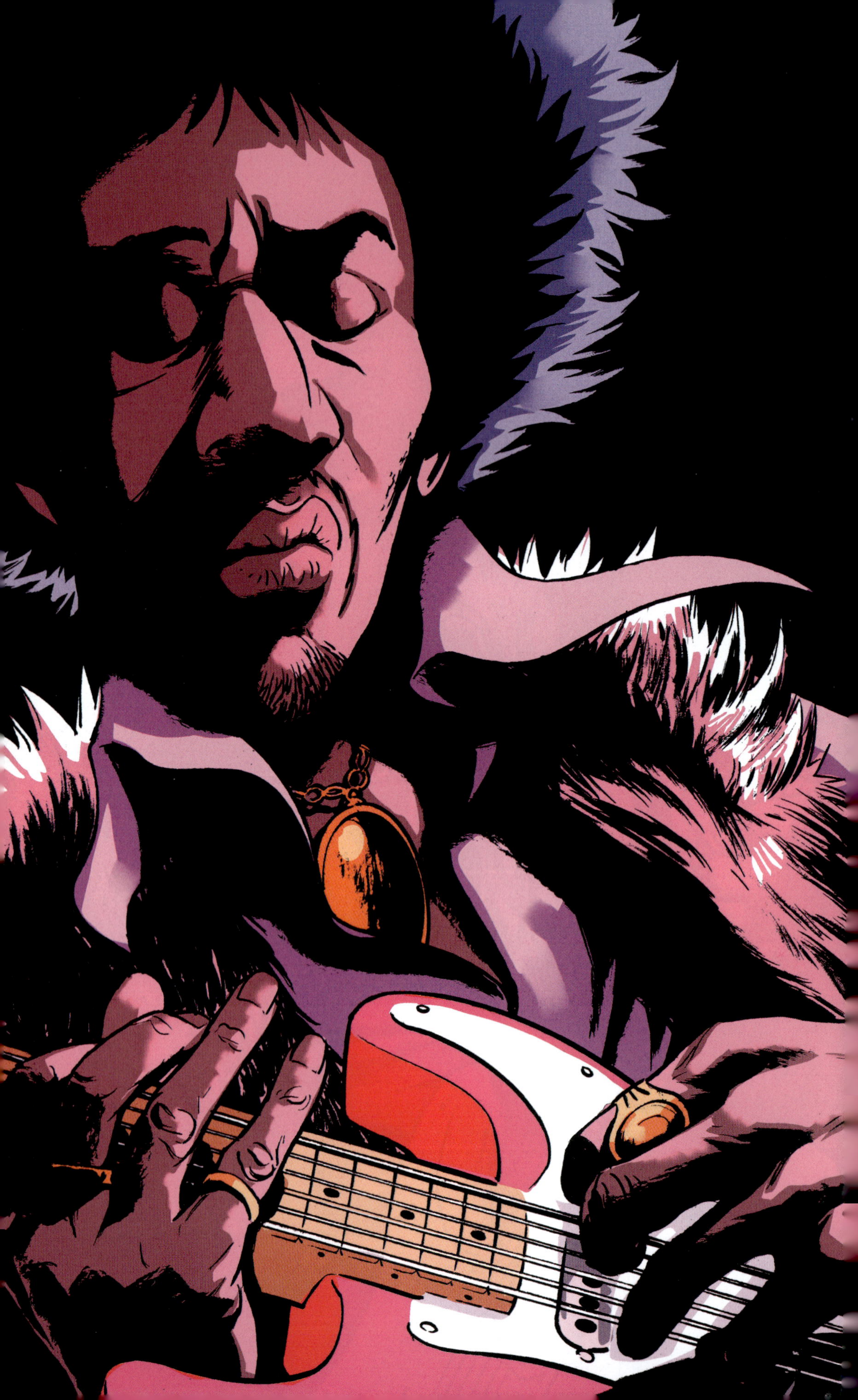

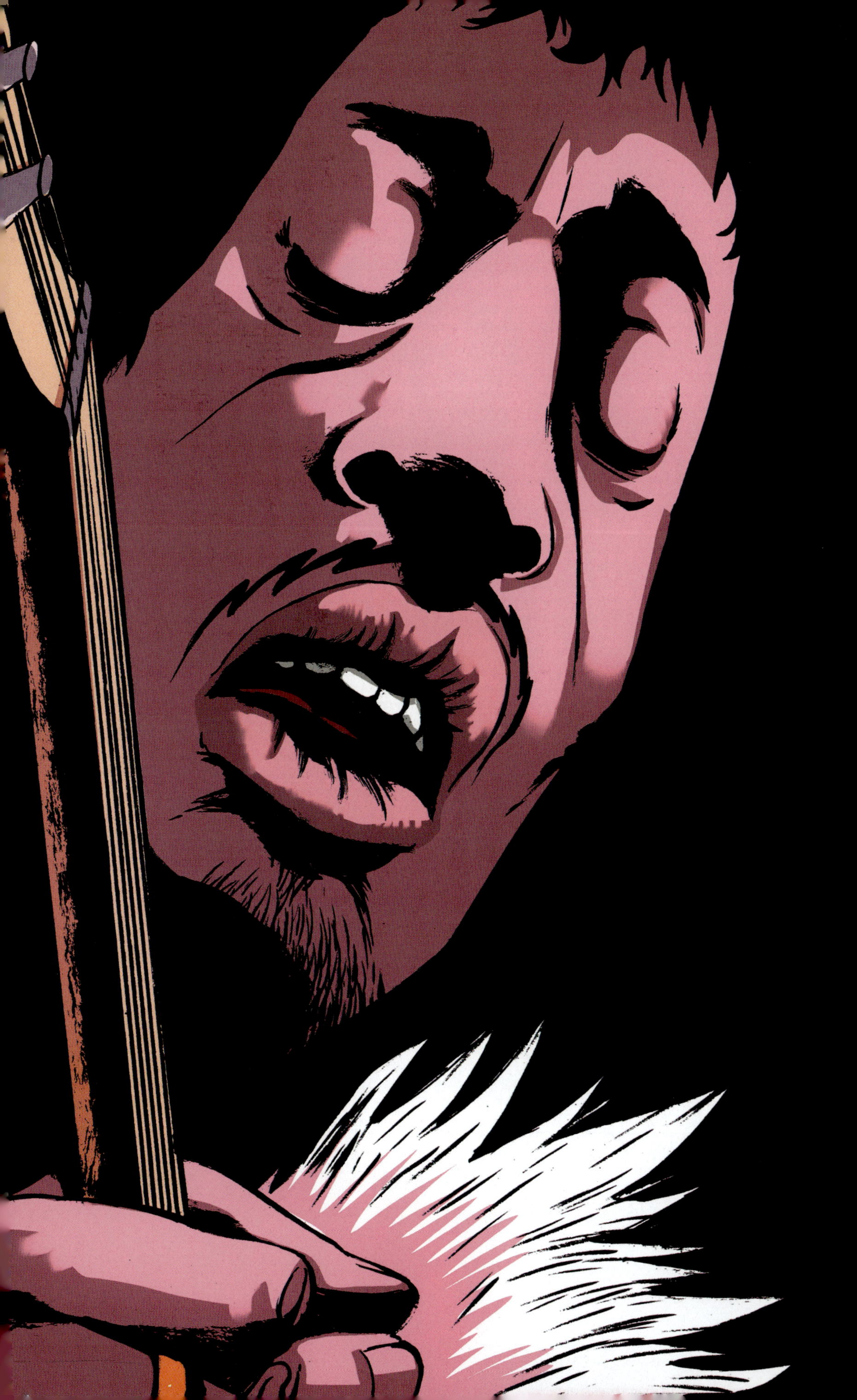

Now is the time to make real the promise of democracy.
Now is the time to rise from the dark and desolate valley of segregation
to the sunlit path of racial justice. Now is the time to lift our nation
from the quicksand of racial injustice to the solid rock of brotherhood.
Now is the time to make justice a reality to all of God's children.

It would be fatal for the nation to overlook the urgency of the moment
and to underestimate the determination of its colored citizens.
This sweltering summer of the colored people's legitimate discontent will
not pass until there is an invigorating autumn of freedom and equality.

There will be neither rest nor tranquility in America until the colored
citizen is granted his citizenship rights. The whirlwinds of revolt will
continue to shake the foundations of our nation until the bright day of
justice emerges.

But there is something that I must say to my people who stand on the warm
threshold which leads into the palace of justice. In the process of gaining
our rightful place we must not be guilty of wrongful deeds.

Let us not seek to satisfy our thirst for freedom by drinking from the cup
of bitterness and hatred.
We must forever conduct our struggle on the high plane of dignity and
discipline. We must not allow our creative protest to degenerate into
physical violence. Again and again we must rise to the majestic heights
of meeting physical force with soul force.

And as we walk, we must make the pledge that we shall march ahead.
We cannot turn back.
There are those who are asking the devotees of civil rights: "When will you
be satisfied?" We can never be satisfied as long as the Negro is
the victim of the unspeakable horrors of police brutality.

We can never be satisfied as long as our chlidren are stripped of their
selfhood and robbed of their dignity by signs stating: "for whites only."
We cannot be satisfied as long as a Negro in Mississippi cannot vote and a
Negro in New York believes he has nothing for which to vote. No, no, we are
not satisfied, and we will not be satisfied until justice rolls down like
waters and righteousness like a mighty stream.

I say to you today, my friends, so even though we face the difficulties of
today and tomorrow, I still have a dream. It is a dream deeply rooted in the
American Dream. I have a dream that one day this nation will rise up and
live out the true meaning of its creed: we hold these truths to be
self-evident; that all men are created equal.

I have a dream that my four little children will one day live in a nation
where they will not be judged by the color of their skin but by the content
of their character.

I have a dream today!

And when this happens, and when we allow freedom ring, when we let it ring
from every village and every hamlet, from every state and every city, we
will be able to speed up that day when all of God's children, black men and
white men, Jews and Gentiles, Protestants and Catholics, will be able to
join hands and sing in the words of the old Negro spiritual, "Free at last!
Free at last! Thank God Almighty, we are free at last!"

Martin Luther King, Jr.

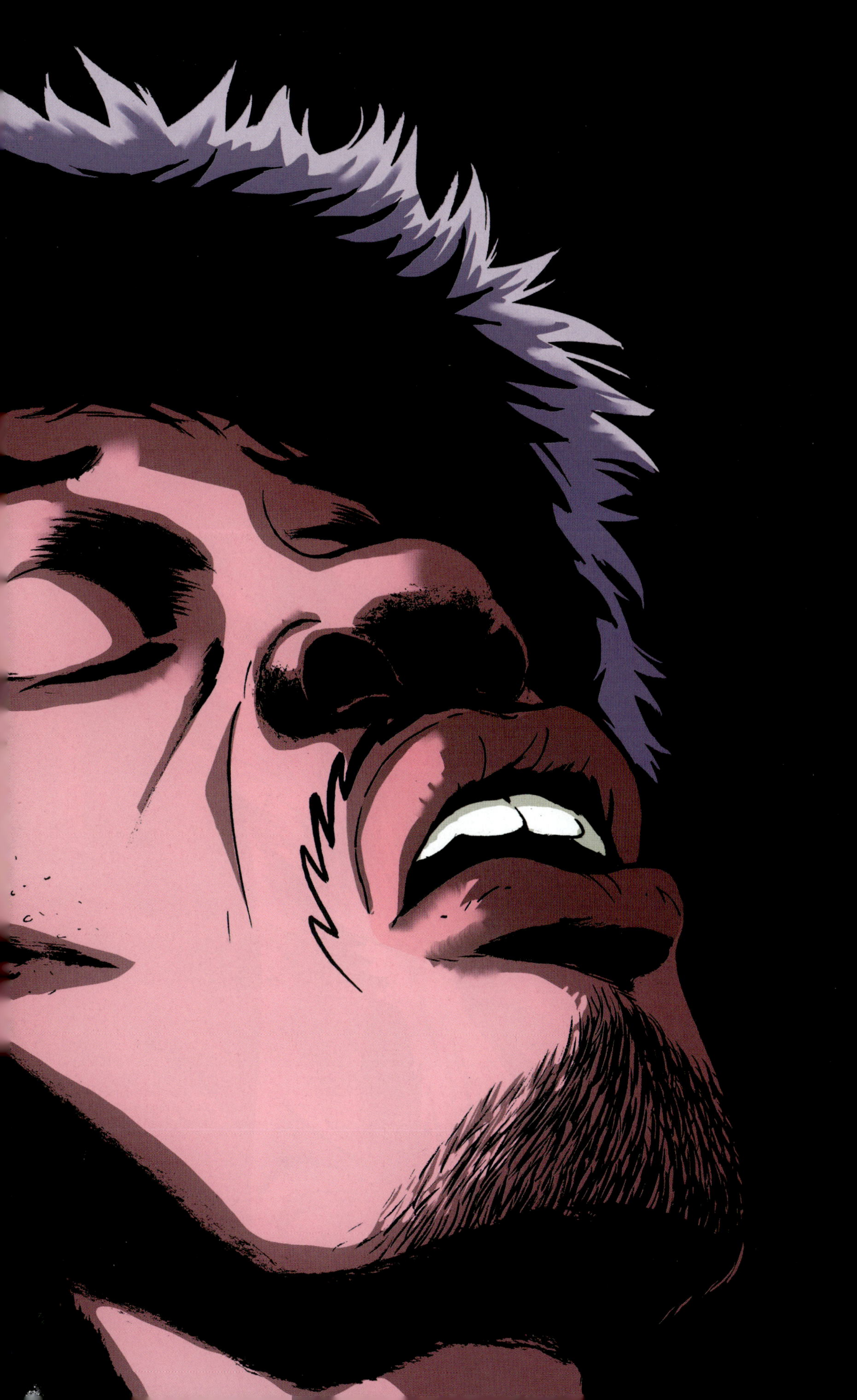

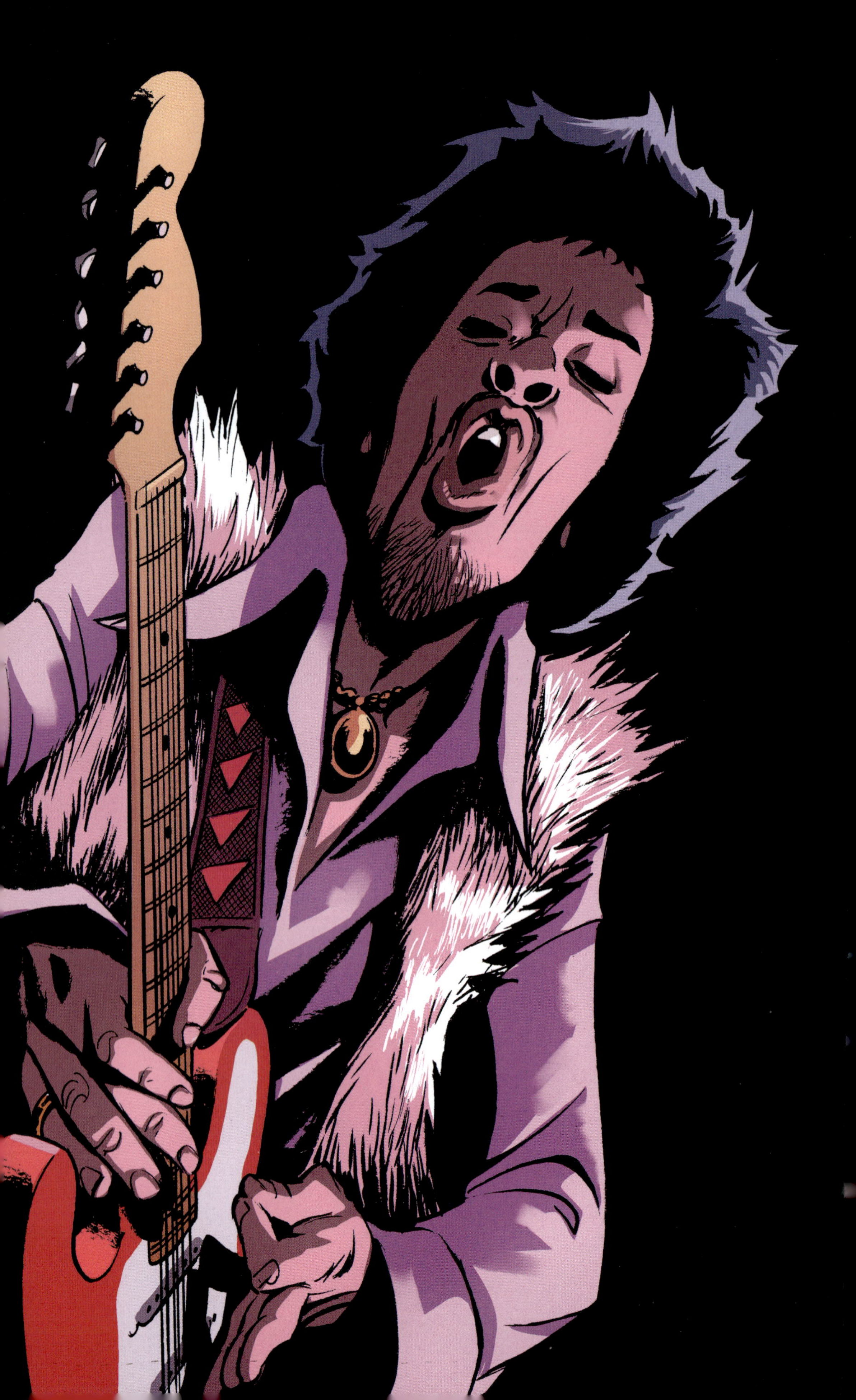

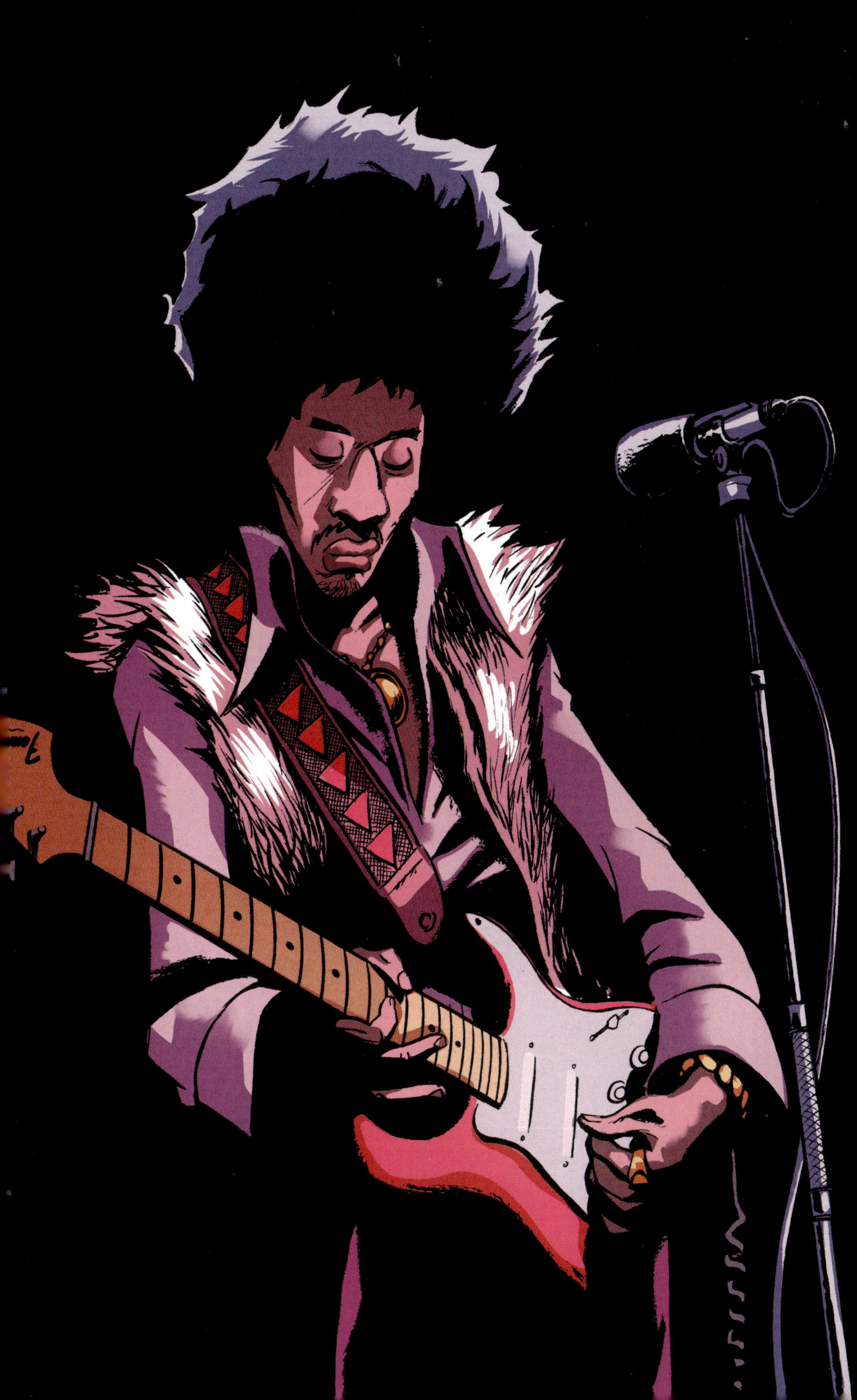

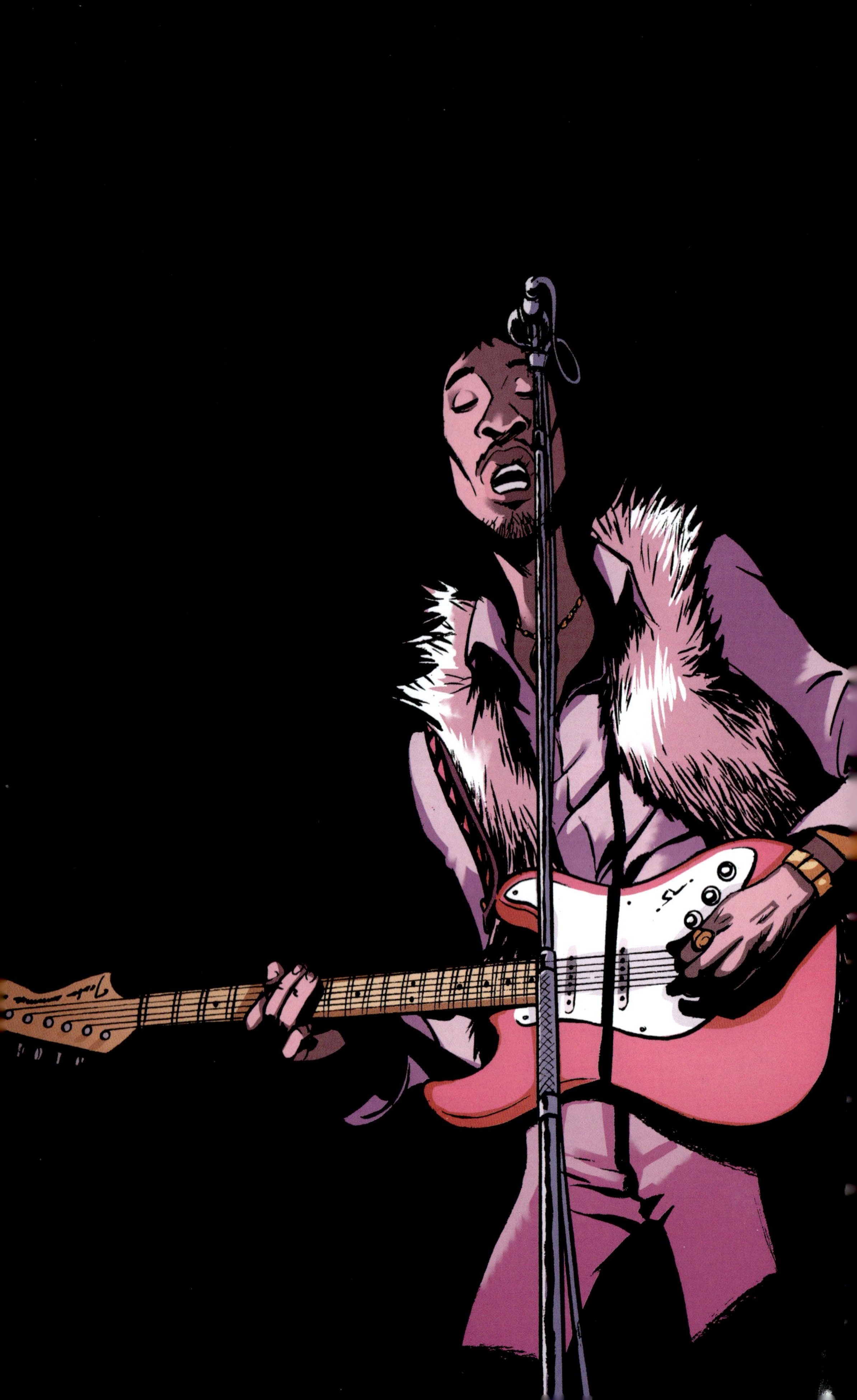

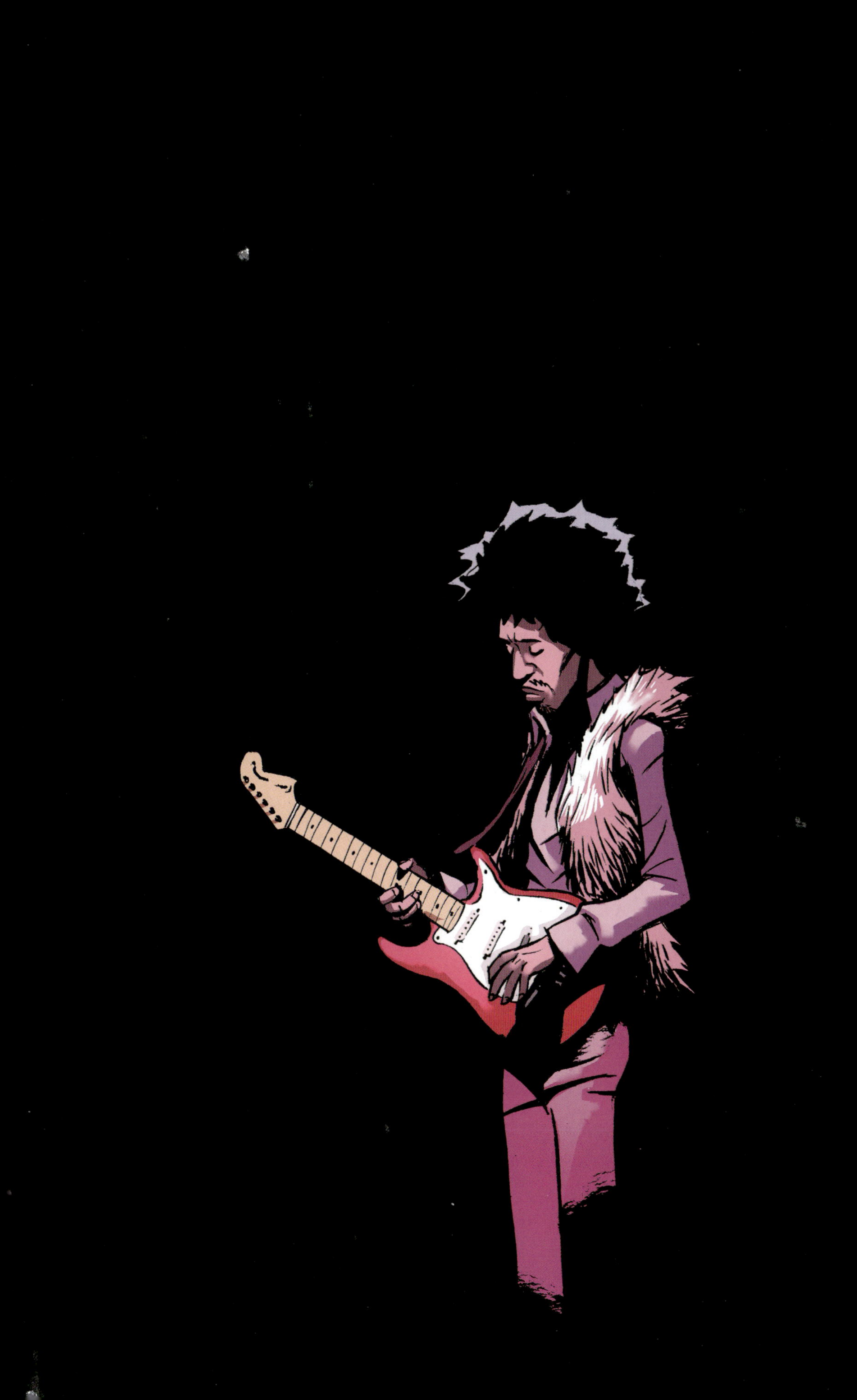

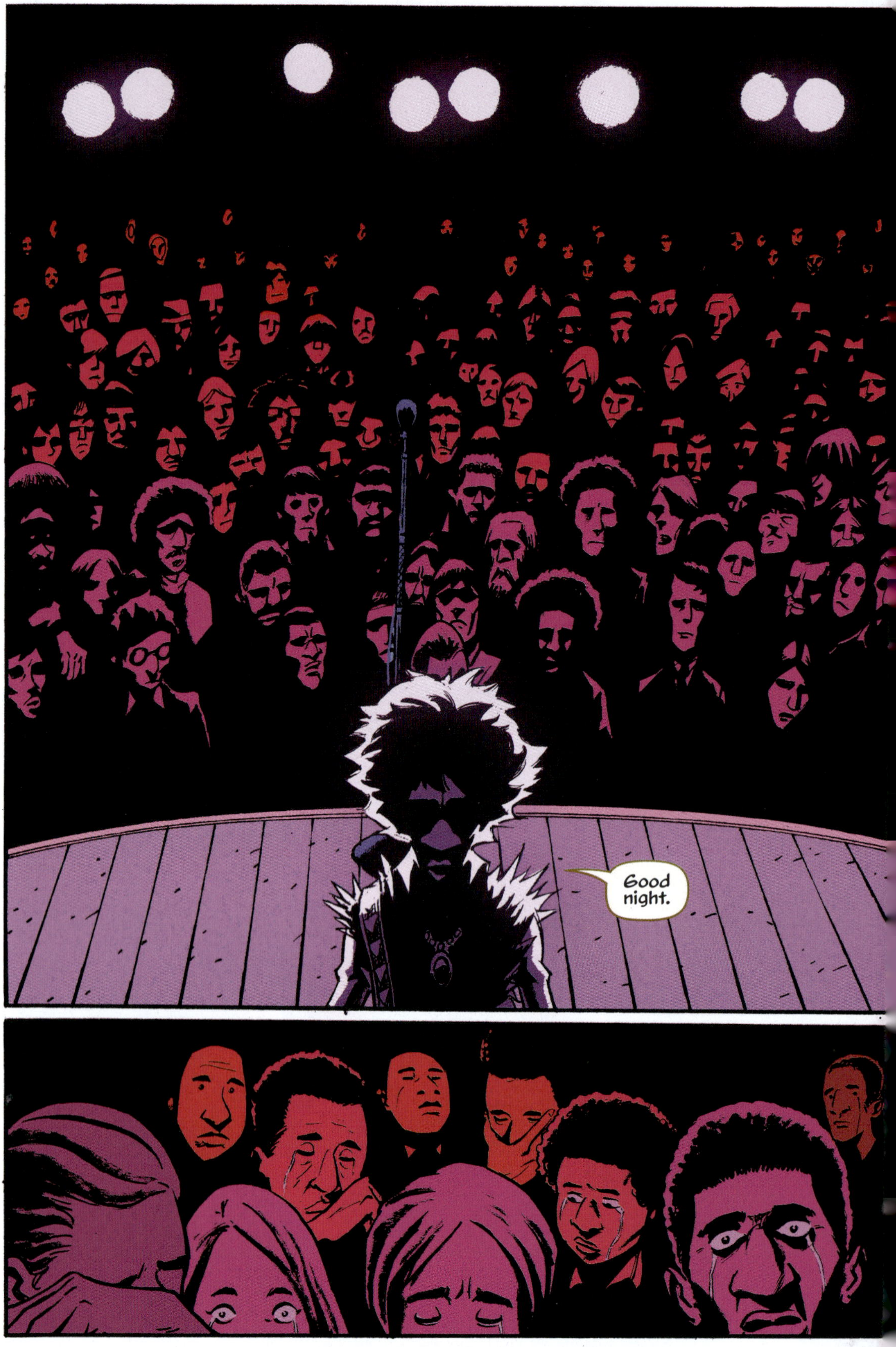
Good night.

# 08.

# HEAR MY TRAIN COMING

After two records and ever-increasing success, in 1969 things started to get complicated for good old James.

On his way to a concert in Toronto, he got arrested for drug possession: hashish and heroin.

Things went on for a long time...

METRO. TORONTO JAMES M. HENDRIX 2.99/69 MAY3/69

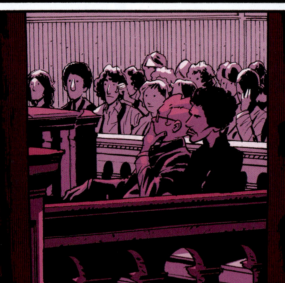

Jimi managed to convince the court that he had no idea how those drugs had ended up in his trunk.

But that was just the tip of the iceberg...

Misfortunes never come alone, they say.

With time, Jimi had become a slave to his perfectionism, which had further alienated the people around him.

His wandering, instinctual attitude made him difficult to manage. So, after much bad blood, while Jimi was building his own recording studio...

...Chas Chandler quit managing the band.

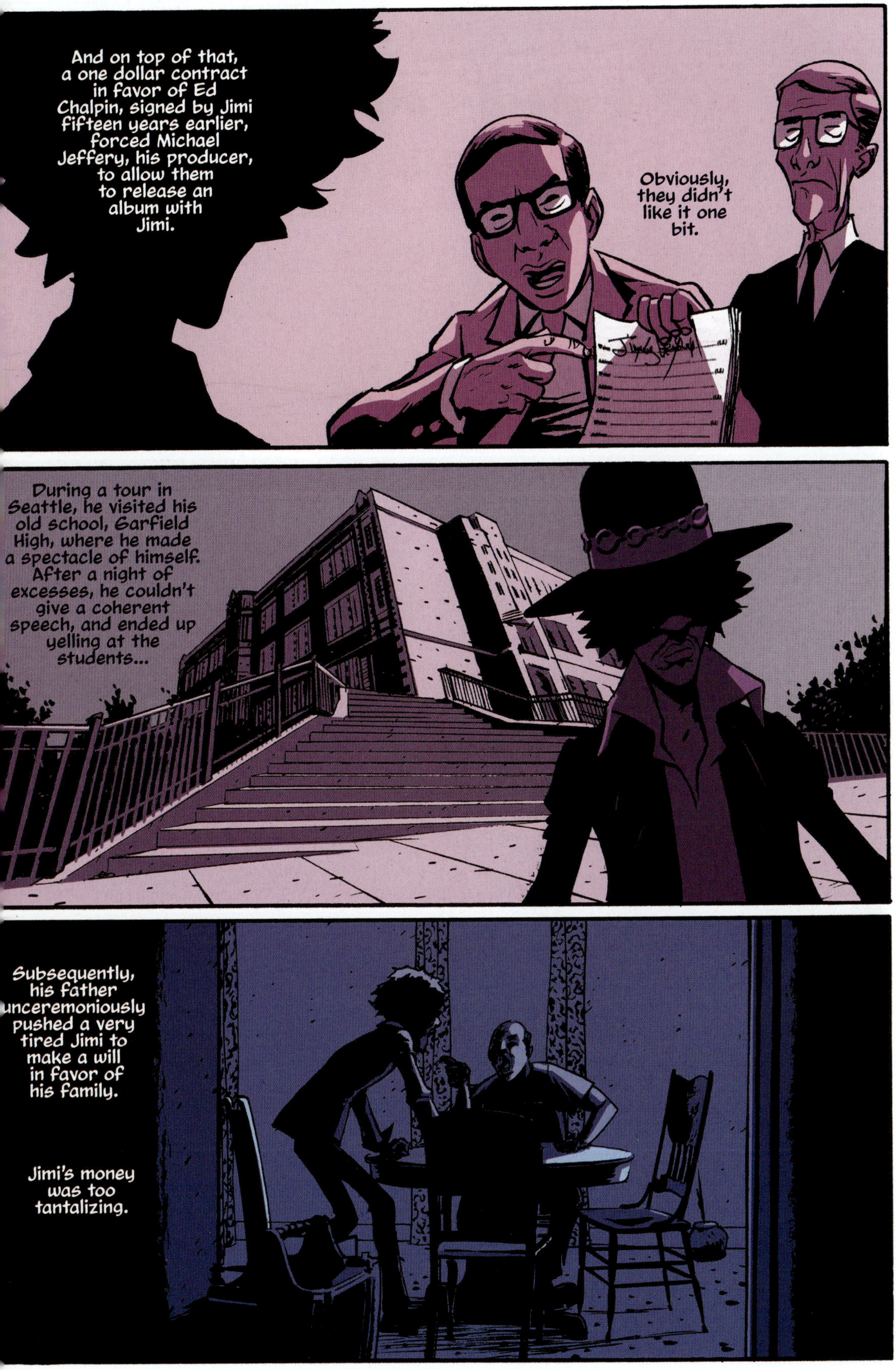

And on top of that, a one dollar contract in favor of Ed Chalpin, signed by Jimi fifteen years earlier, forced Michael Jeffery, his producer, to allow them to release an album with Jimi.
Obviously, they didn't like it one bit.
During a tour in Seattle, he visited his old school, Garfield High, where he made a spectacle of himself. After a night of excesses, he couldn't give a coherent speech, and ended up yelling at the students...
Subsequently, his father unceremoniously pushed a very tired Jimi to make a will in favor of his family.
Jimi's money was too tantalizing.

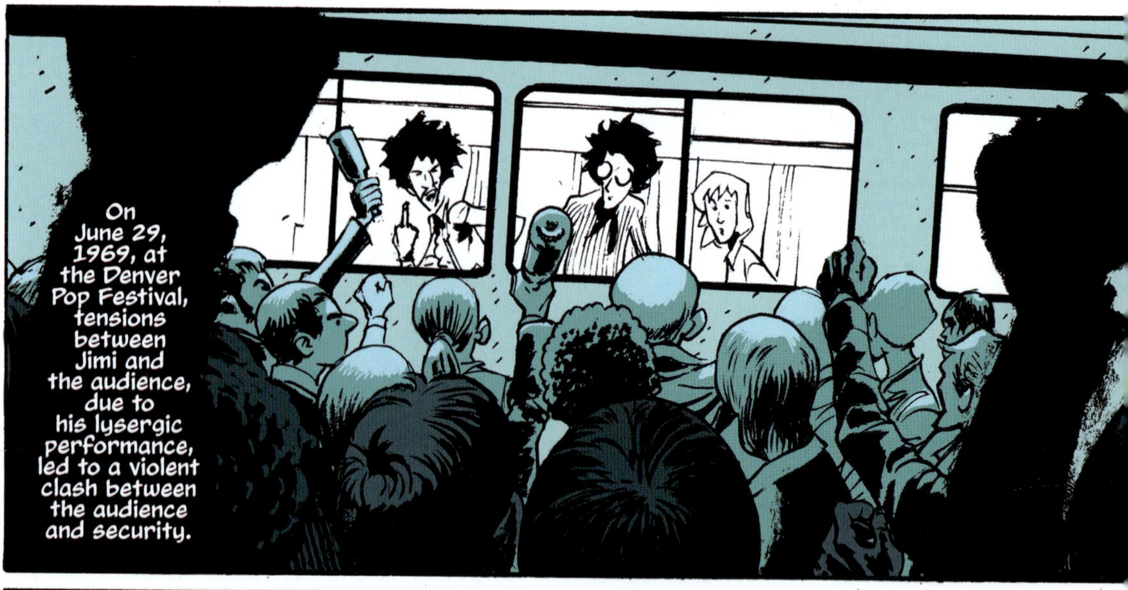
On June 29, 1969, at the Denver Pop Festival, tensions between Jimi and the audience, due to his lysergic performance, led to a violent clash between the audience and security.

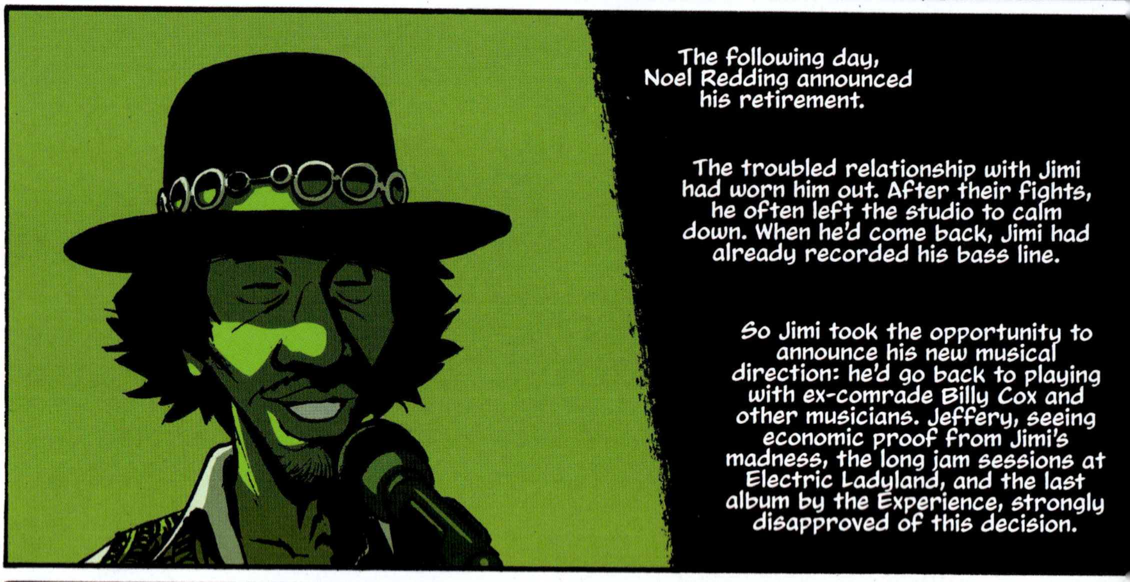
The following day, Noel Redding announced his retirement.
The troubled relationship with Jimi had worn him out. After their fights, he often left the studio to calm down. When he'd come back, Jimi had already recorded his bass line.
So Jimi took the opportunity to announce his new musical direction: he'd go back to playing with ex-comrade Billy Cox and other musicians. Jeffery, seeing economic proof from Jimi's madness, the long jam sessions at Electric Ladyland, and the last album by the Experience, strongly disapproved of this decision.

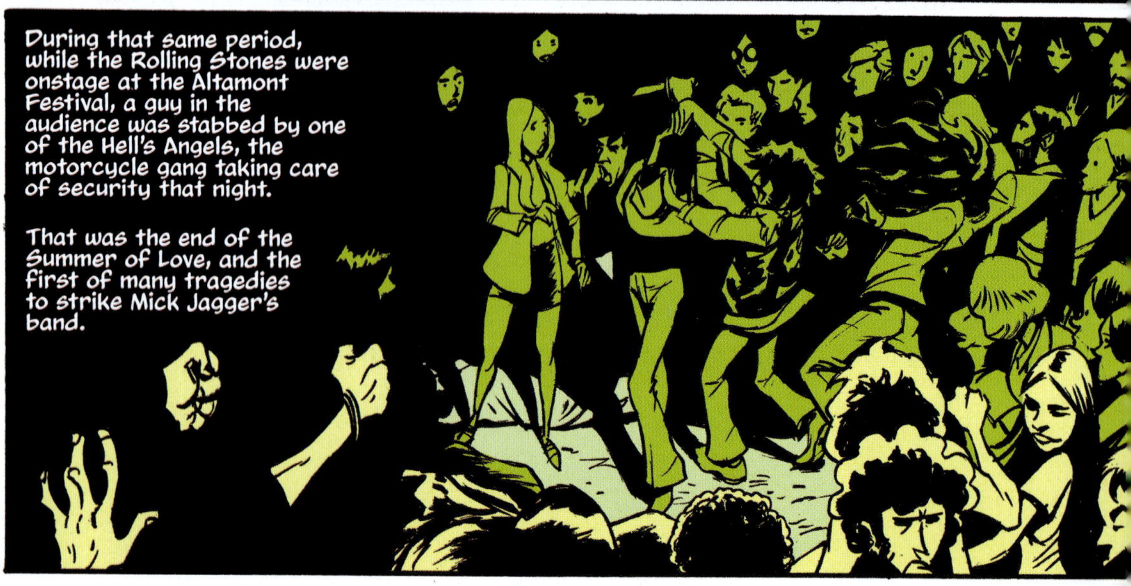
During that same period, while the Rolling Stones were onstage at the Altamont Festival, a guy in the audience was stabbed by one of the Hell's Angels, the motorcycle gang taking care of security that night.
That was the end of the Summer of Love, and the first of many tragedies to strike Mick Jagger's band.

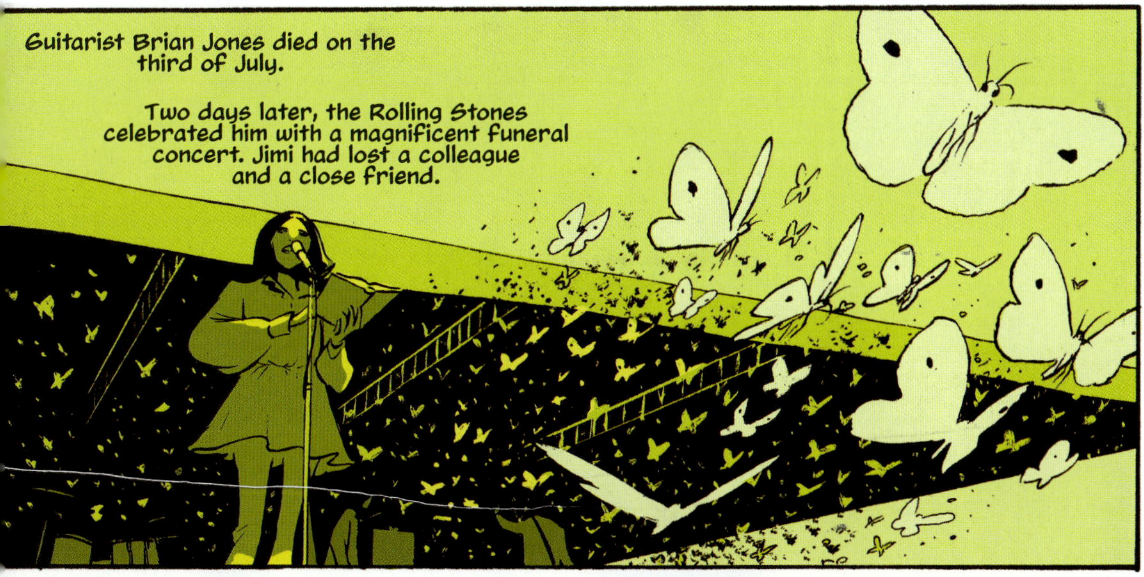
Guitarist Brian Jones died on the third of July.
Two days later, the Rolling Stones celebrated him with a magnificent funeral concert. Jimi had lost a colleague and a close friend.

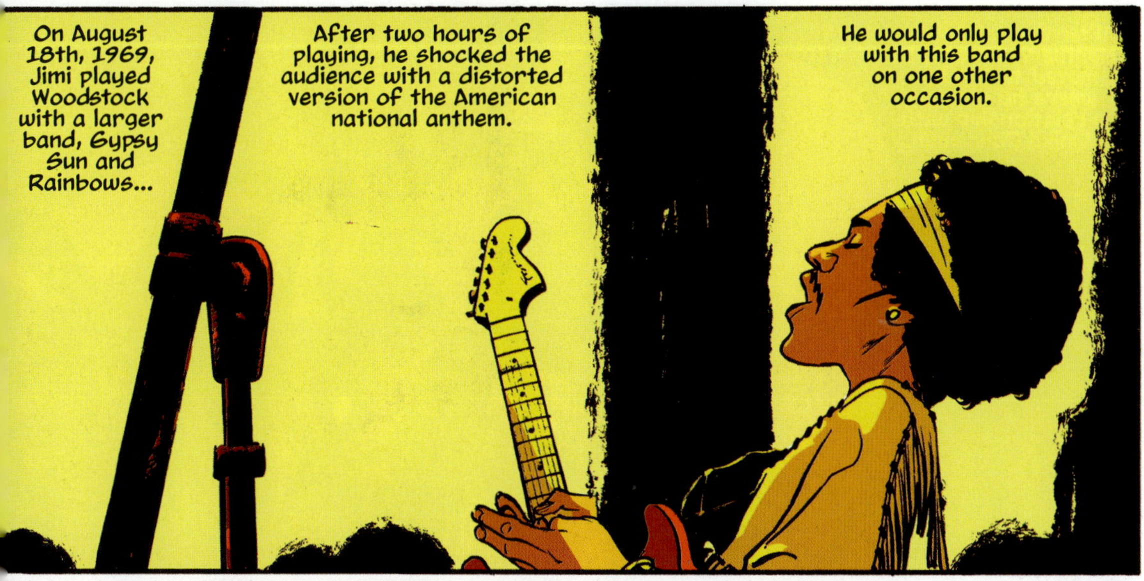
On August 18th, 1969, Jimi played Woodstock with a larger band, Gypsy Sun and Rainbows...
After two hours of playing, he shocked the audience with a distorted version of the American national anthem.
He would only play with this band on one other occasion.

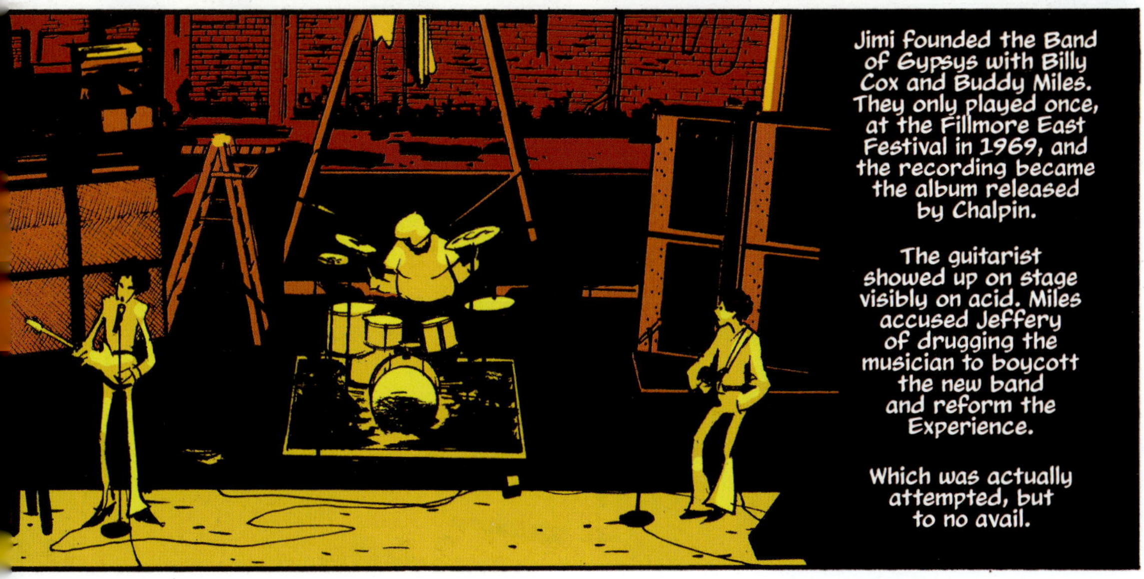
Jimi founded the Band of Gypsys with Billy Cox and Buddy Miles. They only played once, at the Fillmore East Festival in 1969, and the recording became the album released by Chalpin.
The guitarist showed up on stage visibly on acid. Miles accused Jeffery of drugging the musician to boycott the new band and reform the Experience.
Which was actually attempted, but to no avail.

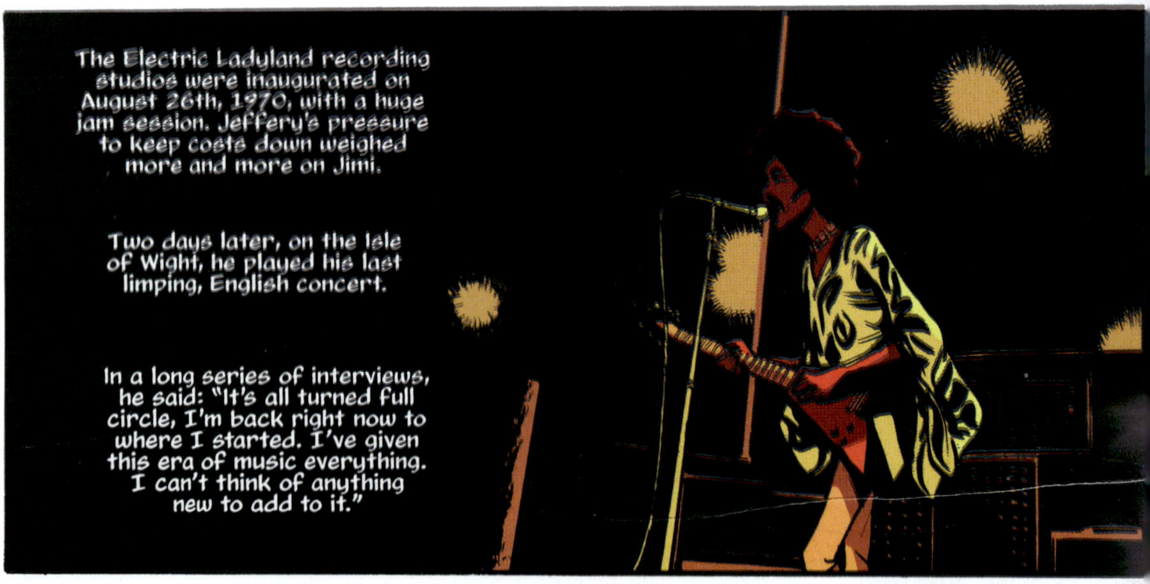
The Electric Ladyland recording studios were inaugurated on August 26th, 1970, with a huge jam session. Jeffery's pressure to keep costs down weighed more and more on Jimi.
Two days later, on the Isle of Wight, he played his last limping, English concert.
In a long series of interviews, he said: "It's all turned full circle, I'm back right now to where I started. I've given this era of music everything. I can't think of anything new to add to it."

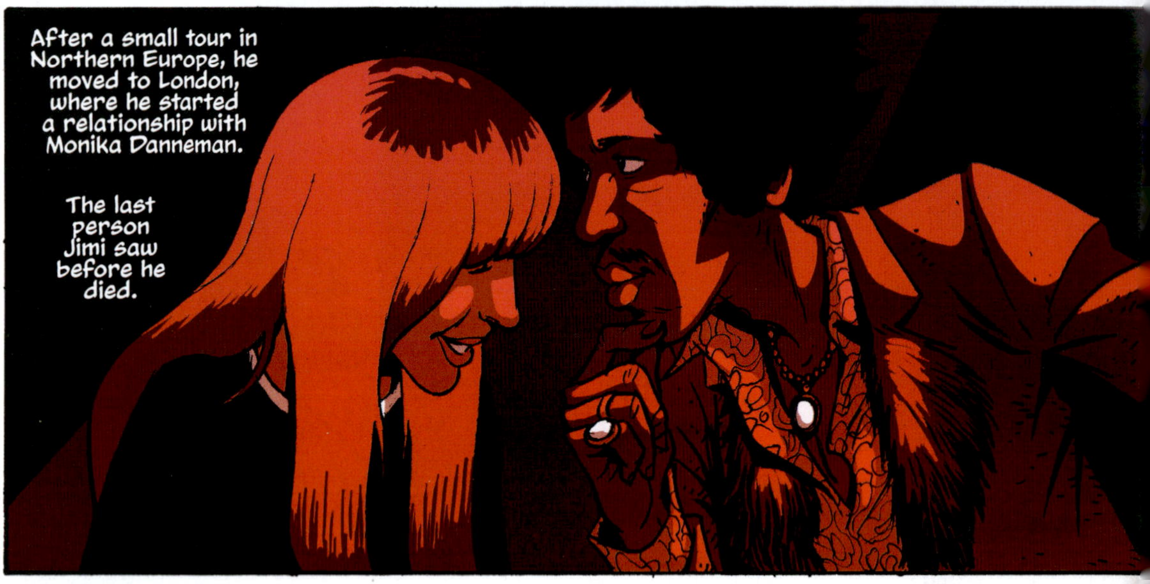
After a small tour in Northern Europe, he moved to London, where he started a relationship with Monika Danneman.
The last person Jimi saw before he died.

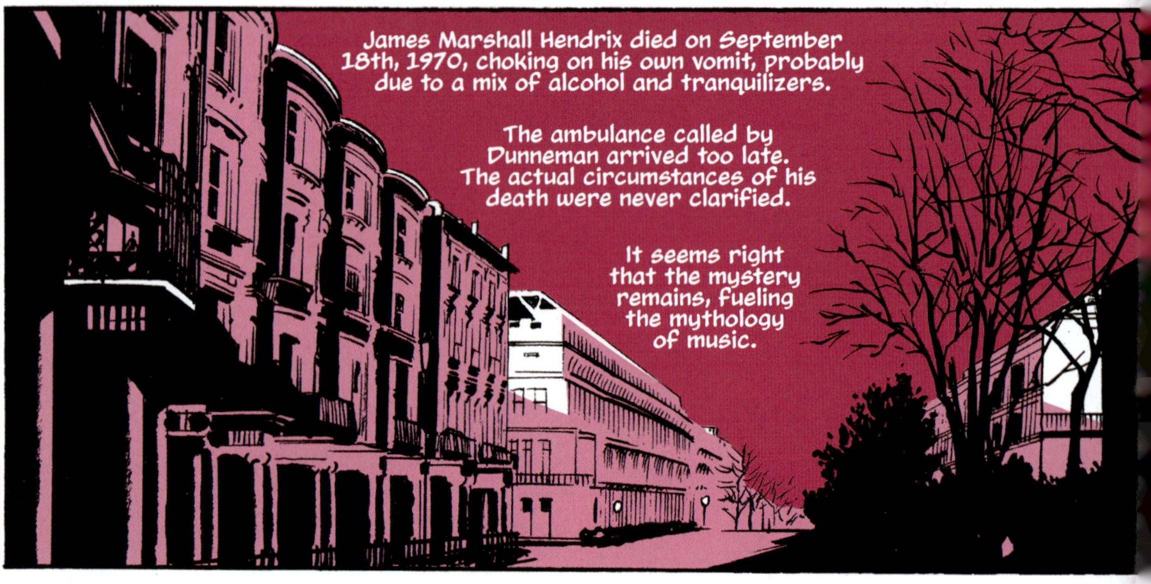
James Marshall Hendrix died on September 18th, 1970, choking on his own vomit, probably due to a mix of alcohol and tranquilizers.
The ambulance called by Dunneman arrived too late. The actual circumstances of his death were never clarified.
It seems right that the mystery remains, fueling the mythology of music.

09.

# VooDoo CHILD

SlighT ReTurn

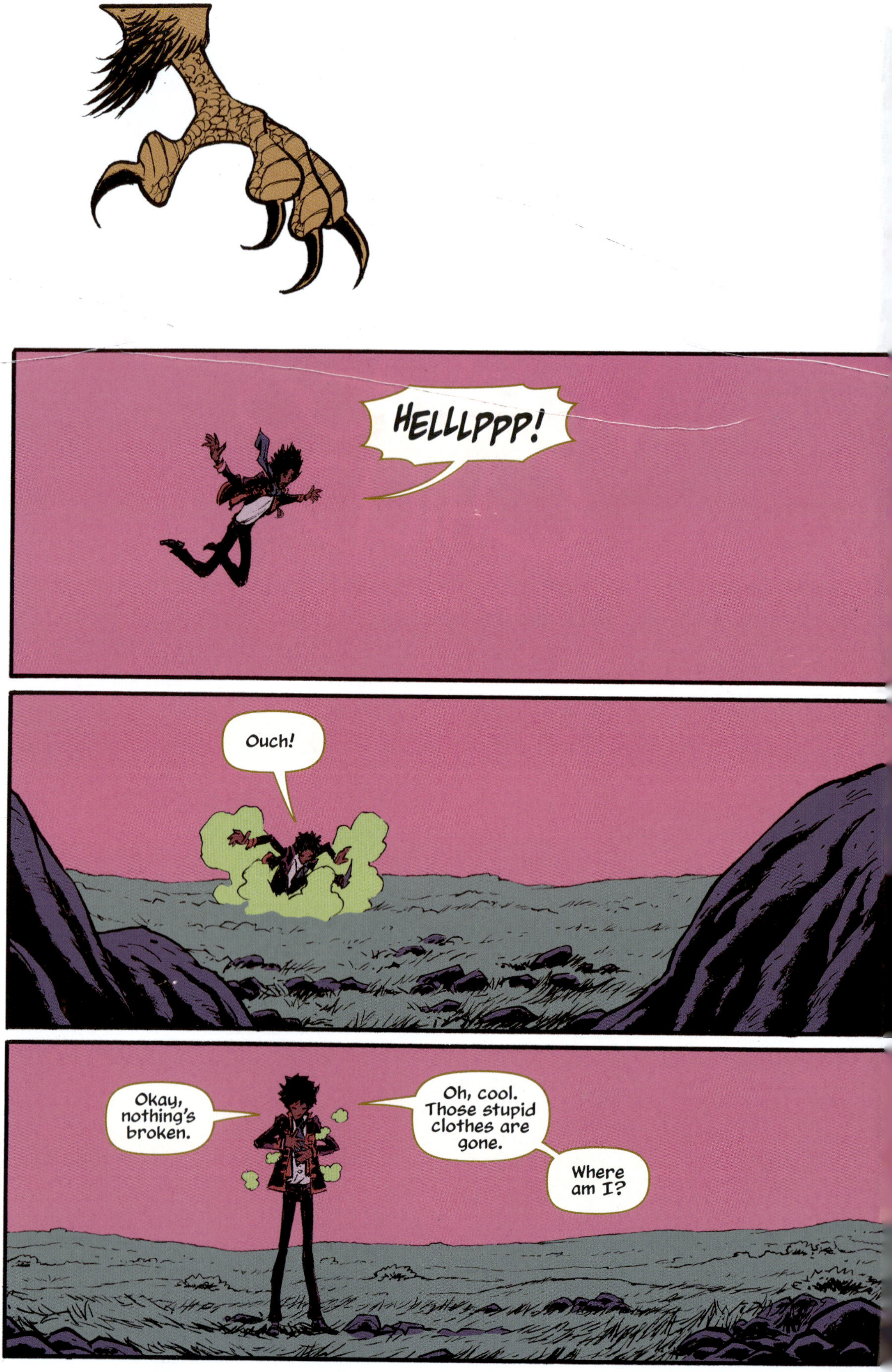
HELLLPPP!
Ouch!
Okay, nothing's broken.
Oh, cool. Those stupid clothes are gone.
Where am I?

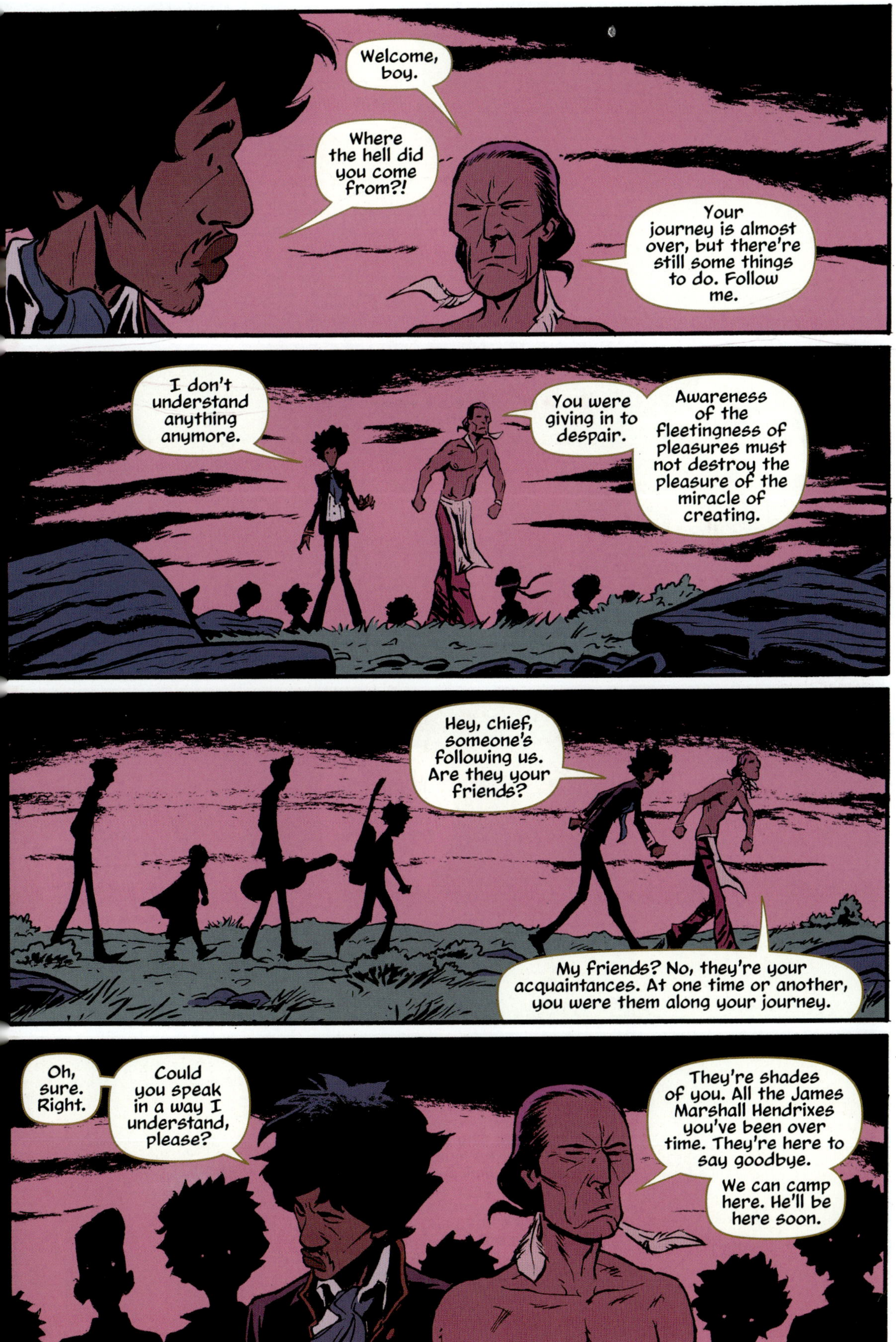
Welcome, boy.
Where the hell did you come from?!
Your journey is almost over, but there're still some things to do. Follow me.
I don't understand anything anymore.
You were giving in to despair.
Awareness of the fleetingness of pleasures must not destroy the pleasure of the miracle of creating.
Hey, chief, someone's following us. Are they your friends?
My friends? No, they're your acquaintances. At one time or another, you were them along your journey.
Oh, sure. Right.
Could you speak in a way I understand, please?
They're shades of you. All the James Marshall Hendrixes you've been over time. They're here to say goodbye.
We can camp here. He'll be here soon.

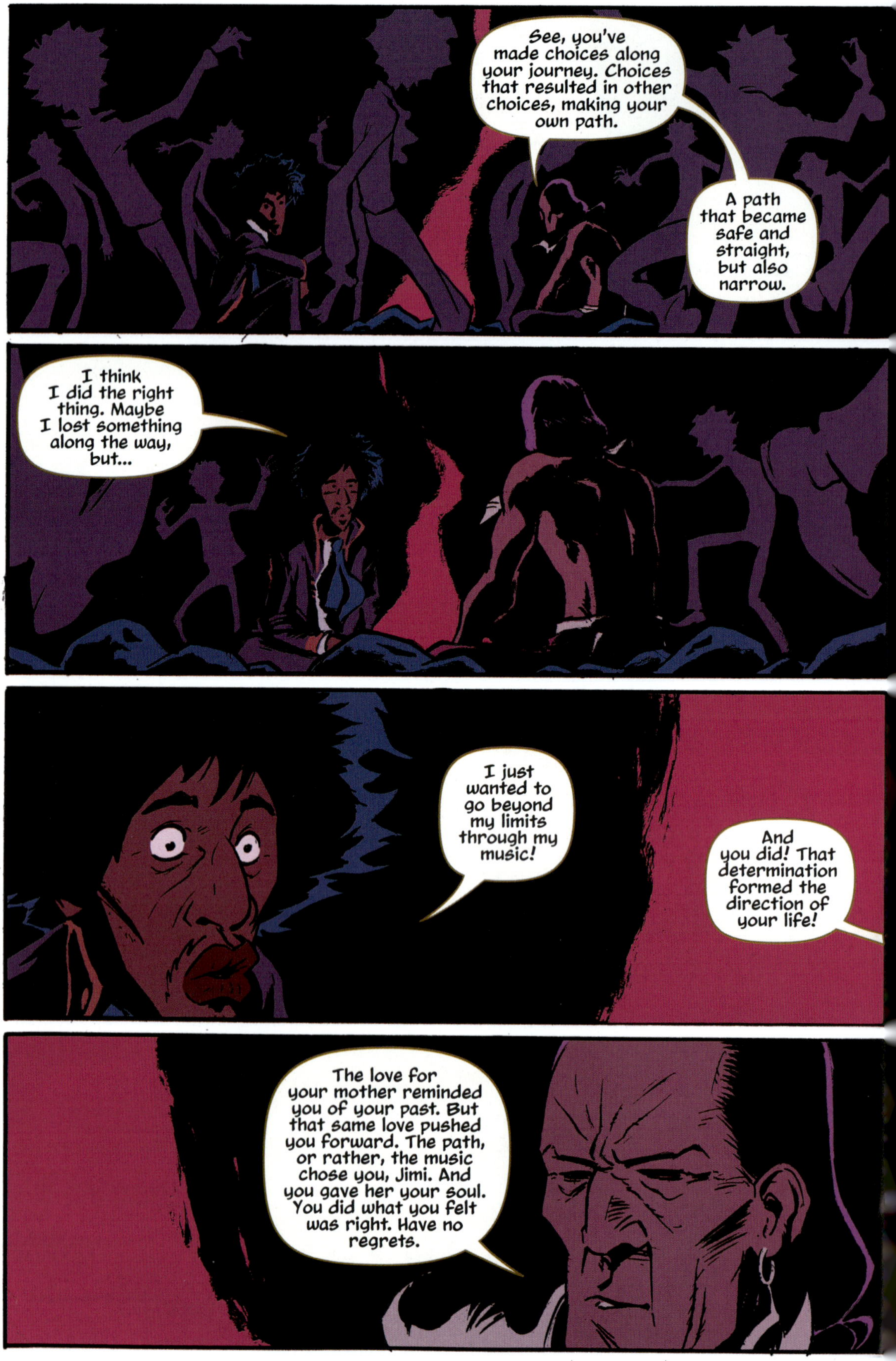
See, you've made choices along your journey. Choices that resulted in other choices, making your own path.
A path that became safe and straight, but also narrow.
I think I did the right thing. Maybe I lost something along the way, but...
I just wanted to go beyond my limits through my music!
And you did! That determination formed the direction of your life!
The love for your mother reminded you of your past. But that same love pushed you forward. The path, or rather, the music chose you, Jimi. And you gave her your soul. You did what you felt was right. Have no regrets.

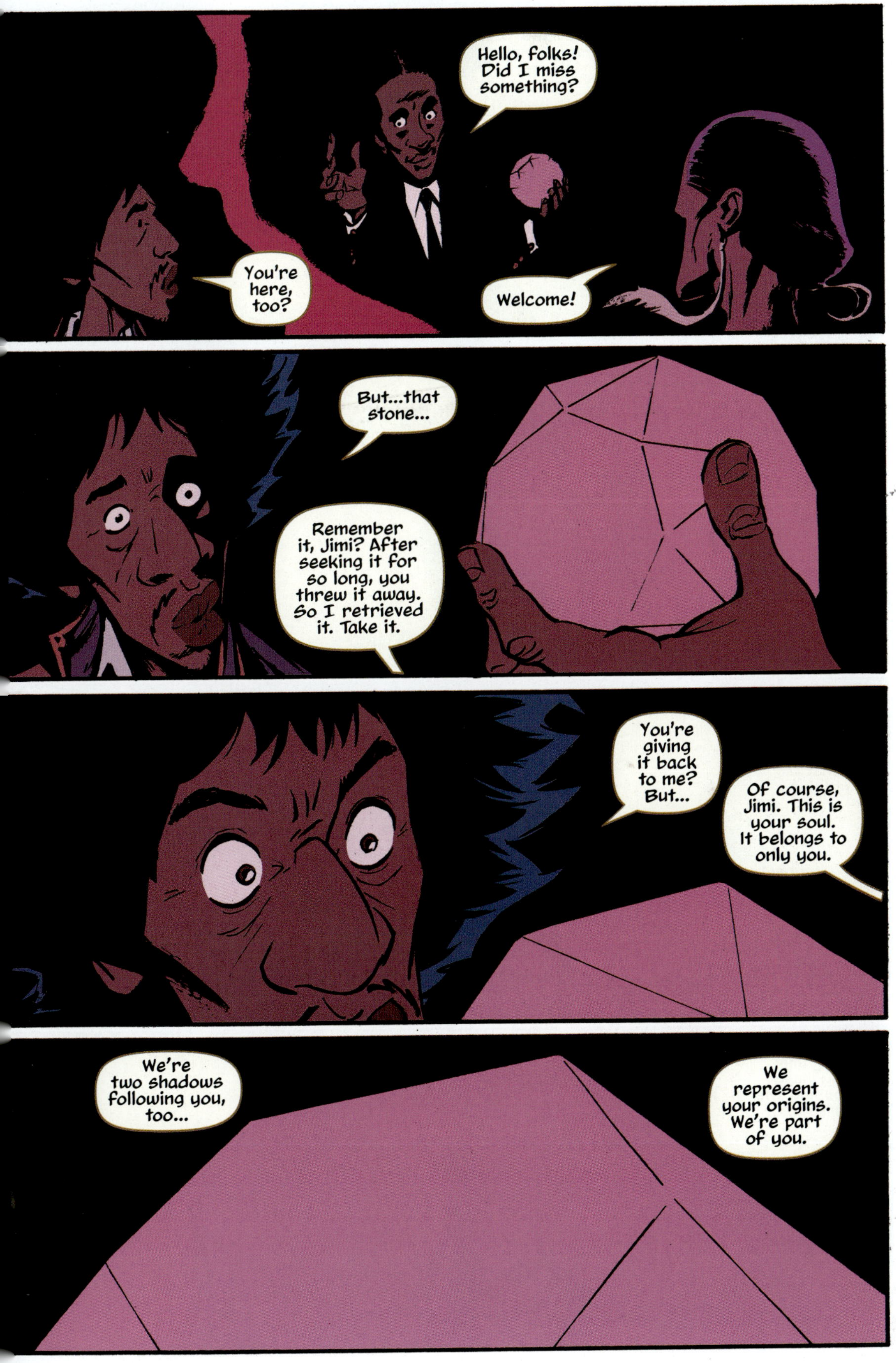

Hello, folks! Did I miss something?
You're here, too?
Welcome!
But...that stone...
Remember it, Jimi? After seeking it for so long, you threw it away. So I retrieved it. Take it.
You're giving it back to me? But...
Of course, Jimi. This is your soul. It belongs to only you.
We're two shadows following you, too...
We represent your origins. We're part of you.

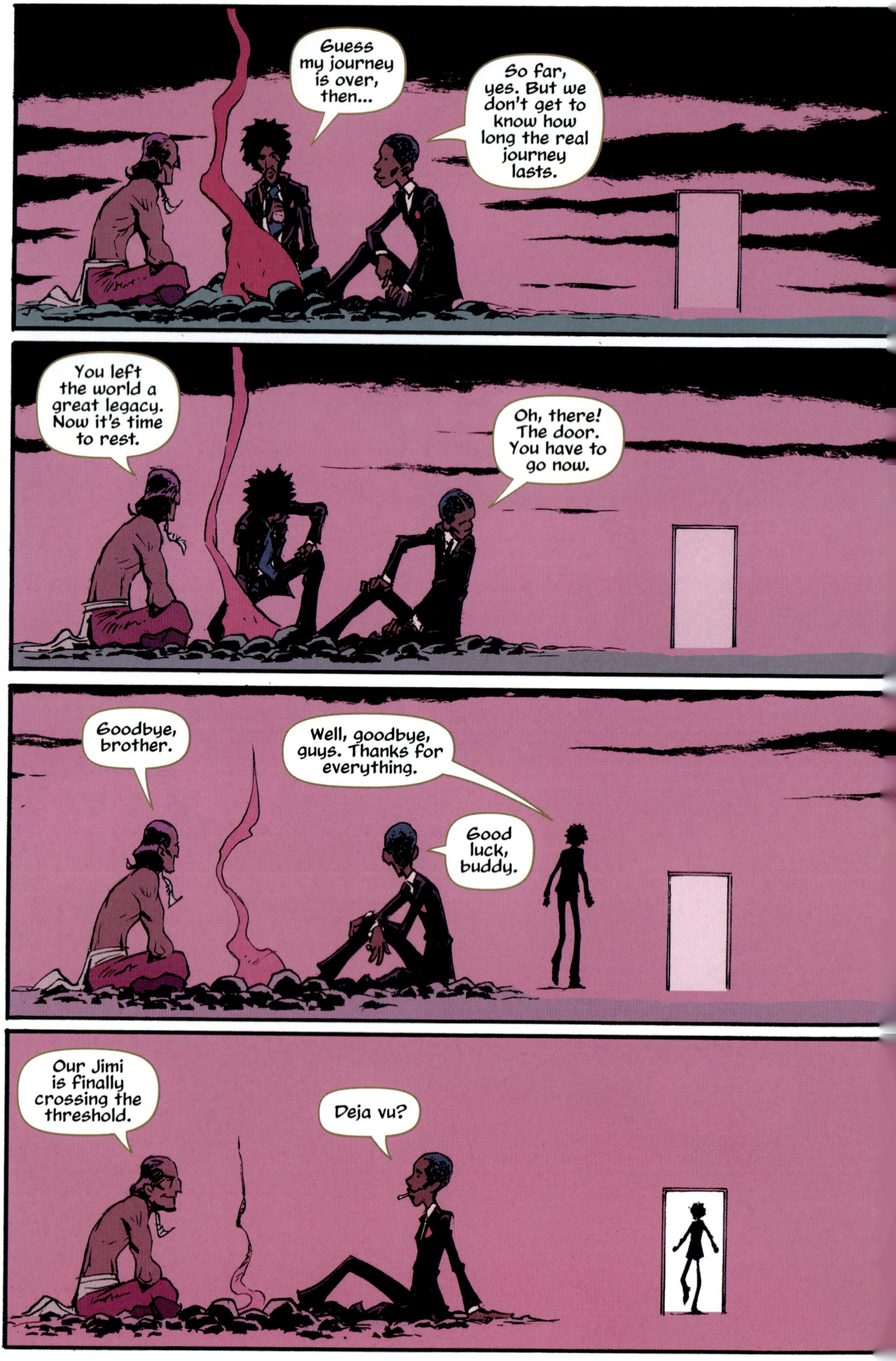
Guess my journey is over, then...
So far, yes. But we don't get to know how long the real journey lasts.
You left the world a great legacy. Now it's time to rest.
Oh, there! The door. You have to go now.
Goodbye, brother.
Well, goodbye, guys. Thanks for everything.
Good luck, buddy.
Our Jimi is finally crossing the threshold.
Deja vu?

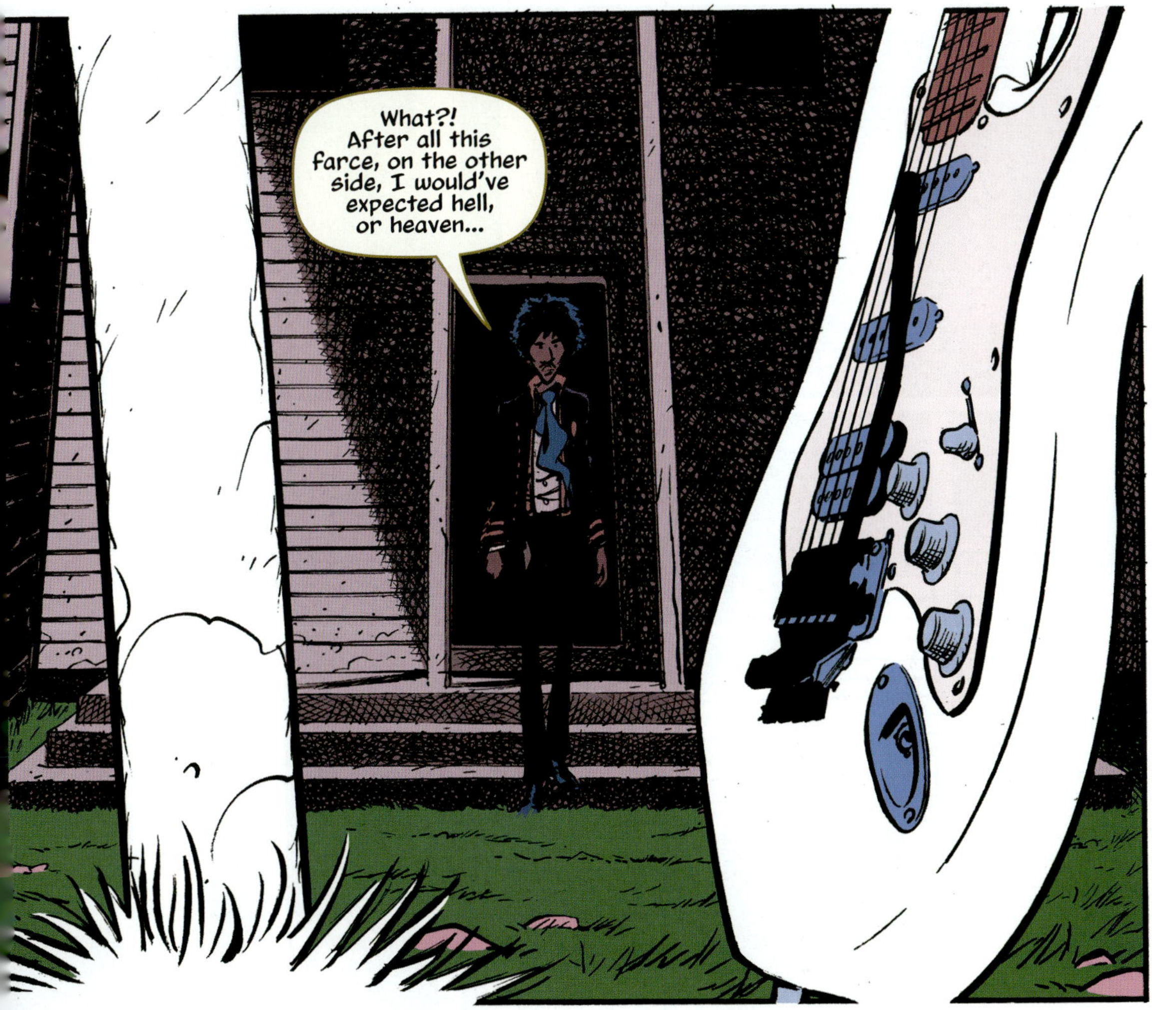
What?! After all this farce, on the other side, I would've expected hell, or heaven...

# EXP-
## epilogue

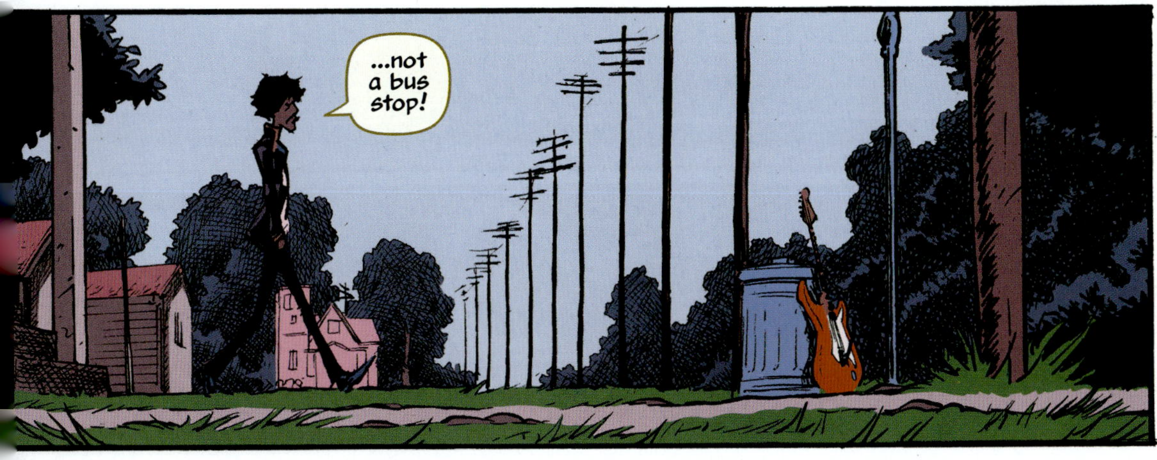
...not a bus stop!

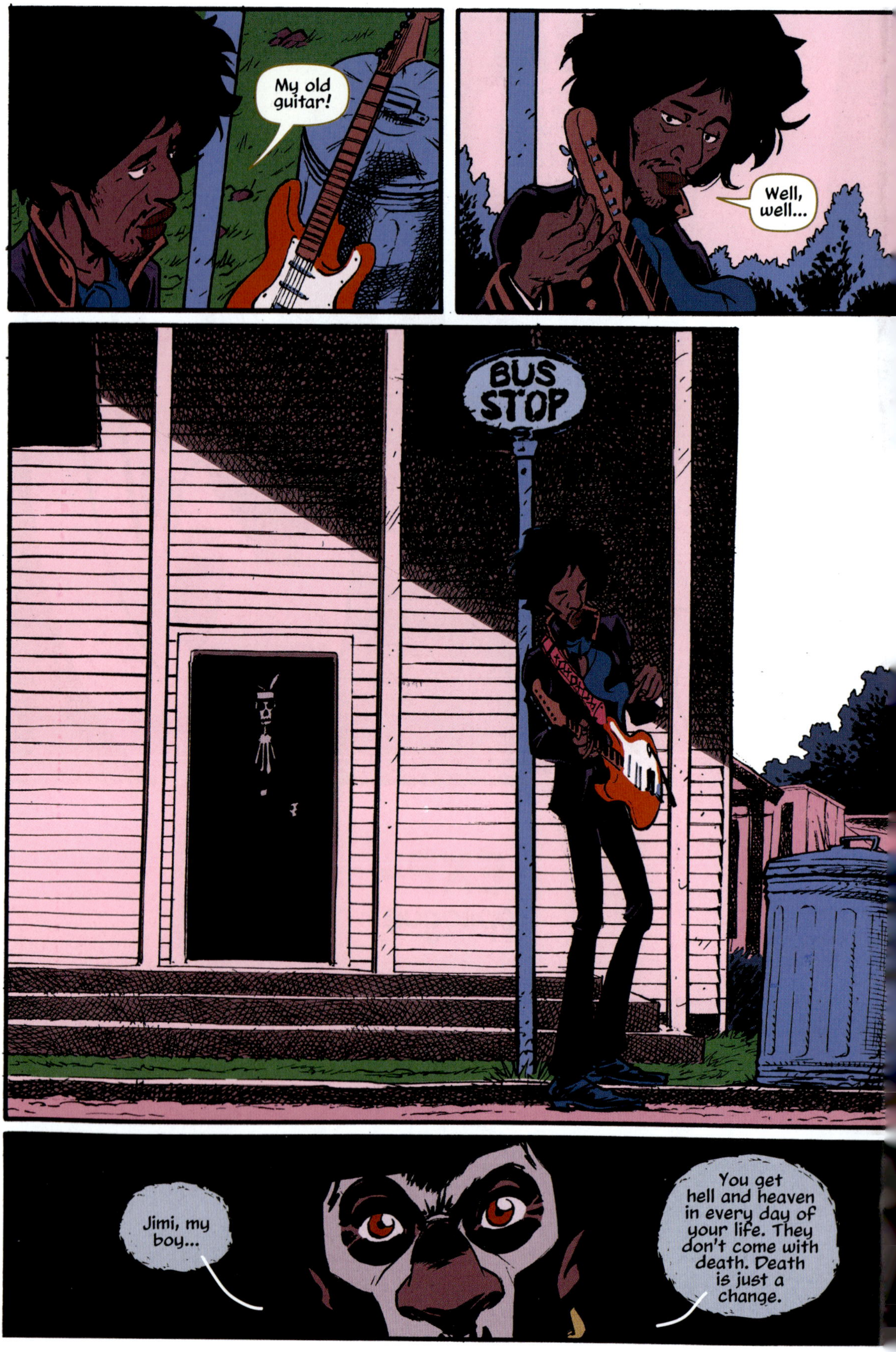
My old guitar!
Well, well...
BUS STOP
Jimi, my boy...
You get hell and heaven in every day of your life. They don't come with death. Death is just a change.

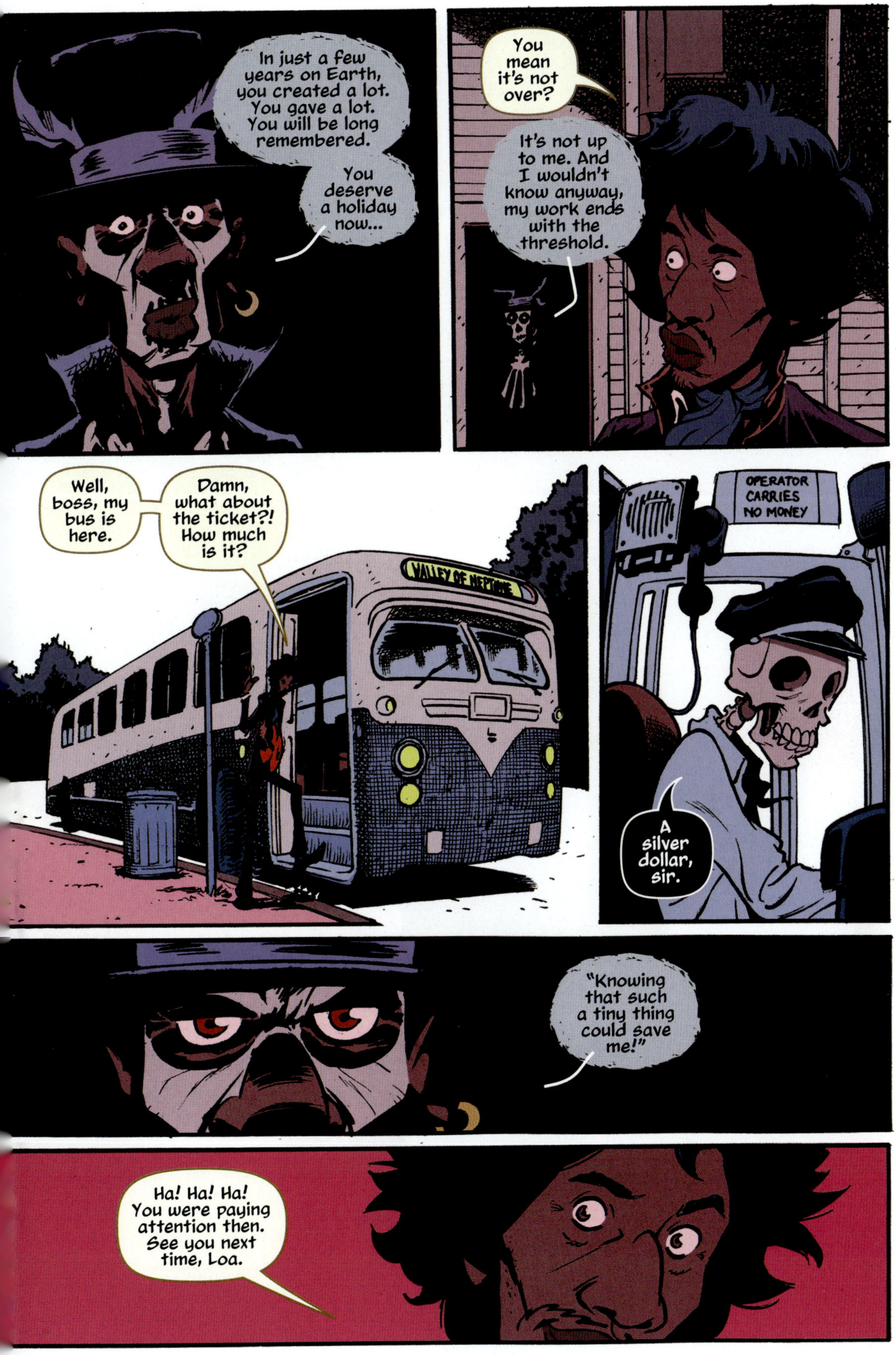
In just a few years on Earth, you created a lot. You gave a lot. You will be long remembered.
You deserve a holiday now...
You mean it's not over?
It's not up to me. And I wouldn't know anyway, my work ends with the threshold.
Well, boss, my bus is here.
Damn, what about the ticket?! How much is it?
VALLEY OF NEPTUNE
OPERATOR CARRIES NO MONEY
A silver dollar, sir.
"Knowing that such a tiny thing could save me!"
Ha! Ha! Ha! You were paying attention then. See you next time, Loa.

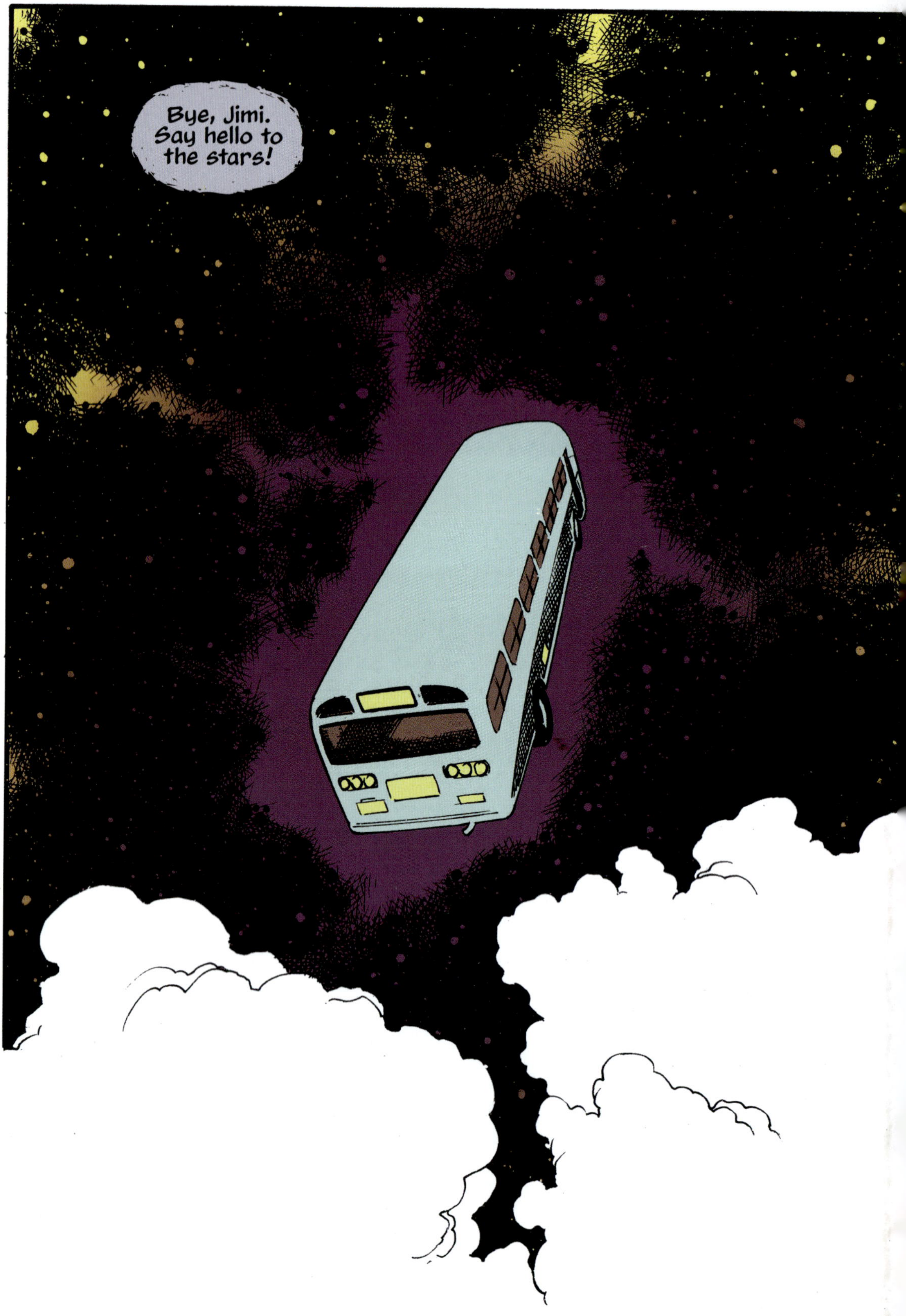
Bye, Jimi. Say hello to the stars!

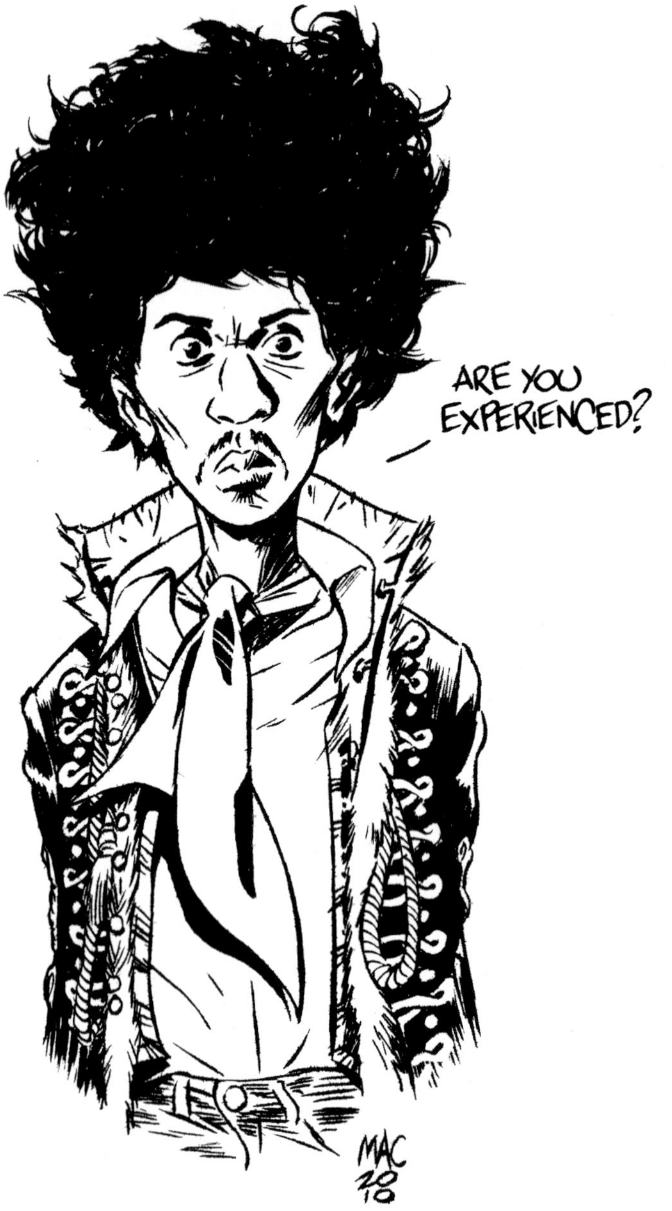
ARE YOU
EXPERIENCED?
MAC
2010

**BIBLIOGRAPHY**

CROSS, CHARLES R., Room Full of Mirrors: A Biography of
Jimi Hendrix, Hyperion, New York, 2005.

LAWRENCE, SHARON, Jimi Hendrix: The Man, the Magic, the Truth, Harper, New York, 2005.

ROBY, STEVEN, Black gold: The Lost Archives of Jimi Hendrix, Billboard Books, New York, 2002.

STUBBS, DAVID, Jimi Hendrix: Voodo Child: The Stories Behind
Every Song, Thunder's Mouth Press, New York, 1992.

LEWISOHN, MARK, Hendrix: Setting the Record Straight, Warner Books, New York, 1992.

SHAPIRO, HARRY, Jimi Hendrix: Electric Gipsy, St. Martin's Griffin, New York, 1995.

HENDRIX, JAMES AL:, My Son Jimi, AlJas Enterprise, Seattle, 1999.

MURRAY, CHARLES SHAAR, Crosstown Traffic: Jimi Hendrix and the Post-
war Rock'n'roll Revolution, St. Martin's Press, New York, 1991.

SIENKIEWICZ, BILL, Voodoo Child: The Illustrated Life of Jimi Hendrix, Penguin, New York, 1995.

## NOTES FROM THE AUTHORS

To write a biography means to condense moments of a life that we have not lived, if not by reflection.

Deciding which are the most significant moments or the mechanisms that guide a person's life is anything but easy.

Keeping that in mind, we tried to make this story as "universal" as possible, shaping our Jimi in such a way that he could talk to anyone. So don't be mad, guitar enthusiasts, if you don't find any astonishing mystery unveiled; and don't be mad, super fans, if you won't find any conspiracy theories.

We tried to play with the rules of comics the way Jimi used to play with musical structures. Each chapter is like a song on a concept album divided into three stylistically different sections: the roots, the climax, and the fall of the music career of the great guitarist.

**pages 3–6:** Jimi never got the chance to fully develop the Electric Church concept, according to which electric music could elevate the emotions by encouraging spiritual maturity, to create and experiment beyond the stereotypes and without the pressure of the music industry.

In our story, it becomes a place out of time in which two spiritual guides, representing Jimi's Black and Cherokee origins, escort him to his judge, Baron Samedi, Loa ("spirit") of hoodoo and ferryman of the souls of the dead.

Various Totentanz ("dances of the dead") decorate the church: among them, "Dead and Monster" by our friend and colleague Alberto Corradi.

**page 12:** In the dream sequences, Jimi dresses as Hal Foster's Prince Valiant, of which he was a big reader as a child.

**pages 14–15:** The images accompanying the songs of the guides refer to important events of the American history of Blacks and Native Americans: the treaty of Fort Laramie, the Sand Creek and Wounded Knee massacres, slavery and the Ku Klux Klan's ignoble deeds.

**page 17:** Since 1920, the Central District of Seattle had been a real community ghetto where a thriving entertainment industry developed. In fact, most of the clubs and dance halls were located in this area. It was there that many African-American artists who later made the history of music, like Ray Charles, Muddy Waters, and Little Richard, began their careers.

**pages 21–22:** The Spanish Castle is actually located in the outskirts of Seattle, very far from the Hendrix's house. It is true, though, that little Jimi went to look for his parents in a club very far from home.

The meeting with the bluesman is obviously fictional.

**page 30:** These are Al, Jimi, and his brother Leon. History has it that the Hendrix brothers didn't go to their mother's funeral. Jimi said his father didn't feel up to it and while the ceremony was taking place, the three stayed in the car outside the cemetery, crying.

We took this poetic license to make the sequence more effective.

**page 33:** There are different versions of how Jimi left the army. The most accepted is that he broke his foot during a parachute jump. But after the desecretion of some military documents, the hypothesis was made that Jimi tried to pass himself as homosexual.

**pages 36-37:** The fictional bluesman talking to Jimi is modeled on John Lee Hooker.

**page 62:** The meeting with Clapton instantly ignited the rivalry between the two. Jimi said that Clapton refused to plug his guitar into the amplifier. The rest of the scene is fictional: the jam session with Hendrix and Cream was actually organized by Chas Chandler.

**page 64:** Noel Redding showed up for an audition as a guitarist for the new Animals by Burdon. Chas Chandler noticed him and proposed him to Jimi as a bass player. Jimi immediately liked him, also because of his big hair.
Noel was a great guitarist and the switch to bass always weighed on him.

**page 65:** Little is known about the meeting between Clapton and Townshend. Clapton said he called Townshend to talk about their mutual admiration for Jimi, but we don't know the actual conversation. We do know that for quite a while they both thought their careers would be over because of Jimi. The movie they went to see is described by Clapton as a "strange italian movie." We picked *Blow Up* by Antonioni because it was running in the movie theaters in London, and it featured a performance by Clapton's former band, The Yardbirds.

**page 68:** The meeting with Michael Jeffery is entirely fictional. Jeffery was said to be in contact with criminal circles, an MI5 (the British Secret Service) spy acting as a double agent for the Russians. His death, in a plane crash in Spain, adds to the mystery around his figure.

**page 70:** The gig at Bag O'Nails actually took place after the supporting gig in France. The gig right after was Saville Theater in June '67, hosted by The Beatles' manager Brian Epstein; Jimi opened with a cover of *Sgt. Pepper's Lonely Hearts Club Band* – the album that had just been released.

**pages 74–75:** Many sources report the argument in Monterey.

**pages 78–79:** This episode is told by Jimi in every detail. The pub was in Liverpool, The Beatles' city. The proximity of a circus forced the owner to take action against those specific customers.

**pages 88–93:** In this monologue, Jimi is dressed as Hamlet played by Laurence Olivier in 1948.

**pages 97–100:** Jimi became most famous the year Stanley Kubrick's *2001: A Space Odyssey* was released.

**page 107:** This episode is reported by several witnesses. However peculiar, we used it to describe Jimi's anticommercial tendency: onstage, he would never play a song the way it was recorded on the album.

SEE PAGE 70 FOR FULL COLOR PAGE OF PEOPLE LISTED HERE

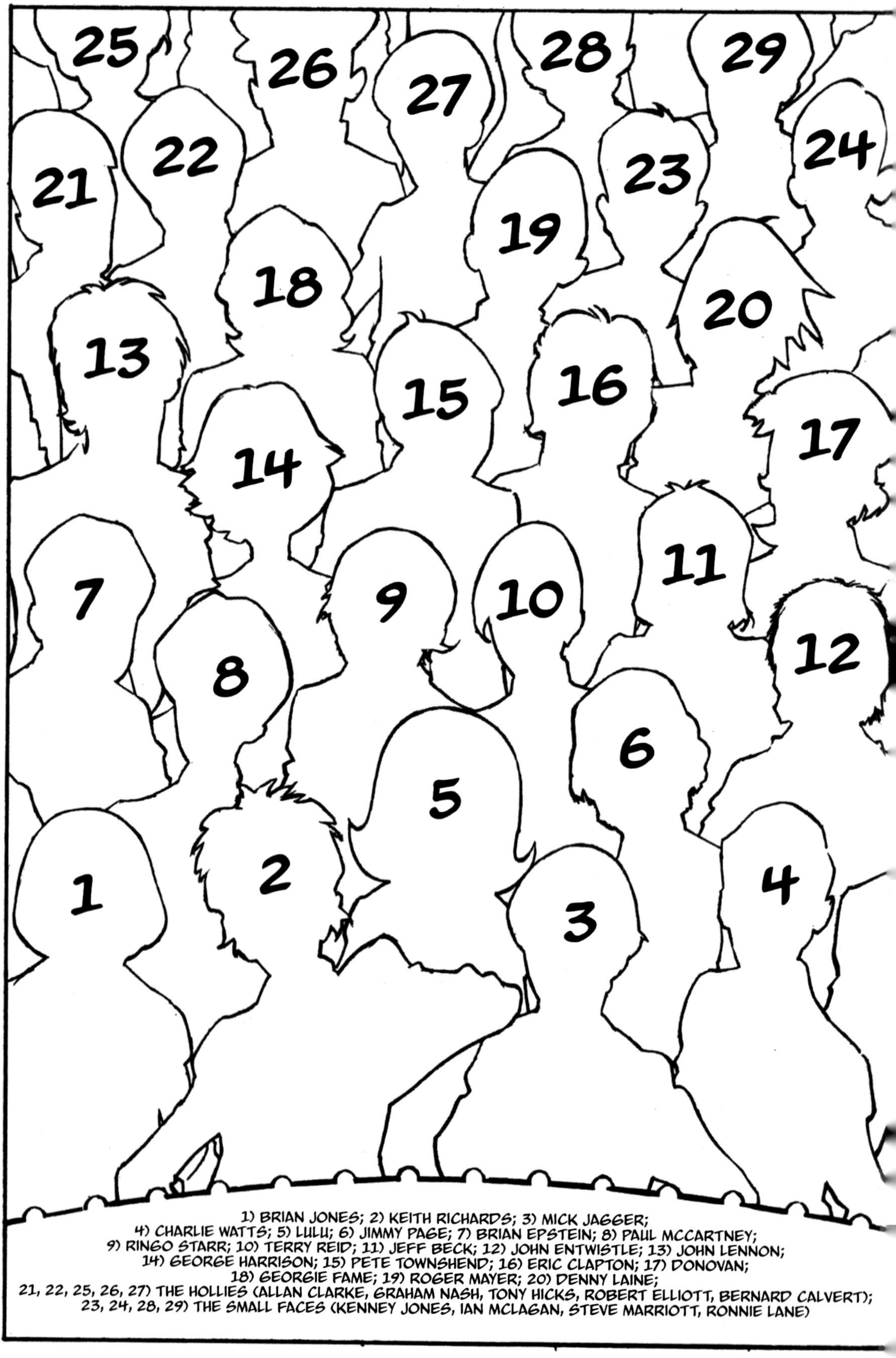
25
26
27
28
29
21
22
23
24
19
18
20
13
15
16
17
14
11
7
9
10
12
8
6
5
2
1
3
4

1) BRIAN JONES; 2) KEITH RICHARDS; 3) MICK JAGGER;
4) CHARLIE WATTS; 5) LULU; 6) JIMMY PAGE; 7) BRIAN EPSTEIN; 8) PAUL MCCARTNEY;
9) RINGO STARR; 10) TERRY REID; 11) JEFF BECK; 12) JOHN ENTWISTLE; 13) JOHN LENNON;
14) GEORGE HARRISON; 15) PETE TOWNSHEND; 16) ERIC CLAPTON; 17) DONOVAN;
18) GEORGIE FAME; 19) ROGER MAYER; 20) DENNY LAINE;
21, 22, 25, 26, 27) THE HOLLIES (ALLAN CLARKE, GRAHAM NASH, TONY HICKS, ROBERT ELLIOTT, BERNARD CALVERT);
23, 24, 28, 29) THE SMALL FACES (KENNEY JONES, IAN MCLAGAN, STEVE MARRIOTT, RONNIE LANE)